Tar Heel Politics

Tar Heel Politics

Myths and Realities

Paul Luebke

The University of North Carolina Press

Chapel Hill and London

Library of Congress Cataloging-in-Publication Data

Luebke, Paul.
    Tar heel politics : myths and realities / Paul Luebke.
      p.   cm.
    Bibliography: p.
    Includes index.
    ISBN 0-8078-1884-4 (alk. paper). — ISBN 0-8078-4271-0 (pbk. :
alk. paper)
    1. North Carolina—Politics and government—1951–   2. Elections—
North Carolina.   3. Political parties—North Carolina.   I. Title.
JK4195.L84   1990   89-14677
975.6'043—dc20   CIP

The paper in this book meets the guidelines for permanence
and durability of the Committee on Production Guidelines
for Book Longevity of the Council on Library Resources.

Manufactured in the United States of America
94 93 92 91 90   5 4 3 2 1

For Theo

Contents

Preface

North Carolina has a reputation as a progressive state. This is true, within limits. The most powerful political forces in North Carolina today represent two economic elites with differing interests. One group, the modernizers, consists of bankers, developers, retail merchants, the news media, and other representatives of the business community who expect to benefit from change and growth. The second group, the traditionalists, includes traditional industrialists (in textiles, furniture, and apparel), tobacco farmers, and others associated with the state's agricultural economy who feel threatened by change and growth. Each group, modernizers and traditionalists, is linked with politicians who represent their interests.

Any progress felt by middle- and low-income North Carolinians has tended to trickle down from actions that modernizers have taken in pursuing their own interests. The political scene has changed substantially since World War II, primarily with respect to the major roles that blacks and Republicans now play compared to four decades ago. Nevertheless, North Carolina remains what V. O. Key called it in his classic book, *Southern Politics* (1949), a "progressive plutocracy." This is the reality of Tar Heel politics.

Two myths stand out about North Carolina politics. The first affords to modernizers a status of "would-be liberalism." That is to say, a Terry Sanford or a Jim Hunt would take more liberal stands, especially on tax reform, education, and public transportation, if only the Tar Heel electorate would allow it. According to this myth, a more egalitarian public policy to assist the less affluent majority is stymied by conservative voters. The reality is that Sanford and Hunt are modernizers, who shape and reflect the dominant ideology of today's North Carolina Democrats. Democrats like Sanford and Hunt have deliberately chosen the moderate-to-conservative, trickle-down path that for the most part is followed year-in and year-out by their fellow Democrats in the General Assembly.

The second myth, with two variations, concerns Jesse Helms. The National Congressional Club version of this myth characterizes "Uncle Jesse" as the defender of a down-home traditionalism that represents the views of most Tar Heels. This traditionalism would have men at the head of the household, mandatory Christian prayer in the public schools, and abortion prohibited by amendment to the U.S. Constitution. According to the Congressional Club, the systematic bias of North Carolina's news media, especially the major dailies, forces Helms and his associates to spend millions of dollars on television advertising at election time in order to set the record straight. North Carolina Democrats hold to a second, conflicting variation on the Helms myth. To Democratic leaders, the state's electorate, while conservative, is not as right-wing as Helms is, and Helms wins elections only because he manipulates the voters with his incessant thirty-second TV spots for months before Election Day.

In fact, Helms's traditionalist ideology is not shared by most Tar Heels. But the Democrats are wrong to perpetuate the myth that Helms has to hoodwink the people to win. He has, after all, been elected three times to the U.S. Senate. The reality is that a clear majority of white voters agrees with at least some of his antichange, traditionalist thinking. Many fundamentalist Protestants vote for Helms because they agree with him about abortion, while many corporate executives support him because he opposes increased government regulation of their businesses. Just as Terry Sanford and Jim Hunt have consciously decided to be modernizers, Jesse Helms is a traditionalist by choice.

I moved to North Carolina in 1975 from Mississippi. Before that, I lived in the Middle East (Ankara and Istanbul, Turkey), West Germany (Cologne and Frankfurt), and New York City. I spent my childhood in Chicago, Detroit, and St. Louis. For me, southern politics, and especially Tar Heel politics, is more engaging than political life in any of the other cities and countries I have known. In North Carolina, I enjoy the interplay of small-town cultural conservatism and the more urbane culture of midsize cities, the beauty of the mountains and the coast, and the friendliness of the people. The struggle of North Carolina blacks and Tar Heel Republicans to gain powerful positions in a state once controlled by white Democrats is both important and fascinating.

I began studying North Carolina politics in 1976, and over the years have published numerous articles on the subject in sociology journals, newspapers, and magazines. Specialists in political sociology, the branch of sociology where I concentrate my energies, are more often than the average sociologist in tune with the stuff of everyday politics.

But while most political sociologists are not themselves active in politics, I thrive on it. The mix of scholarly analysis and practical political involvement has been the driving force behind this book. Throughout my years in North Carolina, I have been active in organized efforts to gain increased political power for the state's less affluent majority. While I doubt that this vision of citizen empowerment will ever be fully realized, I believe it is a worthy goal.

Numerous graduate students in the Department of Sociology at the University of North Carolina at Greensboro (UNCG), where I have been a faculty member since 1976, have provided research assistance for this book. In particular, I thank Ken Shelton, who, with unflagging persistence, tracked down some hard-to-get information during 1987–88, as I struggled to finish the first draft. I also thank UNCG for providing several small Research Council awards and for granting me leave with half-pay during the 1986–87 academic year, when I completed my research and began writing this work.

Many friends, in this state and in Maryland, Wisconsin, and Ohio, read sections of the manuscript. I am especially grateful to three friends and fellow social scientists, not only for reading various chapters at important times, but also for encouraging me to keep going at low points: Mark Hellman in Durham (with whom I attended Valparaiso University in Indiana in the mid-1960s as well as countless political meetings in the 1970s and 1980s); Bill Woodward in Chapel Hill; and Bill Markham, my colleague in the Department of Sociology at UNCG.

Most of all, I want to thank my son Theo, now a fourth-grader at E. K. Powe public school in Durham, for being such a loving child and for tolerating his Dad's penchant for numerous phone calls and political meetings. Theo probably knows more about Tar Heel Democrats and Republicans than most North Carolinians twice his age—in part, because he has watched me "breathe and eat" politics for as long as he can remember. As Theo can attest, my morning ritual is incomplete without a big dose of local and state politics from the *Durham Morning Herald* and the *News and Observer* to go along with a cup of good coffee. This book is for Theo.

Durham, North Carolina
January 16, 1989

Tar Heel Politics

1

The Heritage of the Democratic Party Elite

North Carolina has long been considered a progressive southern state. Although the term is often ambiguous, the general notion of "progressivism" conveys an image of North Carolina as more committed than other southern states to economic and racial change. In fact, the closer North Carolina has been studied in recent years, the more researchers have come to question the label (Beyle and Black 1975; Bass and DeVries 1976; Ferguson 1981).

In the first half of the twentieth century, however, North Carolina Democrats led the South in their commitment to public school and university education, a state highway network, and industrialization. The dominant interpretation of actions taken by Democratic governors and legislators to achieve such ends is positive (cf. Lefler and Newsome [1973] for a conventional view). Two aspects of this positive interpretation are significant. The first, which few dispute, is that North Carolina's development of an activist state government was unusual for the South. Thus, its reputation among the southern states as relatively more committed to political and economic change seems secure.

The second aspect of North Carolina's favorable image is more controversial. It hinges on the content of the Democrats' programs. In the dominant view, these state investments were positive because they made industrialization possible. Expressed vaguely in history books and in the speeches of successful Tar Heel politicians, progressivism created an environment in the early decades of the twentieth century that enabled North Carolina's manufacturing economy to become the largest in the South.

An alternate view is more critical of progressivism in the early twentieth century. It does not assume that government activism is in itself positive. Rather, it asks: who benefited from the state investments? It focuses on the close ties between industrialists and the Democratic party leadership. It notices the relative powerlessness of workers and the absolute exclusion of blacks from political life. The alternate view, then, suggests that "progressivism" can be a misleading term; it masks the fact that the state's power holders, even as they invested in educational and transportation improvements, were serving the interests of a narrow economic elite (Finger 1981, 12–13).

Political scientist V. O. Key (1949) subscribed to the alternate view of North Carolina's political economy. Although he praised the state's moderate race relations, he emphasized that North Carolina's economic progressivism was in fact conservatism, not liberalism. He characterized the state as a "progressive plutocracy" whose power was subtle but complete:

> Industrialization has created a financial and business elite whose influence prevails in the state's political and economic life. An aggressive aristocracy of manufacturing and banking, centered around Greensboro, Winston-Salem, Charlotte and Durham, has had a tremendous stake in state policy and has not been remiss in protecting and advancing what it visualizes as its interests. Consequently a sympathetic respect for the problems of corporate capital and of large employers permeates the state's politics and government. For half a century an economic oligarchy has held sway (p. 211).

This book adopts Key's definition of progressivism. According to Key, a North Carolina progressive is committed to economic change and believes that corporate leaders should control this change in order to benefit the state's business community. The public prospers when business does (Key 1949, 214–15). As background to this book's analysis of contemporary Tar Heel politics, this chapter examines briefly some major political events in North Carolina from the late nineteenth century to the mid-twentieth century. Two points are central. First, North Carolina's moderate reputation in race relations during the early twentieth century ignores the white leadership's harsh repression of black political participation just before 1900. Second, the Tar Heel interest in industrialization says nothing about the economic and political conditions faced by the growing numbers of factory workers. The reality is that business control of laborers went hand in hand with political control of black protest.

Industrialization as Progress and the Crisis in Agriculture

North Carolina's industrialization in the late 1800s was mostly in cotton textiles. It took place primarily in the state's central region, from Durham in the east to Shelby, west of Charlotte, in the western Piedmont. The raw material was nearby in the cotton-growing counties, mainly in the east (Lefler and Newsome 1973). In these early years, North Carolina's affluent citizenry underwrote the cost of mill start-up (Sitterson 1957). Indeed, sociologist Dwight Billings (1979) has concluded that direct continuity existed between the large landowners of the pre–Civil War period and the textile capitalists of the later nineteenth century. Workers, virtually all of them white, abandoned farming to search for higher income in the factory (J. Hall 1987). The mill relied more on child and women's labor than men's. In part because such a labor structure was cheap, mills in the years before 1900 were highly profitable (Lefler and Newsome 1973, 508–9, 514–15; Durden 1984, 313–14). A major feature of mill life for workers was the mill village, a closed community where housing, food, and religion were available but political conflict was taboo (Pope 1942).

The mill village, which survived in many North Carolina towns until after World War II, was the cornerstone of textile paternalism. Uncle Ben on the hill took care of "his" workers in the mill (Roy 1975). Such a closed social system had clear significance for labor relations in the mill. Workers who came to view their life in the village as family were far less likely to protest about working conditions at the factory (Pope 1942). Those who did protest found it difficult to win majority support from fellow employees. Preachers at mill churches often castigated union organizers as heathen. The religious message, primarily fundamentalist Protestantism, stressed the importance of other-worldly salvation rather than collective action in this world. In short, emphasis was placed on individual responsibility and obedience (Earle, Knudsen, and Shriver 1976; Pope 1942; Durden 1984, 314).

The development of labor control through the mill village structure patently benefited textile employers at the workplace. Workers taught from early on to obey their mill supervisors seldom engaged in political protest activities. At the mass level, then, the industrialization of North Carolina resulted in a disciplined labor force not initially inclined toward unionization. Yet desperate economic times would later change this pattern.

North Carolina's tobacco industry boomed in the years after the Civil

War. R. J. Reynolds started his company in Winston while Washington Duke became the most successful tobacco entrepreneur in Durham. Both cities were built on tobacco prosperity. Increasingly, farmers in the western and eastern Piedmont as well as on the Coastal Plain began growing bright leaf tobacco to meet the demands of the tobacco manufacturers. But tobacco manufacturing never employed as many Tar Heels as did the textile industry (Durden 1984, 311–13).

Despite the great publicity that accompanied industrialization, most North Carolinians in the closing decades of the nineteenth century remained on the land. For them, economic conditions were dismal. Forty percent of white farmers, and a majority of black farmers, did not own their own land. Under the crop-lien system, they were continually in debt to the merchants who provided credit. In the late 1880s, an economic populist group, the Farmers' Alliance, began organizing in North Carolina and spread "like wildfire across a parched and wind-swept forest" (Durden 1984, 316). By 1890, the alliance had more than 2,100 local chapters and 90,000 members statewide. Although alliance members focused their anger primarily on the national economic program of the Republicans, they also criticized the policies of the state Democratic party.

The Democrats, in close alignment with the growing business class, saw no need to respond to the farmers' protests. The Farmers' Alliance opposed the Democrats' disproportionate reliance on the taxation of farmland, their neglect of public education, and their use of ballot fraud and violence to maintain political power. Most of all, Democrats relied on white racism to keep Republicans from winning elections. The unwillingness of Democrats to undertake political reform in the 1890s provided the potential for a political alternative (Durden 1984, 316). This alternative joined the Populist and Republican parties in a coalition against the Democrats.

The Populist-Republican alliance, which became known as "fusion," depended on black participation in politics. Although white Populists and Republicans recognized that this gave the Democrats a continuing issue of "negro rule" (Crow 1984, 340), only the combined totals of blacks and whites interested in political and economic reform could oust the Democratic party. In 1894, the fusion forces won two-thirds of the seats in the General Assembly. They passed a wide-ranging election law that limited Democratic fraud and allowed illiterates to participate by having colored ballots for each political party; returned home rule, which had been restricted by Democrats, to the counties; increased funds for public education; and limited interest rates (Crow 1984, 338). In 1896, fusionists won a similar majority in the General Assembly and elected a reform-minded Republican governor. Blacks held eleven seats in the General Assembly, their largest total in more than a decade.

The fusion forces foundered, however, on an issue that would permeate North Carolina politics a century later. How much should the General Assembly control business? Was the public interest better served by regulating and taxing business, or by giving business a relatively free hand? The new Republican governor, Daniel Russell, proposed an economic program to help farmers and small-business people who were hurt by the high freight rates of the railroads. This was in response to a ninety-nine-year lease that the Democratic governor in 1895 had granted to J. P. Morgan's Southern Railway. The lease, which today's Tar Heel politicians must renegotiate with the Norfolk Southern by 1994, gave the Southern Railway control over track from Gastonia northbound to Danville, Virginia, and from Greensboro eastward to Morehead City.

Although farmers and small-business people favored Governor Russell's antirailroad stance, most Republicans objected to the antibusiness tone of their governor, and the 1897 session resulted in a standoff between Populists and some Republicans versus the probusiness stance of the Democrats and most Republicans. As a result, Russell joined Populist leader and U.S. Senator Marion Butler in proposing a strong program of economic reform in the 1898 election: nullification of the ninety-nine-year lease, increased taxation on railroad property, and stricter state regulation of rail rates (Crow 1984, 340).

The Democrats countered the Populist economic program with a violent white supremacy campaign. This campaign was led by Furnifold Simmons, who would subsequently dominate the North Carolina Democratic party for three decades while serving in the U.S. Senate. Simmons and other Democrats organized White Government Unions and established paramilitary units known as Red Shirts and Rough Riders. The Red Shirts and Rough Riders harassed Populists, Republicans, and especially blacks. Historian Jeffrey Crow summarized the Democrats' 1898 campaign this way: "Armed men broke up fusionist political rallies, disrupted black church meetings, whipped outspoken blacks, and drove black voters from the polls. Simmons enlisted the financial support of business people and manufacturers in the state by promising not to raise taxes. But the cry of 'negro rule' led by Josephus Daniels's (Raleigh) *News and Observer* overwhelmed any public discussion of the economic issues involved in the campaign" (Crow 1984, 340).

The worst violence took place in Wilmington, where black and white Republicans controlled local government and a black-owned newspaper, the *Wilmington Record*, was published. Democratic leaders in Wilmington secretly trained Red Shirts in the months before the November election. The antiblack sentiment was so strong that Governor Russell was persuaded to withdraw the local fusion ticket for the General Assembly. Nevertheless, the violence continued. Two days after the election, the Democrats began the so-called Wilmington Race Riot. The *Record*'s offices were burned, black and white Republicans were dragged to the train station and sent out of town, and the local Republican government was forced to resign. Democratic replacements were sworn in on the spot (Crow 1984, 341). Only days after the election, the *News and Observer* commented that "Negro rule is at end in North Carolina forever. The events . . . at Wilmington and elsewhere place that fact beyond all question" (Lefler and Newsome 1973, 559).

Halting Economic Reform and Institutionalizing White Racism

The Democrats successfully used the race issue to regain a majority in the General Assembly in 1898 (Lefler and Newsome 1973, 559). Beginning in the 1899 session of the General Assembly, they repealed the election reform laws of the fusionists. This ensured the demise of the Populists' economic reform program because, under the new restrictions, the poor biracial majority could not win many elections. Virtually all blacks and many whites were disfranchised by a new election law together with a restrictive suffrage amendment that instituted a poll tax and a literacy test for all voters. The amendment included a grandfather clause allowing illiterates to vote only if their grandfathers had voted before 1867. Since blacks did not have the vote in 1867, the grandfather clause permitted illiterate whites but not blacks to register. With passage of the suffrage amendment, the Democrats institutionalized for decades by law what the Red Shirts had achieved by violence in 1898: the denial of political rights to black Tar Heels (Parramore 1983, 86–92; Crow 1984, 341).

Business interests were also pleased. Their goal of industrialization could now proceed with little danger that economic reformers would attempt to restrict their activities. The Populist movement, which had begun as the nonelectoral Farmers' Alliance in the 1880s and achieved some goals through electoral fusion in the 1890s, was politically dead by the turn of the century. The coalition of business people and Democrats, shaken by the Populist challenge, used white supremacy to regain power. Black political participation would be an undebated issue in North Carolina politics for the next fifty years.

Charles B. Aycock: The "Education Governor"

The Democrats realized the Populist party had selected issues that mattered to the state's farmer majority—for example, public education and health. On his election in 1900, which coincided with the election of another Democratic majority in the General Assembly and ratification of the suffrage amendment, Charles Aycock sought greater education spending in North Carolina. Although he openly acknowledged that superior resources should go to white schools, he nonetheless supported spending for black schools as well. Popular history in North Carolina remembers Aycock as the "Education Governor." Ironically, he could also be labeled the "Segregation Governor." Aycock was a prominent advocate of white supremacy both in the 1898 and 1900 elections. Social harmony necessitated that blacks be disfranchised, he argued. His education programs were supposed to eliminate illiteracy among whites so they could more easily register to vote (Lefler and Newsome 1973, 561). Thus, the education program, as presented by Aycock before the 1900 election, was intended to win support for the suffrage amendment. He did not propose that it help blacks regain the vote. Historian Helen Edmonds has argued that the Democrats promoted education in the 1900 campaign only because illiterate whites threatened to vote against the disfranchisement amendment. In short, were it not for their white supremacy goals, the Democrats might not have even promised educational improvements (Edmonds 1951).

The electoral changes achieved by the Democrats had a major effect on political participation by both races after 1900. Overwhelmingly, blacks were disfranchised. But poor whites who could not pay the poll tax also lost the vote. The number of eligible voters dropped after 1900, and, within this smaller group, only 50 percent voted in the 1904 gubernatorial election. This compared to 87 percent participation by eligible voters in 1896, when the biracial fusionist coalition elected Daniel Russell governor.

Historian Paul Escott has pointed out that the growing domination of the Democratic party after 1900 by corporate interests, coupled with the poll tax, drove poor and working-class whites from the voting booths. These representatives of the economic elite, who had funded the white supremacy campaigns at the turn of the century, restricted the state's political agenda to issues of benefit to them. Economic and political reform to empower the white majority was simply unthinkable. Accordingly, many of these whites lost interest in North Carolina politics (Escott 1985, 261). In Escott's view, the success of Democratic white supremacy shaped both economic and racial politics in North Carolina for many years:

> Elite Democrats did more than beat back the challenge of the Populists, disfranchise black people, and stigmatize cooperation between Tar Heels of both races. They imposed an undemocratic electoral system so complete and effective that all future political discourse had a restricted character. The new system excluded a large segment of the population from participation and thereby eliminated a broad spectrum of opinion. Subsequent generations learned their politics within a highly constricted, conservative frame of reference. In this way the events of the 1890s froze political thought and kept it from evolving for decades (p. 265).

Governor Aycock's education reforms are best viewed in this context. Corporate leaders joined Aycock in a "crusade" for public education. The crusade was successful. Never before in North Carolina had more monies been allocated for school construction. The school year was extended to a minimum of four months, and 800 high schools—650 for whites and 150 for blacks—were planned. But the various reasons behind this school expansion are significant. First, Democrats believed education improvements were necessary, at least initially, to overcome any anti-Democratic organizing among reform-minded whites. Having destroyed the Populists, the new education crusade represented a pragmatic effort by Democrats to claim the mantle of political reform. In fact, Aycock's education programs differed from the Populists' in that Aycock viewed business as the appropriate direct beneficiary of government policy. Literacy could trickle down to the masses, but they were not to share political power with the elite. The activist government under Aycock and future Democratic governors pledged progress for North Carolina. Nevertheless, this progress "tended to enhance the interests of the business community primarily and to reinforce the existing social, political and economic order." (Crow 1984, 342).

More Progressive Policy: The "Good Roads State"

The second major area in which Democrats involved state government prominently was highway construction and maintenance. It is another example, beyond education, of how government investment provided the infrastructure that enabled North Carolina to lead the South in industrialization during the early twentieth century.

Although the General Assembly did not make a major investment in roads until 1921, business began laying the groundwork for state support almost as soon as the automobile was available. In 1902, textile manufacturer Phillip Hanes became the first president of the North Carolina Good Roads Association. The association called for the establishment of a State Highway Commission and state maintenance of highways. Before state involvement, wealthier urban counties built roads by assessing a county road tax. But in 1910 more than 90 percent of North Carolina's "roads" were little more than mud tracks when it rained. In 1915, the General Assembly established a State Highway Commission to cooperate with counties in road construction (Lefler and Newsome 1973, 587–88).

As the number of automobiles rapidly increased, from 2,000 in 1910 to 150,000 in 1921, so did the political pressure of the Good Roads Association. Heavily lobbied, especially by association secretary Harriet Morehead Berry but also by Governor Cameron Morrison, the General Assembly gave the State Highway Commission responsibility for both highway construction and maintenance. North Carolina soon gained a national reputation as the "Good Roads State." The road building took place because of the state's willingness to finance a bond issue, to be paid for primarily with revenues from a new tax, the gasoline tax (Lefler and Newsome 1973, 587, 600).

Also in the early 1920s the General Assembly continued its commitment to public education. Most importantly, it increased the minimum school year from four months to six, and established standards for school certification and teacher salaries. The legislature also made large commitments to higher education, primarily to the state's major white campuses at Chapel Hill, Greensboro, and Raleigh (Lefler and Newsome 1973, 600–601).

Progressive Finance: Taxation in the 1920s and 1930s

By the second decade of the twentieth century, many North Carolinians realized that the length of the public school term could not be increased without an expanded source of state revenue. Like most other states at the time, North Carolina relied on a state property tax that required fair tax valuations at the local level. But counties had a self-interest in keeping valuations low in order to pay less to the state treasury (Liner 1979, 46).

In 1913 the General Assembly had proposed constitutional amendments to abolish the state property tax, assigning that tax to local government, and to limit state taxation to income, franchise, and inheritance taxes. Voters rejected these amendments in 1914, but, faced with the prospect of higher property taxes after a statewide revaluation in 1919–20, they strongly endorsed the amendments in 1920. Accordingly, the 1921 General Assembly established two new state-administered taxes, an individual and a corporate income tax. North Carolina became one of the first states to end its reliance on the property tax and establish an income tax instead (Liner 1979, 46). As part of the Good Roads program, it also imposed a one-penny-per-gallon gasoline tax.

The Democrats' decision to establish new state taxes, including a corporate income tax, underscored the leadership's commitment to progressive ideology. Business could not prosper if state government was unable to provide services, so new tax revenues had to be found. It is a hallmark of future-oriented business people that they are willing to pay taxes as a last resort in order to fund government programs, although they would prefer that legislators keep business taxes at a minimum.

By the early 1920s, then, state government services included support for both public education and highways. In the interest of efficiency, the Good Roads program of 1921 assumed total responsibility for inter-town road building. Schools, however, still depended on local as well as state taxation. To avoid raising property taxes, many local governments issued bonds to pay for services. This led to high bond indebtedness on the part of many Tar Heel counties and cities. In 1928 the state ranked second in the nation, after New York, in total bond debt, four and one-half times the national average. When the impact of the Great Depression hit in the early 1930s, North Carolina faced a major fiscal crisis (Liner 1979, 48).

Once again, an energetic governor seized the initiative. O. Max Gardner, a textile industrialist, had been elected in 1928. Independent of the financial problems caused by the depression, Gardner believed in efficiency based on centralization (Stoesen 1984, 383). Perhaps because of his strong beliefs, no other state during the depression "transformed its system of governmental finances as radically as North Carolina" (Liner 1979, 47).

Following recommendations of a report that Governor Gardner had commissioned in 1930 from the Brookings Institution, both state and local governments became more centralized. The 1931 General Assembly assumed control of county roads, prisons, and the public schools. At this time, no state except Delaware was totally responsible for public schools, and no state took responsibility for all road construction and maintenance (Liner 1979, 47). The legislature also established a Local Government Commission to supervise local finances and especially to restrict bond indebtedness (Stoesen 1984, 383).

The consolidation of state government took the pressure off the local property tax, which had become especially burdensome for farmers during the depression (Key 1949, 211). But the 1931 General Assembly deadlocked over how to raise additional state revenues. Gardner sided with the farmers, who opposed the sales tax and favored a luxury tax (Lefler and Newsome 1973, 608). The General Assembly enacted neither tax in 1931, and instead passed temporary taxes as well as budget reductions.

The legislature faced another fiscal crisis in 1933. The newly elected governor, J. C. B. Ehringhaus, was handpicked by Gardner (Key 1949, 213). In 1932 he had campaigned against both the sales and luxury taxes. But once in office, Ehringhaus concluded that, given the state's financial problems, the sales tax was the only option. Otherwise, North Carolina would be required to continue borrowing over the short term to meet its long-term obligations (Ehringhaus 1934). Further, the new revenues would allow the General Assembly to finance extension of the mandatory school term to eight months instead of six.

Ehringhaus justified the sales tax as if taxes on business or the wealthy were not possible: "If it is a choice between a sales tax on one hand and a decent school on the other, I stand for the school" (quoted in Lefler and Newsome 1973, 613). But in fact, Ehringhaus and a majority of the General Assembly were ignoring the recommendations of the state Tax Commission, which had been established by the legislature in 1927 to "digest all available data on taxation" and submit policy proposals (Lefler and Newsome 1973, 604). The Tax Commission opposed the sales tax as "unsound, unfair, and unwise." Instead, it recommended budget cutbacks and a 20 percent increase in income, franchise, and license taxes. These tax increases would have burdened business and primarily the wealthy (few Tar Heels earned more than the $4,000 in taxable income, which triggered the income tax; the governor's salary, for example, was $6,390 in 1933) (Lefler and Newsome 1973, 612; Liner 1981, 34). The increases also would have permitted the repeal of a temporary statewide property tax that had been passed to keep public schools open.

The insurance and tobacco industries led the campaign against the Tax Commission plan. Insurance companies insisted that North Carolina's insurance taxes were already the nation's highest, and tobacco lobbyists, speaking for all industry, noted that corporations already paid 57 percent of all Tar Heel income taxes. Merchants as well as the *News and Observer* spoke out against the sales tax. The Merchants' Association called it "the last resort of despotism" and brought anti-sales tax petitions to the General Assembly, while editor Josephus Daniels campaigned for a luxury tax. In the end, the insurance-tobacco-Ehringhaus position prevailed. The General Assembly accepted the Tax Commission's recommendation to end the statewide property tax, but rejected the idea of replacing the revenue with taxes on business or the wealthy. Instead, it passed a 3 percent sales tax (Lefler and Newsome 1973, 612–13; Liner 1981, 33).

In retrospect, the outcome of the 1933 tax debate is remarkable because it set a pattern that Democratic politicians would often follow throughout the remainder of the twentieth century. In effect, business persuades the Democratic majority that it cannot afford to pay any more taxes. The sales tax is a lucrative alternative. The lower-income majority, which pays a higher percentage of its income in sales taxes because it spends a higher proportion of its income on necessities, lacks the political organization and clout of corporate lobbies. Democrats who want to modernize North Carolina are known for their willingness to tax in order to provide necessary services like schools and highways. Significantly, as in Ehringhaus's justification, Tar Heel Democrats will usually argue that the end—adequate schools—justifies the means—a regressive tax. This happened when Terry Sanford, as governor in 1961, advocated reimposing the 3 percent sales tax on groceries (groceries had been exempted in 1941) to improve public education, especially community colleges. It also occurred in the 1980s when Democrats raised the local option sales tax from one cent to two cents, tying both half-cent increases to specific local government investments to aid school and sewer construction.

The tax structure established in 1931 and 1933 still serves as the basis for state finance. Indeed, the 6 percent flat rate of the corporate income tax did not change until 1987, when it was raised to 7 percent. The 7 percent top rate in the individual income tax, established in 1937 for net income above $10,000, has never changed, even though inflation has fundamentally changed the meaning of $10,000. The 3 percent state sales tax has remained the same, but all one hundred counties also collect a local 2 percent sales tax. Over time, however, businesses' share of state taxes dropped dramatically. Between 1935 and 1978, for example, the total taxes business paid into the North Carolina General Fund dropped from 60 percent to 20 percent, primarily because the individual income tax had grown much faster than the corporate income tax (Liner 1982, 40–41; see also Chapter 3). In effect, a once progressive individual income tax had become much less so a half century after its initial implementation.

Democrats and Unions: From 1900 to the Great Depression

Another component of the Democratic heritage is its antagonism toward organized labor. In fact, the state already enjoyed a reputation as antiunion in the early twentieth century. Not surprisingly, most Democrats, closely aligned with big business, were openly opposed to unions. The key contribution of Democratic governors was to mobilize the National Guard in order to break workers' strikes.

Beginning around 1900, the American Federation of Labor (AFL) tried but failed to organize textile workers in Gibsonville, Durham, Raleigh, and Fayetteville. Labor's losses had a sobering effect. Although skilled workers succeeded in establishing unions in a few dozen places around the state, both the AFL and its textile affiliate, the United Textile Workers (UTW), largely gave up on North Carolina until the national labor unrest immediately following World War I. The reason was not lack of interest by workers, but rather the virulent opposition of mill owners. When the UTW conducted a South-wide organizing campaign from 1913 to 1918, it specifically exempted North Carolina because of "strong anti-union sentiment" (Lefler and Newsome 1973, 584).

The actions of three governors between 1921 and 1934 (Morrison, Gardner, and Ehringhaus) illustrate the pattern of elite antiunionism. These governors, directly or indirectly tied to industrialists in the cities and small towns of the western Piedmont, believed unions interfered with progress. The ideology of progressive North Carolina excluded labor organization just as it opposed black political participation.

The position of a fourth governor, Thomas Bickett, who was elected in 1916 from agrarian eastern North Carolina, constituted an exception that proved the rule of antiunionism. In 1919 Bickett refused to take sides during bitter confrontations between workers and mill owners in and around Charlotte, and pressured the dismayed mill owners to reach a settlement (J. Hall 1987, 188–89).

When Cameron Morrison, the "Good Roads Governor," was elected in 1920, industrialists had a friend in Raleigh. Morrison was linked professionally and through family ties to the Piedmont business elite. Further, he had begun his political career as a Red Shirt, harassing blacks in the eastern Piedmont counties near Rockingham just before 1900 (J. Hall 1987, 194; Abrams 1978, 426). In 1921, striking union members in Charlotte and Concord asked Governor Morrison to mediate their dispute with management, but he refused to meet with them. Shortly afterward, at the request of Cannon Mills owner Charles Cannon, he called out the National Guard. When the Guard allowed strikebreakers to enter the mills, the strikes were broken (J. Hall 1987, 194).

Max Gardner's term as governor from 1929 to 1933 was punctuated by strikes both before and after the depression began. Gardner was generally considered to be more progressive than Morrison, who had defeated Gardner in the 1920 gubernatorial primary. But Gardner, himself an industrialist, consistently sided with the mill owners. In 1929 he sent the National Guard to Gastonia, where a Communist-influenced union was organizing a strike, as well as to Marion, where the anti-Communist UTW was involved. Both strikes were broken (J. Hall 1987, 215).

During the depression, mill owners' plans to cut back wages often met with resistance from workers. The strikes were usually spontaneous and received little assistance from national unions like the UTW. Cone Mill workers in Greensboro in 1931 appealed to Gardner to intervene in their dispute, but he refused. In 1932, strikes in textile and furniture factories in the High Point area were so serious that a local newspaper editor and state legislator asked the governor to mediate. Under those circumstances, Gardner did oversee a labor-management settlement. In the same year, again recognizing serious conflict during a textile strike in Rockingham, Gardner was willing to intervene, but backed off when local mill owners refused to negotiate (Bell 1982, 31–39).

Two years later, Governor Ehringhaus responded to the General Strike that took place across North Carolina, primarily in textile mills, by mobilizing 14,000 National Guardsmen. Some mill owners, grateful for the troops, drew a parallel between worker rebellion in 1934 and black political participation before 1900. (J. Hall 1987, 332–34). In the eyes of business, blacks and unionized workers were equally illegitimate political actors.

North Carolina workers in the first third of the twentieth century could win labor-management battles only if a neutral governor were willing to pressure recalcitrant industrialists into negotiating with unions. This rarely happened. More commonly, when the governors sided with the owners, the owners could wait out the strike since the strikers ultimately faced starvation. While the strike went on, the National Guard's presence allowed management to try to resume production with strikebreakers.

In the half century following the 1934 General Strike, the National Guard would intervene in a major labor dispute just one more time. In 1958 Governor Luther Hodges, himself a former executive of Fieldcrest Mills, sent Guardsmen to Henderson during a strike at Harriet-Henderson Yarns, the effect of which was to help strikebreakers cross the picket line. As in the case of Governors Morrison and Ehringhaus before him, Hodges's loyalties to industrialists spelled doom for the local union.

W. Kerr Scott: Progressivism in the Post–World War II Era

Max Gardner became a dominant force in the Democratic party after his election as governor in 1928. His political organization, dubbed the "Shelby Dynasty" after his hometown located west of Charlotte, controlled the governor's office for two decades. But in 1948, Kerr Scott defeated the Dynasty's candidate by advocating greater concern for the state's farm population. Governor Scott's "Go Forward" program included a $200 million bond issue for secondary road construction, a huge amount for that time. Scott also promoted measures to improve schools, public health, and rural electrification (Lefler and Newsome 1973, 627). His administration expanded the Democratic party's progressive ideology to include neglected areas of society. Identifying social needs, the General Assembly appropriated the funds, through bond issues and direct expenditures, to allow state government to assume additional responsibilities.

Two other events marked the Scott administration. First, a young Fayetteville lawyer named Terry Sanford got his start in politics working for Scott. Second, in 1949 the governor appointed North Carolina's leading liberal, University of North Carolina President Frank Graham, to a vacancy in the U.S. Senate.

Frank Graham's Defeat: The Limits of Progressivism

At the time of his Senate appointment, Frank Graham had been president of the University of North Carolina for nineteen years. Scott and other political observers were convinced that Graham, as the "best-known and best-loved man in North Carolina" (Ashby 1980, 257), would win the special election scheduled for 1950. But they failed to consider the political realities: Graham was a genuine economic and racial liberal in a state whose elite generally tolerated neither.

In the 1920s Graham had supported collective bargaining for workers, and in the 1930s he had advocated both the Social Security system and federal aid to education (Ashby 1980, chap. 11). Further, Graham played a prominent role in the few interracial conferences that took place in the South. Although he opposed mandatory federal civil rights legislation, he did not hide his distaste for racial segregation (Ashby 1980, chap. 12). Conservatives at both the national and state levels continually accused Graham of being "soft on Communism." Even some of his allies, such as U.S. Senator Clyde Hoey, a former governor of North Carolina, conceded on the Senate floor that Graham had been "careless in association with certain organizations" (Ashby 1980, 245).

Graham was thus vulnerable to the charge that his commitment to economic and racial reform was out of step with the beliefs of most North Carolinians. Willis Smith, a Raleigh lawyer serving at that time as president of the American Bar Association, became Graham's major opponent. Graham led in the first primary with 48 percent of the vote; Smith received 42 percent, while two minor candidates shared the remaining 10 percent.

Smith almost declined to call for a runoff, but changed his mind after supporters converged on his front lawn just before the deadline. One of the rally organizers was a young man from Raleigh named Jesse Helms. Smith's supporters had used plenty of dirty tricks in the first primary. Among them was a fraudulent postcard mailed to whites in every part of the state. Allegedly from the "National Society [sic] for the Advancement of Colored People," it thanked "Dr. Frank" for all he had done "to advance the place of the Negro in North Carolina." Smith supporters produced leaflets and ads that declared Graham a Communist sympathizer because of some of his associations over the years (Ashby 1980, 262, 268).

Smith's campaign benefited from a U.S. Supreme Court decision that was handed down between the May and June primaries. In *Sweatt v. Painter*, the Court ruled that the state of Texas had to admit a black student to the previously all-white University of Texas law school. For segregationist Smith backers, the Court's decision symbolized the danger of Graham's racial views (Ashby 1980, 262).

Although Smith took the high road in criticizing Graham, leaving the dirty work to campaign staff, his comments paralleled the campaign slurs. On the stump, he asserted that Graham's election would mean desegregation. Between the first and second primaries, the Smith campaign attacks on Graham became virulent. Reminiscent of the Democratic rhetoric of 1898, one newspaper ad listed the first primary results in selected black precincts around the state and asked, "Are we going to throw away the work and accomplishment of all those patriotic men who freed our state from Negro domination?" Another declared, "White People WAKE UP Before It Is Too Late. . . . Do you want Negroes working beside you, your wife, and your daughters in your mills and factories? . . . Frank Graham favors mingling of the races" (Ashby 1980, 265).

The racial theme succeeded in reversing the results of the first primary. Especially in eastern North Carolina where few blacks voted but where they comprised more than one-third of the population, Graham lost counties that he had won in the first election. But Graham also lost to Smith in the affluent precincts of the urban Piedmont. In short, parallel to 1898 and 1900, a white elite successfully mobilized white voters to defeat an economic reformer. The Communist and race issues were used to thwart a candidacy sympathetic to both economic and racial equality.

For North Carolina progressives like Kerr Scott, who were not strongly opposed to gradual racial change, Graham's defeat was sobering. Smith's victory indicated that, for a majority of voting Tar Heels, racial and economic liberalism was too threatening, even in the person of "best-loved" Frank Graham.

The 1950 election also highlighted the emerging conflict for Tar Heel Democrats. North Carolina's moderate racial reputation had always been predicated on no serious challenge to the racial status quo. Graham's lifelong commitment to racial change made him an unacceptable symbol to many white Democrats. But to others, the party should be heading in that direction. More than any other issue, race would tear apart the party in the decades to come. During the 1950s and 1960s, racial segregation faced a growing challenge from blacks even as the other key aspect of progressivism—an activist, procorporate state government—encountered only occasional opposition from Tar Heels.

2

Competing Ideals in North Carolina Politics

Since the early 1970s, two ideologies have competed for dominance among Tar Heel politicians and members of the business community. The first, the modernizer ideal, emphasizes the importance of economic expansion for the state's future. Social changes that accompany economic growth, such as suburban sprawl, traffic congestion, or greater demands for day-care, are viewed as less worrisome than missing the opportunity for prosperity. The second ideology, the traditionalist ideal, is skeptical of further economic change given its potential for social disruption and economic competition. Modernizers believe that economic development can only benefit North Carolina, while traditionalists see merit in maintaining the status quo.

In North Carolina during the 1970s and 1980s, modernizers and traditionalists fought for control of government policy in order to implement their particular values. U.S. Senator Terry Sanford and former governor Jim Hunt on the one hand, and U.S. Senator Jesse Helms on the other, stood as prime promoters of modernizer and traditionalist ideology. Modernizers are usually Democrats. Helms, a onetime Democrat, is a Republican, and many rural or small-town Democrats are traditionalists. A third ideal, populism, has virtually no institutional support within North Carolina. However, it stands in marked contrast to traditionalism and modernism in contending that government policy should benefit directly the less affluent majority rather than large corporations and the wealthy.

Traditionalism

Traditionalist ideology is rooted in the culture of North Carolina's small towns and rural areas. Economically, traditionalism is associated

18

with agricultural production and historic industries like textiles and furniture. This relationship is not accidental. Traditionalism is not opposed to economic change, but changes that allow the established social relations to continue are preferable. Thus, cotton mills with their adjacent mill villages were desirable because they provided workers continuity with the small-scale rural community from which they had migrated (Pope 1942). In the 1980s, traditionalists believed that the arrival of high-tech industry to North Carolina was less than ideal for two reasons. First, the industry promised to bring large numbers of outsiders to North Carolina. Second, high technology would make it more difficult for existing low-wage industries such as textiles and furniture to prosper. Traditionalism holds that policymakers should have a primary commitment to corporations that have long invested in the state's economy; they should not spend state money trying to woo new national or multinational firms to North Carolina.

Traditionalism's ideal community is based on fundamentalist Protestantism, especially Baptist denominations, which permeates North Carolina. A deferential relationship should exist both between employer and employee and between husband and wife. Traditionalists consider labor unions and collective bargaining as disruptive of the workplace. Even though high percentages of North Carolina women are in the low-wage labor force, the ideology of patriarchy, not feminism, remains paramount. Ideally, for traditionalists, blacks would not challenge white authority. Gains of the civil rights movement have forced traditionalist ideology to tolerate racial desegregation. Yet affirmative action programs, for either blacks or women, are unacceptable.

The implications of social traditionalism for North Carolina politics are many. First, for either traditionalist elites or their mass followers, egalitarian social movements promoted by blacks, women, or labor organizers are anathema because they challenge the established order. Second, a political candidate who runs against specific manifestations of these movements—such as the Equal Rights Amendment (ERA) or a paid holiday honoring Dr. Martin Luther King—can be assured of a certain core support. Third, the strength of traditionalist deference among working-class whites in North Carolina (Botsch 1980) makes the campaigns of either populist politicians or of union organizers more difficult, because a certain percentage of the white population does not believe in challenging authority.

Traditionalist ideology is both antitax and anti–big government. Ideally, government should not seek an active role in economic development, but allow the free market to reign. As legislators, traditionalists normally vote against tax increases. Even though it is virtually impossible to say so publicly, traditionalists question privately whether more government spending for primary and secondary schools will solve economic problems. Ideologically, traditionalists hold that responsibility for learning lies more with the parents than with the state. Finally, the state does not need to regulate corporations or government agencies to protect the consumer. Such notions of consumer rights imply an economic conflict that traditionalists believe does not, or should not, exist (Black and Black 1987, chap. 2).

North Carolina traditionalists have promoted an antichange ideology in both economic and social policy. But because of North Carolina's legacy as an activist state, going back to Governor Charles B. Aycock's education spending program of 1901, traditionalists have enjoyed more political success in the General Assembly implementing their social views. In response to student activism during the early 1960s, primarily on the Chapel Hill campus of the University of North Carolina, traditionalists in 1963 imposed the Speaker Ban Law. This statute prohibited state-supported colleges from allowing as a campus speaker any Communist, any advocate of the overthrow of federal or state government, or anyone who had "pleaded the Fifth Amendment to the Constitution in refusing to answer any question with respect to Communist or subversive connections or activities." In 1968, a federal court declared the Speaker Ban unconstitutional (Lefler and Newsome 1973, 699–701). But traditionalist influence continued well into the late 1980s. Defeat of the ERA in six General Assembly sessions between 1973 and 1982 (cf. *Greensboro Record* 1977), strong antipornography legislation passed in 1985, and restrictive laws in many counties on liquor-by-the-drink or beer and wine sales all suggested the sustaining power of social traditionalism.

Modernism

Modernizer ideology values individual economic achievement, whether as an entrepreneurial or a corporate activity. By promoting growth, modernizers envision prosperity for all through an expanded economic pie (Elazar 1972; Cobb 1984). Unlike traditionalism, modernism places no special value on existing social relations. Indeed, economic change is presumed to alter the old social order, but modernizers do not assume that change means loss of economic or political control

(Luebke 1989). North Carolina modernizers continually seek to diversify the state's economy. In particular, in contrast to traditionalists, they are committed to reducing the state's dependency on low-wage industries like textiles or apparel (Goldman and Luebke 1985).

Modernizer ideology is more secular than traditionalism, and it is rooted in the major cities of the North Carolina Piedmont. People who relocate in the Tar Heel state, especially those in business, are far more likely to be modernizers than traditionalists. Modernizer politicians are usually North Carolina natives, often graduates of the University of North Carolina at Chapel Hill or North Carolina State University. The faith in public education is high, and the commitment to improve education is mandatory for a modernizer politician.

Like traditionalism, modernizer ideology has been shaped by affluent white males. Yet, unlike traditionalism, modernism does not reject demands from blacks, women, or unions out of hand. In the interests of social stability and economic gain, modernizers seek an accommodation with such groups. Significantly, modernizers are more sympathetic to social changes in race or gender relations than to economic changes advocated by unions. North Carolina modernizers are less threatened by the integration of a few blacks and white women into the modernizing elite than by the challenge they feel from workers' organizations (Goldman and Luebke 1985).

Black and women's issues constitute an important point of conflict between modernizers and traditionalists. The King holiday, the ERA, and abortion rights are three examples of controversy. Modernizers acknowledge the necessity of federally required affirmative action policies for blacks and women, even if they themselves would not initiate such policies. Modernizers do not wish to maintain the deferential social structure preferred by traditionalists. Their ideal society is dynamic and growing.

To fuel the "growth machine" (Molotch 1979), modernizers want an active state government. For existing businesses to expand or new national or international capital to invest in North Carolina, the state's infrastructure of schools, community colleges, universities, highways, airports, and sewer and water lines must also be expanding (Black and Black 1987). Consequently, modernizers believe in taxation. Even though traditionalists in principle are antitaxation, if a tax increase seems inevitable, the traditionalist will join the modernizer in preferring a regressive tax such as a sales tax. Both modernizer and traditionalist politicians have contributed in recent years to a shift in North

Carolina's tax burden away from business and toward lower-income consumers. Taxation policy provides an example of what the two ideologies share—in contrast to a third ideal, economic populism.

Neopopulism

A century ago, both in the South and across the Midwest, farmers organized against what they viewed as the monopolistic power of the large banks, railroads, and other economic forces (Goodwyn 1976). Although ultimately unsuccessful, populism challenged the dominant political-economic elite with the counterargument that the marketplace should not be unfairly controlled by a few large corporations. Government's job, according to populist ideology, was to ensure economic fairness for the "little guy" (Clotfelter and Hamilton 1972).

In North Carolina, the populist movement in the 1880s and 1890s was strong enough to elect a U.S. senator. Aligned with blacks in the Republican party, the Populist party challenged the power of the Democrats who constituted the establishment party. Indeed, Charles Aycock's turn-of-the-century education reforms were taken with an eye to eliminating political challenges from Populists and Republicans, and to reestablishing the hegemony of the Democrats.

"Neopopulism" is the term usually applied to contemporary populist ideology. Raised on occasion by politicians of the 1970s and 1980s, especially in the South and the Midwest, neopopulism argues that government remains improperly in the hands of the economic elite and their politician allies. The less affluent majority, whom Black and Black (1987) term the "have-nots" and the "have-littles," should elect politicians with an alternate redistributive vision. This alternative ideology advocates more direct government benefits to the majority and higher taxes on the affluent minority and large corporations. At the national level, the strongest advocates of economic populism during the 1980s were three Democrats: Iowa Senator Tom Harkin, a leader of the congressional populist caucus; Texas Agricultural Commissioner Jim Hightower; and presidential candidate Jesse Jackson.

Both traditionalism and modernism oppose neopopulism, because neopopulism challenges the dominant position of big business in the political system. The populist alternative has no established power base in North Carolina politics. But if neopopulism does not blossom in the Tar Heel state, neither does it altogether wither. In recent years, urban Democrats, especially from the statehouse, have challenged business selectively on finance companies' interest rates, insurance companies' attempts to limit their liability in civil cases ("tort reform"), and utilities' construction plans and rates. A variant on neopopulism, citizen-action ideology, gained a weak footing in the General Assembly during the late 1980s. Citizen-action ideology encompasses disparate visions of greater political equality for citizens along racial and gender as well as economic lines, and less power for the entrenched political and economic elite. Environmentalists, who ordinarily do not consider themselves populists, are often in conflict with corporations and fit under the rubric of citizen activism. Citizen-action ideology shares with neopopulism a desire for greater equity in politics, but does not always view the economic and political power of large corporations as the central issue.

It is tempting to view traditionalism and modernism as synonymous with conservatism and liberalism, but that is inaccurate for several reasons. First, although traditionalists can usually be termed conservatives, modernizers are not in fact liberals on either economic or social issues. Especially concerning taxation and ties to big business, modernizers are at best moderate-conservatives. Economic equity, a key element of liberalism closely associated with Democrats since Franklin Roosevelt's New Deal, is not important to modernizers. Modernizers are more sympathetic to racial and gender equality, particularly the former, than to economic equality. But on these social issues, a liberal would most likely initiate change. Tar Heel modernizers, by contrast, are open to change but are likely to undertake it only when pressured by blacks or feminist women.

In recent North Carolina history, four elections have accentuated the prominence of traditionalism and modernism. Jesse Helms's first election to the U.S. Senate in 1972 underscored the power of traditionalism, while Jim Hunt's victory in the 1976 gubernatorial race affirmed the appeals of modernism. Their bloody battle for Helms's Senate seat in 1984 exemplified the clash between traditionalism and modernism. Republican Jim Martin's election to the governor's office in the same year demonstrated the political appeal of a blend of traditionalist and modernizer ideologies.

The Traditionalist Politician: Jesse Helms

The year 1972 was an important watershed in North Carolina politics. Richard Nixon swept the state with 69 percent of the vote against

George McGovern. Significantly, for the first time in the twentieth century, voters elected a Republican governor and U.S. senator. Both statewide victors no doubt benefited from Nixon's coattails. But the winning Republican governor, Jim Holshouser, and senator, Jesse Helms, ran different campaigns, because they represented important differences in the style and substance of Tar Heel Republicanism. Holshouser, a lifelong "Mountain" Republican, typified those who had toiled for decades to build a two-party system (Stevenson 1975). His campaign emphasized the inefficiencies of one-party Democratic rule. Similar to the pattern increasingly common in the 1970s among Republican gubernatorial candidates across the South (Black and Black 1987), Holshouser argued that a future-oriented state needed a break from the political oligarchies of the past. He campaigned in vague terms as a modernizer against the alleged traditionalism of the Democratic party. In fact, his Democratic opponent, Hargrove ("Skipper") Bowles, was a modernizer. But Holshouser won anyway as a result of his particular strength among Democrats in urban counties. In emphasizing his willingness to modernize the state through both government efficiency and expenditures, Holshouser set a tone for what has become mainstream Republicanism in North Carolina. As in 1984, disunity reigned within the 1972 Democratic party because of divisive gubernatorial primaries. Many Democrats felt that Bowles, in winning the runoff primary against Lieutenant Governor Pat Taylor, had usurped the nomination from its rightful heir. Holshouser's successful appeal to Democrats in 1972 foreshadowed Jim Martin's victory in 1984.

In contrast to Holshouser, Jesse Helms had built his political base among whites in eastern North Carolina. Helms ran as a traditionalist. His message was above party lines. Indeed, he had remained a registered Democrat until 1970, even though he says he had never voted for a Democratic presidential nominee. But his campaign for the U.S. Senate seat received a big boost long before he filed in 1972 as a Republican candidate.

Helms had became a household word to North Carolinians during the 1960s when he served as the television editorialist for WRAL in Raleigh, eastern North Carolina's most powerful station. Besides appearing daily on a five-minute spot at 6:25 P.M., Helms was heard across the state on radio's Tobacco Network. At a time when egalitarian movements rooted in the nation's larger cities and college campuses were thriving, Helms affirmed the values of traditionalism. He provided North Carolinians with the vision of a society that should not change.

Helms sympathized with Alabama's Governor George Wallace, urged Richard Nixon during the 1968 presidential campaign to stand firm on law and order against "weak-kneed liberals" like his Democratic opponent, Senator Hubert Humphrey, and regularly condemned "pinkos," black militants, and "hippies" as threats to the American way of life. His charismatic style made him a hero in the eyes of thousands of white Tar Heels, who admired him for standing up for what was right against the advocates of what they saw as radical change.

It was much more than political hyperbole that led Helms to oppose liberal reform so strongly. Helms is the archetypal traditionalist, the quintessential foe both of modernizers like Jim Hunt and of more radical political critics. Like other traditionalists, Helms considered the egalitarian movements of the 1960s a fundamental challenge to his value system. He found anti–Vietnam War students, especially the activists at the University of North Carolina at Chapel Hill and at Duke University, particularly offensive. Such students would often watch his 6:25 P.M. broadcast as a bit of political humor. But Helms regarded his editorials as a serious effort to sustain his ideology. He sought to reassure his Tar Heel admirers that it was "the militants"—the liberals, radicals, Yankees, northeastern media, blacks, and, later, women's liberationists—who were off base (Nordhoff 1984, 27). In short, the simple message of the virtues of old-time religion and old-fashioned values struck a responsive chord with white North Carolinians who felt threatened by demands for racial equality in their hometowns as well as by calls for other far-reaching changes reported on the nightly national news.

In 1971 Helms's political confidante, Raleigh lawyer Tom Ellis, convinced him to consider running as a Republican in the upcoming U.S. Senate race; his condition was that Ellis find financial backers. Those business people willing to promote Helms were, not surprisingly, themselves traditionalists, skeptical that big government could do any good. His largest single supporter was Hugh Chatham, scion of a wool-blanket manufacturing family from Elkin and son of a former Democratic congressman, who loaned Helms $50,000. Chatham's ideological commitment to North Carolina Republicanism came at a time when the GOP had yet to elect a candidate to a statewide office in the twentieth century. Subsequently, especially by 1984, many business people from the low-wage textile, apparel, and furniture industries could optimistically support Republicans as an alternative to the Hunt administration's emphasis on higher-wage, high-tech economic development.

But in 1972 Chatham was a pioneer because Helms was hardly a front-runner. Most North Carolina business people at that time played it safe by supporting Democrats for both the U.S. Senate and state-level offices even while voting Republican for president. But Helms appealed to business on the basis of economic traditionalism. The unfettered free enterprise system needed to be protected from the liberals who sought to hamstring business with regulation. For Helms, liberalism was just a step away from socialism. Moreover, he strongly advocated a balanced federal budget. His traditionalist appeal to business avoided direct references to the social upheaval that had preoccupied him as an editorialist. Helms emphasized economic traditionalism's commitment to low taxes and limited government.

Social traditionalism provided Helms with a broader mass appeal. He promised to say no to busing and other liberal racial reforms. Although Helms in the past had defended segregation, his campaign messages used codes like "forced busing" that could not be easily tagged as racist. He opposed world communism as a moral threat to Christianity. Thus, his support of the Pentagon took on both patriotic and religious overtones (Helms 1976; Luebke 1983).

Helms had the good fortune to run against a modernizer Democrat, Nick Galifianakis, a Durham congressman who had upset the aging traditionalist Democrat, B. Everett Jordan, in the May 1972 primary. By North Carolina standards, Galifianakis's voting record was relatively liberal. Galifianakis symbolized the politics of the fast-growing metro Piedmont, while Jordan, from a tiny textile town near Burlington, represented rural values. Helms missed no opportunity to link Galifianakis to Democratic presidential candidate George McGovern, labeling him at times "McGovernGalifianakis" (Bartley and Graham 1975, 176). Further, he ran on the ethnocentric slogan, "he's one of us," suggesting that Galifianakis was not (Furgurson 1986, 100). Was it Galifianakis's Greek-American ethnicity, his non-Baptist religion, or his occasional questioning of Pentagon budget requests that made him an outsider? Helms also ran unabashedly on Nixon's coattails, mailing thousands of would-be supporters a postcard picturing Helms with "Nixon needs him" printed along the bottom. Finally, Helms promised that he would mince no words in the nation's capital; his outspokenness as a TV editorialist would continue on the Senate floor.

In winning comfortably over Galifianakis, 54 to 46 percent, Helms had built a coalition of social traditionalists, economic traditionalists, and straight-ticket Republicans. Once in Washington, D.C., he provided a strong voice for traditionalism. Indirectly but significantly, he also legitimated traditionalist politics at state and local levels within North Carolina.

The Modernizer Politician: Jim Hunt

In winning the governor's office at age thirty-nine, Jim Hunt was determined to be an enthusiastic progressive Democrat in the spirit of Charles Aycock, Kerr Scott, and Terry Sanford. For loyal Democrats, Hunt's victory was especially important because, after Republican Jim Holshouser's upset win in 1972, gubernatorial power was now restored to its proper owners. Hunt's election also represented a victory for modernism. Both economic development and racial change would be part of this new elite ideology.

Jim Hunt typified several strains of Democrat. His father, a populist-leaning New Dealer from Wilson County in eastern North Carolina, inculcated in him the idea of the FDR Democrats, portraying the party as the friend of poor farmers and workers. While somewhat mythological, of course, especially at the level of North Carolina politics, this vision of the party did propel Hunt into the political upper-mobility route followed by countless would-be governors: college Democrats, Young Democrats, and membership on the state executive committee. Such aspiring politicians became yellow-dog Democrats, ignoring ideological differences within the party and supporting the entire ticket even if Democratic candidates included, as the saying goes, a couple of "yellow dogs."

When Hunt was a college Democrat at North Carolina State University in the late 1950s, the party hardly represented national liberalism. First, Democrats still endorsed Jim Crow segregation. Second, they agreed with Tar Heel business that economic diversification was good for North Carolina, but labor unions should not be part of that change. In general, the Democratic party, although progressive in terms of economic change, in large part was dominated ideologically by racism and antiunionism.

The national turmoil of the 1960s, beginning with the civil rights movement and followed, with less impact on North Carolina, by the antiwar and women's equality movements, generated conflict within the state Democratic party where there had previously been little. The old North Carolina progressive ideology previously sustained by a set of traditional social values began splitting apart in the early 1960s. The most salient changes centered on noneconomic issues, primarily race relations. Beginning in 1960 with Terry Sanford's decision to tie his gubernatorial general election campaign to the presidential bid of John F. Kennedy, leading Tar Heel Democrats moved away from a century-long commitment to institutional racial inequality (Chafe 1981, 103). Sanford and Kennedy both carried North Carolina in November 1960, but by smaller margins than Democrats had achieved in statewide races four years earlier. By 1964, in a climate of racial turmoil, Richardson Preyer, Sanford's political ally and a Kennedy appointee to the federal bench, was unable to win the Democratic gubernatorial nomination against the combined forces of militant and moderate segregationists.

The cautious endorsement of federally induced racial change was the core position of a new social ideology within the Democratic party. Modernizer ideology rejected Jim Crow segregation as interfering with meritocratic attempts to change society. Modernizer Democrats argued in the late 1960s and 1970s that it was either futile, wrong, or both to try to prevent the demise of segregation (Chafe 1981). In a crucial linkage to economic development, modernizers came to see segregation as impeding the influx of capital that could reduce North Carolina's dependence on textiles and tobacco (Cobb 1984; Luebke 1989). Modernizers, then, differed from the progressives in their acceptance of changes in race relations. Modernism constituted an evolution of progressivism when it was no longer possible to graft economic development ideology upon status-quo social ideology. Modernizer Democrats, not surprisingly, lived disproportionately in the metro Piedmont, the cities of the Piedmont crescent ranging from Charlotte near the South Carolina border, through Winston-Salem and Greensboro in central North Carolina, to Chapel Hill, Durham, and Raleigh at the Piedmont's eastern edge.

When Jim Hunt decided in 1970, at thirty-three, to run for lieutenant governor, he was well-positioned ideologically to win. He was one of the youngest modernizer Democrats, who linked the state's future economic development to the gradual elimination of Jim Crow institutions. At the same time, he shared traditionalists' values regarding social issues other than race. For example, he personally opposed abortion and was a teetotaler. Hunt lacked a strong background in state government, but he made up for it by winning the backing of Bert Bennett, a master Democratic power broker. A college classmate of Terry Sanford at Chapel Hill, Bennett played the de facto role of campaign manager of Sanford's successful quest for the 1960 Democratic gubernatorial nomination. Bennett strongly espoused the Sanford-Kennedy link during the fall 1960 campaign. A well-to-do Winston-Salem businessman, he epitomized the urbane, elite orientation of the emerging modernizer Democratic ideology. With Bennett's help, Hunt established a coalition based on old-fashioned, county-by-county personal networks, and his 1972 campaign blurred ideological differences between traditionalism and modernism.

Modernizer Democrats stand an excellent chance to win Democratic primaries as long as too many of them do not divide the same political base. (Too many modernizers competed in the 1984 Democratic gubernatorial primary, which contributed to the party's disunity in the November 1984 election.) A model modernizer campaign is straightforward. First, from a base in the party center, the modernizer builds support networks around a commitment to an activist state government and economic progress. Especially critical here are business people, party loyalists, and state employees. Second, relying on a commitment to racial progress and related programs like improved educational funding, the modernizer seeks the votes of blacks and whites in the party's citizen-action wing. Third, as the modernizer and citizen-action bases solidify, the modernizer ventures into the traditionalist wing of the party with various appeals to old-fashioned values. A modernizer's goal is to capture the party center, limiting the appeal of candidates on the party's left and right wings.

In 1976, Jim Hunt followed this program religiously. He pledged to reestablish the Democratic party as a friend of business investment. In light of the embarrassing fact that North Carolina had fallen to fiftieth place in national industrial wage rankings, Hunt promised to seek new, higher-wage jobs from out of state. Central to Hunt's thinking was the notion of trickle-down, not redistributive economics. If business prospers, so will workers.

As Hunt expressed support for civil rights and the ERA, he argued pragmatically with blacks and whites to his left that no other candidate with a chance to win cared as much about their concerns. At the same time, he pitched his media campaign to traditionalist Democrats. In his most memorable TV spot of that year, Jim Hunt promised that he would lock up the criminals as the camera zeroed in on the slamming of a prison cell block door. In campaign appearances in rural North Carolina, he reminded voters that he was a teetotaler and did not support liquor-by-the-drink.

Hunt's modernizer campaign against three opponents, bolstered by his special appeals to both traditionalist whites and black and white citizen activists, worked. His 57 percent vote in the August 1976 primary made him the first Democrat in two decades to avoid a runoff by winning an absolute majority. In November, he defeated his Republican opponent by nearly two to one, while Jimmy Carter won the state with 56 percent over Gerald Ford.

During his first term, Hunt underscored the modernizer commitment to state investment, public-private partnership, and efficient government. One efficiency was his initiative to establish uniform sentencing for criminals. This had the added benefit of alleviating the traditionalists' concern that he might not be "tough enough" on that issue.

Hunt demonstrated his commitment to economic development in three interrelated ways. First, he convinced the General Assembly to place a $300 million transportation—read: highway construction—bond issue on the November ballot. Second, with much fanfare, Hunt beefed up the industrial recruitment division of the state Department of Commerce, with the mandate to raise North Carolina's average industrial wage by recruiting high-wage employers into the state. Third, he launched a legislative campaign to improve the quality of public school education by reducing classroom size and establishing minimum competency levels for graduating high school seniors.

Hunt's agenda also focused on gubernatorial succession. He argued, in the name of efficiency, that governors ought to be able to develop a leadership plan for several years without immediate lame-duck status, in contrast to legislators, who were not restricted to one term. Applying the succession amendment to himself meant that he and incumbent Lieutenant Governor Jimmy Green could run for reelection in 1980. Hunt also would have liked to establish a gubernatorial veto, but Democratic legislators agreed to only the former change (Beyle 1981). Voter approval of the succession amendment in November 1977 gave Jim Hunt, a young politician with national aspirations, more time to build a record of achievement as governor and develop a greater set of national political contacts.

Hunt's support within the business community came disproportionately from growth-oriented sectors: bankers, real estate developers, truckers, and executives of multinational corporations. Such capitalists have an unambiguous interest in economic growth and recognize the importance of politicians who believe in government-financed infrastructure like highways, schools, and water/sewer lines. At Hunt's 1977 conference on state economic development, held in Charlotte, the keynote speaker was Wachovia bank president John Medlin. In 1979, Hunt organized the North Carolina Council of Management and Development, a who's who of the state's business elite, which provided Hunt with a sounding board for his proposals and gave key corporate leaders ready access to his office (Hunt 1982, 446–47). It is indicative of modernizer ideology that Hunt developed such close mutual ties with business, but that labor leaders or environmentalists usually would not enjoy such a close relationship with the governor.

Hunt's first-term agenda, contrasted with the positions taken by Helms, set the stage for their subsequent modernizer-traditionalist encounter along party lines. But not all Tar Heel Democrats and Republicans fall neatly into these categories. Many Democratic legislators, especially from outside the metro Piedmont, are traditionalists. A few metro Piedmont Republicans are sympathetic to modernism. Most importantly, Republican Jim Martin's election as governor in 1984 reflected an amalgam of traditionalist and modernizer ideology that is sometimes at odds with Helms's traditionalism.

A Traditionalist-Modernizer Blend: Jim Martin

Since the political rise of Jesse Helms, North Carolina Republican politicians have more often than not reflected traditionalist rather than modernizer values. In 1980, Jim Hunt's reelection campaign assembled an impressive coalition of political interest groups, from traditionalist business to the AFL-CIO, none of which wished to oppose an incumbent governor. To challenge Hunt, Tar Heel Republicans chose I. Beverly Lake, Jr., a former Democratic state senator from Raleigh whose father was a North Carolina Supreme Court justice and the Democratic segregationist candidate in the 1960 and 1964 gubernatorial primaries. Lake ran an underfinanced, pure-traditionalist race, supported by Helms's National Congressional Club, which attacked Hunt as a big-spending liberal who would assuredly raise taxes. In 1981, Hunt did in fact advocate and receive an increase in the gasoline tax from the General Assembly. To raise sales taxes to provide transportation infrastructure is good modernizer strategy, but a policy that relies on such flat taxes is in fact economic conservatism, not economic liberalism. The Congressional Club's campaign attacks on Hunt had little effect on the 1980 outcome.

Hunt's crucial asset in the 1980 race was the breadth of his coalition,

which made him invulnerable to serious attack in either the May gubernatorial primary or the November election. Republican Lake won just
38 percent of the vote, even though Ronald Reagan carried the state
over Jimmy Carter. But in 1984, the Democratic party demonstrated
anything but unity, as eight candidates, three of them well financed,
fought bitterly for the right to succeed Hunt as governor.

Sensing opportunity, Jim Martin, a six-term congressman from Charlotte, agreed to run, even though, in early 1984, winning that race
seemed like a long shot. A GOP gubernatorial candidate would clearly
benefit from President Reagan's place on the November ballot, and
Helms's race against Hunt assured high voter interest. But Martin, to
his credit, ran a strong campaign in his own right. Martin grafted
modernizer appeals, both substantive and symbolic, onto the traditionalist base of the GOP. This Republican traditionalist-modernizer blend
has served Martin well, because it attracts moderate Democrats to the
Republican party.

Martin, a Ph.D. chemist once on the faculty at Davidson College, had
amassed a strong economic-conservative voting record in Congress that
won him the admiration and support of big-business political action
committees. In his North Carolina campaign, he courted textile, apparel, and furniture industrialists, many of whom had become disenchanted with Hunt's emphasis on out-of-state high-tech economic recruitment. Martin promised these traditionalist business people, who
had long been sympathetic to national Republicans but had stuck with
Democrats in state elections, that he would end the perceived bias
against Tar Heel firms if they would take a chance on his long-shot
candidacy. At the same time, he assured modernizer business people,
such as those in the banking industry, that he would be a pro-growth
governor. Thus, the Martin campaign made major inroads among both
modernizer business people who, four years before, perhaps only pragmatically, had stuck with Hunt, and among traditionalist business people who were increasingly unhappy with the spending programs of
state Democrats.

On social issues, Martin held two strong cards. First, his 1983 vote
against the Martin Luther King federal holiday (he was the only North
Carolina congressman to do so) improved his standing with the National Congressional Club and won him support among white racial
traditionalists. At the same time, he took care to develop a modernizer
image. For example, when a state GOP direct mail campaign in summer
1984 suggested that whites should vote Republican to send Jesse Jack-

son a negative message, Martin disassociated himself from the tactic. Cynics correctly noted that the disclaimer never would be seen by the overwhelming majority of traditionalist whites to whom the anti-Jackson mail had been targeted.

Martin's other appeal to traditionalist voters focused on abortion. He promised that, if elected, he would try to eliminate the state abortion fund, a Hunt-supported budget item that allowed low-income women to abort a pregnancy even if they could not afford the cost of the operation. This assured Martin support from right-to-life groups, including recently politicized fundamentalist pastors often referred to as the New Christian Right. Like his vote against the King holiday, Martin's antiabortion stand provided another link to the Congressional Club. Yet Martin did not highlight his social traditionalism in his television advertising. On the contrary, his media campaign presented him as an urbane, pragmatic modernizer whose strength was not specific issues but rather quality of leadership. Martin's overall image resembled Jim Holshouser's in 1972.

Although his decision to run for governor in 1984 originally was risky, Martin in fact won easily, 54 to 46 percent. (By contrast, in the same election Helms defeated Hunt by just 51 to 49 percent.) North Carolina Democrats often argue that Martin was elected either because of Reagan's coattails or because many Democrats refused to unite around their candidate, state attorney general Rufus Edmisten, who narrowly won a bitter runoff battle. While these factors mattered, such analyses fail to credit the Martin campaign for developing the traditionalist-modernizer mix that can appeal to traditionalist and modernizer Democrats while holding onto the core Republican vote. The Martin campaign will be the GOP formula for statewide victories over the next decade.

As governor, Jim Martin elaborated on his campaign themes. He highlighted his social traditionalism in 1987 by opposing a paid state holiday to honor Martin Luther King. But his traditionalist position on this issue did not prevent him from making conciliatory gestures toward blacks. Although there are few black Republicans in North Carolina, Martin appointed some of them to state boards. Further, he participated annually in the voluntary King holiday program for state workers, and he met with Coretta Scott King when she visited North Carolina to lobby for the King holiday.

Martin made good on his promise to fight the abortion fund and to establish an office within the state Department of Commerce to support Tar Heel "traditional industries." His appointments to boards and commissions have demonstrated a greater ideological commitment to social and economic traditionalism than to modernism. For example, his nominees to the state Industrial Commission, where workers' compensation claims are handled, have been strongly tilted toward management, and his appointees to the state Day Care Commission all voted in 1985 to allow day-care centers to use corporal punishment. In the latter instance, the commission's Democratic majority, following party lines, voted to prohibit spanking. Here, and in the case of the state Social Services Commission, which has sought to limit state-funded abortions, Martin tended to appoint Republican traditionalists, whereas Hunt usually named modernizer Democrats.

While Martin played the traditionalist tune on social issues, his economic agenda recognized the realities of an active state sector. Nowhere were Martin's sympathies for modernism clearer than in his support for an increased gasoline tax in 1986. Growth-oriented businesses expressed concern that the state highway fund would soon be bankrupt and unable to provide the road infrastructure they needed. In contrast to the Congressional Club, which has always opposed such tax increases, and similar to Hunt's gubernatorial program, Martin advocated higher gasoline taxes and reached a compromise with leading Democrats in the General Assembly.

At the same time, Martin led the fight from 1985 onward to reduce taxes on business inventories and intangible wealth, two levies that are especially disliked by traditionalist business people. Martin succeeded in underscoring to the business electorate that Democrats were far less willing than he and Republican legislators to cut business taxes. Democrats in the General Assembly countered that the tax dollars were needed to implement critical state government programs. This debate represents the classic disagreement between traditionalist and modernizer ideology. The former assumes that many taxes lead to unnecessary spending, while the latter contends that a thriving economy requires state programs and thus state taxes.

Public school spending needs represent another area where Martin assumed a modernizer position. He and the Democrats disagreed on specific spending details of the Basic Education Plan, but Martin resisted the antieducation label that Democrats wanted to affix to him. Finally, Martin energetically involved himself in the recruitment of out-of-state firms to North Carolina. Following Hunt's pattern, he traveled to Europe and Asia to promote the state's business climate. Despite his symbolic gesture to the traditionalist textile-furniture sector, Martin was firmly committed to non–North Carolina capital investment.

From 1985 to 1988 Martin continued his partisan assertion that Democrats were thwarting his attempts to lead the state. Although Democratic legislators have been unwilling to give any governor, regardless of party, veto power (the only one of the fifty governors not to have the veto), Martin sought to frame the issue as an example of anti-Republican bias.

The Elite Consensus: Say No to Equity

The differences between modernizer and traditionalist ideology are substantial in their social and economic goals for North Carolina. The significance of race and gender equality within each ideology constitutes one key distinction. A second focuses on the size and activism of state government. But these ideologies share a common vision concerning equity. Both reject the premises of economic liberalism and populism that government should decrease the tax burden of low- and middle-income citizens and at the same time increase government benefits to those groups. While critics of economic-liberal ideology have argued that the actual amount of redistribution to the working-class majority in American politics—for example, during the New Deal—has been limited, a dominant quality of Tar Heel politics is that neither leading ideology advocates the redistribution of the costs and benefits of state government (Luebke 1981b).

Modernizer ideology is often confused with economic liberalism. North Carolina's decision in 1961 to place a sales tax on food offers clear evidence of the economic-conservative tendencies of modernizers. As governor in 1961, Terry Sanford believed that the state needed to invest more in its public school system, including community colleges. Facing resistance from antitax traditionalists, Sanford found that the revenue source with the greatest prospects for legislative approval was the reimposition of the sales tax on groceries. (A 3 percent sales tax on most retail items became law in 1933, but the General Assembly exempted groceries in 1941.) The sales tax is regressive because it taxes everyone from pauper to millionaire at the same flat rate.

If Sanford were an economic liberal, as is often claimed by his political enemies, he might have sought to raise the state individual or corporate income tax, both of which placed relatively greater tax burdens on high-income families and corporations. Alternatively, the legislation might have earmarked the food tax revenues for education and included a sunset provision so that, when certain educational benefits were provided, the tax would be repealed. In fact, Sanford advocated neither, and the General Assembly's 1961 legislation was in the late 1980s still generating unspecified revenues for the General Fund. Sanford's defenders claim that without the food tax none of the educational investment would have been made. That point remains debatable. But undoubtedly reimposition of the food tax was consistent with modernizer ideology. If modernizers believe that certain investments will benefit a majority of the state's citizens, then such legislative programs are enacted regardless of whether the burden of funding and implementation is disproportionately placed on poor and middle-income citizens.

Investment in the state's future, even if financed by regressive taxes, was a hallmark of Democratic party policy in the 1970s and 1980s. Under Governor Jim Hunt, and, after 1984, with Lieutenant Governor Bob Jordan as the state's leading Democrat, the modernizer ideology held sway. From the early 1970s to the late 1980s, while Democrats controlled the General Assembly, sales taxes went up and business taxes were reduced. As a consequence, the state's tax burden shifted toward low- and middle-income Tar Heels.

The traditionalist ideology prefers no new taxes. But faced with a choice of increasing individual income or sales taxes, traditionalists— whether Democrat or Republican—favor the sales tax. Although in principle opposed to new taxes, the traditionalist legislator, who like other legislators makes about three times the income of the average North Carolinian (*Greensboro News and Record* 1987a), may pragmatically vote on the basis of self-interest. If new revenue were raised via the income tax, the high-income legislator would have to pay a larger share than, say, a low-income textile worker. By contrast, the burden of the sales tax falls on families making less than $30,000 annually. In 1986, 82 percent of Tar Heels fell into that category, compared to 8 percent of General Assembly members (ibid.).

Modernizer Democrats certainly recognize the risks of campaigning as protax politicians and, of course, never do so. Yet modernizer ideology so dominates the Democratic party that no major candidate for a statewide office campaigns on a traditionalist platform of across-the-board tax repeal. By contrast, Republicans have offered clear antitax policies. In 1984, for example, Martin promised to work for repeal of the state's inventory, intangibles, and food taxes. In fact, as Democrats predicted, he lost interest in food tax repeal shortly after taking office (*Greensboro News and Record* 1985a).

But the traditionalist antitax program, including Martin's attack on the food tax, may have been a critical piece of that many-faceted campaign to convince registered Democrats to cross over to the GOP. It remains a strong ideological weapon for North Carolina Republicans to use against modernizer Democrats. Ironically, Tar Heel Democrats have become bigger defenders than Republicans of regressive taxes like the sales tax.

The occasional victories of populist-leaning Democrats over business interests, whether finance companies or the insurance industry, suggest that at least some sentiment remains among legislators for an egalitarian alternative to either the traditionalist or modernizer political ideals. But the fact that this populist alternative lacks cohesion in the General Assembly or in the populace has important policy consequences. The absence of an organized populist presence in the state Democratic party ensures that the kinds of economic policy advocated by well-financed and well-organized business lobbies are more likely to prevail in the legislature.

3

The General Assembly: Partisan and Ideological Politics

The social forces that struggle over political goals in North Carolina play themselves out ultimately in the state legislature. The General Assembly divides into the 120-member house of representatives and the 50-member senate. Because North Carolina is the only state without a gubernatorial veto, consensus between house and senate means that a bill becomes a law. North Carolina's legislature is one of the nation's strongest, even though the governor maintains many significant appointment powers.

Crucial to an understanding of the General Assembly is the state's guiding ideology. V. O. Key noted forty years ago that an economic oligarchy prevailed in North Carolina whose interests were often served "without prompting" and that those elected to office were "fundamentally in harmony" with the oligarchy's viewpoint (1949, 211). In the 1980s, the relationship between capitalists and the legislature became more complicated. Competing groups of business people differed on the question of how activist state government should become. Nevertheless, a dominant view emerged, similar to Key's findings about the 1940s. Without articulating their ideology explicitly, legislative leaders of the 1980s continued a major commitment to infrastructure development in North Carolina. The purpose of this investment in infrastructure was to meet businesses' needs for transportation, education, and the like. In short, what was good for business, was good for North Carolina.

This ideology is conservative, in that it argues that direct benefits to business will result in indirect benefits to a majority, as the majority takes jobs offered by an expanding private sector. The dominant ideology is also modernizing, in that it recognizes the importance of gov-

38

ernment investment to support economic change. The General Assembly, then, can be viewed as committed to conservative modernization (cf. Moore 1966; Billings 1978). This book calls these beliefs "modernizer ideology."

Traditionalist economic ideology, a belief that the legislature should restrict both taxes and expenditures, has historically been rejected in North Carolina. North Carolina's growth as an industrial economy was tied in the 1920s and 1930s to state government spending for highways and the public schools. Indeed, during the Great Depression, many county school systems would have gone bankrupt if the General Assembly had not decided to assume funding costs.

Traditionalist ideology, however, has fared much better in the social or noneconomic agenda. Such issues as liquor-by-the-drink for years reflected the impact of small-town and rural values in the General Assembly. Modernizing business people who sought to promote North Carolina's quality of life were frustrated until the late 1970s by the unwillingness of the legislature to give metropolitan areas the local option for mixed drinks. Also in the 1970s and early 1980s, the General Assembly on six occasions failed to pass the Equal Rights Amendment. These votes reflected the strength of traditionalist values in the noneconomic sphere.

The procorporate agenda of the General Assembly is highlighted by the kinds of bills that do not become law. With a minor exception, no Tar Heel public employees have the right to engage in collective bargaining with their employers. Public school teachers and other state employees therefore must accept whatever salaries the General Assembly approves in its annual budget session. Further, North Carolina workers do not have to join the union that engages in collective bargaining with their employer (the so-called right-to-work law). Anti-unionism is such a fact of life in the General Assembly that the state AFL-CIO does not even include repeal of the right-to-work law on its legislative wish list.

North Carolina continues to be one of eight states in which compensation from an accident is *not* parceled out by the degree of fault, the doctrine of comparative fault. The General Assembly throughout the 1980s supported the rule of contributory negligence, the legal course favored by insurance companies and other big business enterprises, which denies individuals all rights to a damage claim if they have contributed in the slightest way to an accident. Until the 1985 session, when the legislature began the gradual process of liberalization, North

Carolina had perhaps the strictest worker compensation statutes of the fifty states. In short, the procorporate tilt of consumer and labor law exemplifies the ideological hold of business on the General Assembly.

Southern Democrats and the One-Party State

Democrats overwhelmingly controlled the General Assembly from the turn of the century until 1972. Only a handful of Republicans, virtually all from the western Piedmont and the Mountains, held seats in Raleigh. This changed when the Nixon landslide generated both a Republican governor and fifty GOP legislators. In 1974, however, the Watergate aftermath helped the Democrats reestablish their nine-to-one margin. In 1984, Republicans benefited from the Reagan landslide, electing a GOP governor and fifty legislators. But significantly for North Carolina's evolution into a two-party state, Republicans held their own in the 1986 mid-term election. Although the Republican governor had hoped for a voter rebellion against Democratic control of the General Assembly, the 1986 election did demonstrate that voters in those areas of the state that went Republican in 1984—primarily the western Piedmont, the Charlotte and Triad areas of the metro Piedmont, and the Mountains—were steadfast in their support.

Despite Republican success in winning a substantial minority of the seats in the General Assembly, the reality is that Democratic party domination continues. If Republicans claim an issue for their party, Democrats will usually reject that issue, regardless of its merits, unless they can transform it into a Democratic initiative.

Democratic control of the General Assembly obscures the many differences among Democrats. Although modernizing ideology shapes the budgetary priorities of the legislature and traditionalism has a major impact on noneconomic items, individual Democratic members can use their position in the legislative structure to pass bills that do not neatly fit the overall trend. One such example was the attempt of several metro Piedmont house members to strengthen the workers' compensation reforms of 1987 by easing regulations for hernia victims. North Carolina's existing hernia provisions were the strictest in the nation, meaning that employees had a difficult task qualifying for workers' compensation if they suffered a hernia. But for the state's major business lobby, the North Carolina Citizens for Business and Industry (NCCBI), this hernia-compensation rider went too far because it had not been part of an earlier senate bargain. NCCBI, which seeks to reconcile both modernizer and traditionalist views within its state-wide membership, had previously accepted some change in a senate-passed workers' compensation law, acknowledging that certain provisions were either too strict or appeared that way compared to those of the other forty-nine states. This acceptance of reform, even while fighting to limit its extent, is typical of modernizer politics. Most modernizer legislators supported the earlier compromise worked out in the senate. But metro Piedmont legislators sympathetic to citizen activism in general and organized labor in particular saw a chance to win more on the house floor.

The debate on the hernia-compensation amendment between Democratic representatives highlighted the conflict between traditionalists from the small towns and a handful of citizen-action legislators from the state's larger cities. Bill Alexander, representing the Cannon Mills district in the western Piedmont, made the classic traditionalist argument that government was improperly interfering with the private sector and unnecessarily raising the cost of doing business. The bill's key supporters, Sharon Thompson, a Durham white, and Dan Blue, a Raleigh black, responded simply that government ought not pay for health problems originating at the workplace. It was an argument rarely heard in the General Assembly: let business pay its fair share of social costs. The hernia-compensation amendment survived the house by a 55–54 margin. Small-town Republicans and Democrats represented the core of the traditionalist opposition. Metro Piedmont Democrats provided the backbone of support. The senate went along with the hernia provision even though its inclusion annoyed both traditionalist state senators and business lobbyists.

The house debate also accentuated the fact that a strong Democratic majority in the General Assembly can mask the ideological forces at work. Democrat Alexander's arguments could easily have been made by a traditionalist Republican. This raises the question of representation for the Democratic party. Should Alexander emphasize the health needs of his district's blue-collar constituency or the cost factors that trouble Cannon Mills?

While the Alexander versus Thompson-Blue debate underscores the wide variation among Democrats in the General Assembly, the Democratic legislative leaders can and do on occasion ask for party loyalty in certain areas. When the final vote is taken, most Democrats agree on tax policy and on such major expenditures as education and transportation funding. Their differences emerge on consumer and labor legislation like the hernia-compensation amendment, and on social issues such as abortion rights or comparable worth policy for women employees.

A review of some of the votes taken on these economic and social issues during the 1980s reveals the importance of regional differences. Democrats from the western Piedmont and Coastal Plain were most likely to adopt traditionalist positions. Democrats from the metro Piedmont and from other North Carolina cities tended to support modernizer policies as well as the occasional populist political initiative. Modernizer Democrats hailed from every region of the state, but they were most common in the metro Piedmont counties along Interstate 85.

How Democrats Rule

The Democratic leadership in the state house of representatives has long stemmed from the small-town, rural areas of North Carolina where Republicans are weak. The reasons for this are understandable. In the two-party regions of the state, Republican challengers are eager to unseat powerful Democrats. In the one-party regions, fellow Democrats at the local level defer to the successful representatives. For example, House Speaker Liston Ramsey served through the 1980s, having first been elected from his strongly Democratic Mountain district in 1960. His top lieutenant, Billy Watkins, was an eastern Piedmont lawyer who never faced a Republican opponent. In many cases, Democrats from the one-party areas have no campaign costs and require no campaign organization, because they face no opposition in either the primary or the general election.

When Jim Hunt's succession amendment passed in 1977, it became clear that it would affect power relations in the state senate because the lieutenant governor could serve for eight rather than four years. Incumbent Jimmy Green, a traditionalist Democrat from the one-party Coastal Plain region, won reelection and shaped the senate's agenda. Most significantly, as senate presiding officer, he cast the tie-breaking vote in 1982 against ratification of the Equal Rights Amendment.

It was less obvious that gubernatorial succession would change power dynamics in the house, but in fact the succession amendment broke the long-held tradition of one-term speakers. The first multi-term speaker, Carl Stewart, gave up his seat to run unsuccessfully in 1980 against Green for lieutenant governor. His successor, Liston Ramsey, assumed office in 1981 and served an unprecedented four terms. Under

Ramsey, house Democrats found that political success within the General Assembly depended on establishing a good working relationship with the speaker.

In the early 1970s, house and senate Democrats began the process of enhancing legislative power vis-à-vis the executive branch. This effort received impetus after the elections of Jim Holshouser, North Carolina's first Republican governor in the twentieth century, in 1972, and Charlotte-area Republican Congressman Jim Martin in 1984. But legislative Democrats sought additional power even when Jim Hunt was governor from 1977 to 1985. One step was to organize an independent fiscal and research staff so they would not be dependent on the governor's information. Their major mechanism, however, was self-appointment to boards and commissions established by the General Assembly. This was similar to legislators' control of the Advisory Budget Commission, a body of gubernatorial and legislative appointees created by the General Assembly in 1925 to develop the state budget (Orth 1982).

The move to strengthen the General Assembly was slowed in 1982, when the North Carolina Supreme Court ruled that making legislative appointments to the Coastal Area Management Board violated the separation of powers of North Carolina's constitution. Nevertheless, Democrats found legal ways to limit the governor's powers. For example, in 1985 the General Assembly established an Office of Administrative Hearings to review the decisions of state government agencies. The legislation designated that the chief justice of the North Carolina Supreme Court, not the governor's office, would select the chief hearing officer. Since the top positions in state government under a Republican governor of course were occupied by Republicans, this amounted to a special overview of executive policy. Democratic legislators presumed that the elected chief justice of the supreme court would appoint a Democrat, so that, even with a Republican governor, they could be sure a Democrat would review cases and make recommendations to administrative agencies. Similarly, in 1987 the General Assembly made all the appointments to an executive branch commission charged with determining priorities for public education construction, rather than allowing the Republican-dominated State Board of Education to make the selections.

At the end of the 1985 legislative session and again during the 1986 elections, Governor Martin criticized Democratic pork barrel legislation. These bills provided funding for pet local projects of Democratic legislators who were loyal to the house and senate leadership. The pork barrel was merely the most visible layer of a decision-making process in which few legislators participated. The eight-member "supersub," three Democratic members of both house and senate plus the speaker and lieutenant governor, made the crucial choices for the state's $12 billion budget during the hectic closing days of each legislative session. Martin's criticisms had little effect on the 1986 election, although the attack on pork barrel spending by the Democrats would resurface in the 1988 Republican campaign.

The Democrats' emphasis on party and personal loyalty has an important consequence for policy change. Historically, small-town traditionalists have used seniority to promote their political agendas in the General Assembly. As a small group of metro Piedmont Democrats in the house gained seniority in the 1980s under Speaker Ramsey, some of their issues—like expanded worker compensation rights or a ban on phosphates in detergents—could receive serious consideration. To a lesser degree, a similar pattern developed in the senate under Lieutenant Governor Jordan after 1985. Improved worker compensation and the phosphate-detergent ban, two issues previously beyond the parameters of legislative debate, were placed on the agenda and even became law because of the personal standing of certain legislators.

But such consumer or environmentalist legislation remained by far the exception rather than the rule. The procorporate tilt of legislative policy was reinforced by a coterie of lobbyists, many of them former legislators, who worked hard for their clients (North Carolina Center for Public Policy Research 1986, 1988). Overwhelmingly, these clients were corporations or business associations. At election time, the business lobbies supported their favored candidates with contributions from political action committees (PACs). The bottom line remained that the great majority of Democratic and Republican legislators personally supported the business agenda of either the modernizer or traditionalist variety. What modernizers and traditionalists have in common is the belief that government policy should benefit business first. This contrasts with the populist view that government's first job is to help the average citizen, not the large corporation.

In the General Assembly of the late 1980s, Liston Ramsey, despite a certain hostility toward banks which many labeled "Mountain populism," was comfortable with modernizer ideology. Ironically, because of his hard-nosed partisan style, he was immensely unpopular with many business people who, in fact, benefited from legislation that he supported. Bob Jordan, by contrast, was the consummate modernizer politician. First, while strongly committed to highway and school construction, Jordan also endorsed positions important to big business such as opposing comparative fault insurance. Second, Jordan backed key women's issues such as the state abortion fund for low-income women, and black issues such as the Martin Luther King holiday and revisions of the runoff primary law. As the Democrats' leaders in the General Assembly, Ramsey and Jordan symbolized the commitment to modernizer ideology.

Funding Infrastructure: The Modernizer Approach

Today's modernizers have inherited the mantle of North Carolina's pre–civil rights elite. V. O. Key (1949) called the state a "progressive plutocracy" because the commitment to progress served the interests of wealthy capitalists. Nowhere is the theoretical distinction between traditionalist and modernizer ideology clearer than on taxation policy. The traditionalist opposes new taxes on principle, seeks to repeal some existing taxes, and believes that the state budget is padded and needs reduction. Such a position collides head-on with the claims of state government agencies from highways to health care.

Governor Martin campaigned in 1984 as a traditionalist, advocating that the combined taxes on groceries, business inventories, and intangible property be cut by $489 million (Betts 1985, 5). By 1986, however, he sounded like a modernizer when he proposed raising the gasoline tax to help the state's ailing Highway Fund. In general, the antigovernment feature of traditionalism fares better in more symbolic settings like the U.S. Senate. Jesse Helms has been able to vote his traditionalist principles as a protest, while recognizing that a majority of the Senate will pass the spending bills he opposes.

Modernizer taxation policy begins with the premise that funds must be available to pay for an activist state government. The crucial question is, who shall pay for big government? The answer emerges from the self-interest of modernizer business people. Modernizer ideology, whether espoused by politicians or employers, exists to serve the interests of the growth-oriented business. Consequently, modernizers would prefer to place the burden of taxation on other groups in society besides themselves. Two areas require close examination. First, does the tax fall directly on business or on the consumer? Second, is the tax progressive? "Progressive" means that the higher one's income, the higher the rate of taxation. It is not surprising, then, that the preferred tax of modernizers in the 1980s was the sales tax, paid equally by all consumers regardless of income. Because it is a flat tax, the sales tax is regressive, not progressive. A 1987 national study showed that, in percentage terms, the poorest North Carolinians paid four times as much in sales taxes as the wealthiest Tar Heels (CTJ 1987, table 33).

Yet modernizers are not inflexible. When spending needs are urgent but the political climate does not permit higher sales taxes, business taxes can be raised. Although this is a position of last resort, it affirms the modernizer commitment to expansion of the state's infrastructure. In 1987, modernizers raised the state corporate income tax from 6 percent to 7 percent. This was the first increase in fifty-four years. To be sure, the modernizer Democrats also gave business a plum, something traditionalists and some modernizers, including Governor Martin, had been demanding for years: abolition of the tax on business inventories. In effect, a tax increase was exchanged for a tax decrease. Further, the corporate income tax continued to be regressive; the rate was the same for a tiny country store as it was for IBM. Yet business taxes, not consumer taxes, were raised. The major opposition in 1987 to another sales tax increase came from Lieutenant Governor Jordan, who was expected to challenge Jim Martin in the 1988 gubernatorial election. Since the General Assembly had raised the local-option sales tax a half-penny in 1983 and again in 1986, so that sales taxes were 5 percent in all counties, Jordan saw the political risk of facing an opponent like Martin who had successfully campaigned in 1984 as an antitax traditionalist.

The General Assembly's decision to raise the corporate income tax in 1987 emerged from a modernizer recognition that the state's expanding public education program adopted in 1985, the Basic Education Plan, should not be deferred. Legislators recognized the link between educational improvement and hopes for economic development in the poorer counties. (See the discussion of public education policy below.) Although far less fundamental in its implications, the raising of corporate taxes even slightly in lieu of an increased sales tax is somewhat reminiscent of the funding crisis that confronted the legislature during the depression.

When local governments faced bankruptcy during the depression years, the state in 1931 assumed primary funding responsibility for public schools and highways. The individual income tax rates established at the time meant that all but the wealthy were exempt from the tax. Even though the legislature also created a sales tax in 1933, the net effect of the combined business and consumer taxes was progressive.

Business taxes accounted for 60 percent of General Fund revenues in 1934–35, while sales taxes made up 31 percent and income taxes 6 percent. (Liner 1979, 49). In short, facing a crisis, the state's political leaders forced business and the wealthy to pay a significant share of the costs of state government.

Over time, however, the relative shares of business and consumer taxes changed dramatically. The major reason was bracket creep; as a result, middle-income citizens, who had been exempt from the income tax when rates were set in the 1930s, became the financial backbone of the system. Additionally, in 1961 Governor Terry Sanford persuaded the General Assembly to reinstitute the sales tax on groceries in order to provide more funding for public education, including community colleges. This made the sales tax a far more lucrative source of revenues.

Between 1935 and 1978, the business share of General Fund taxes dropped from 60 percent to 20 percent. The personal income tax share rose from 6 percent to 41 percent, while sales taxes stayed about the same (31 percent versus 28 percent). This trend away from business taxes continued in the 1980s. Thus, while modernizers avoided a tax increase for either business or the wealthy (through an adjustment in personal income tax rates), North Carolina was becoming more dependent on the less-affluent consumer for its revenues. By 1980, a once-progressive state tax system was placing a disproportionate burden on the middle-income taxpayer because of bracket creep and increasing sales taxes (Liner 1982, 40–41). In 1985, when income, property, and sales taxes were combined, all North Carolinians—poor and rich alike—paid virtually the same percentage of their income for taxes. (CTJ 1987, table 33). In short, the state's tax progressivity had disappeared.

But there was no public awareness of this shift. On the contrary, as a result of continued and effective lobbying by North Carolina businesses, the only policy thoroughly debated by the Democratic legislative majority in the 1980s was whether business's demands for abolition of the inventory tax and the tax on intangible wealth were affordable.

Modernizers believe that a good policy goal can justify a regressive tax. Terry Sanford, from the time the food tax was reestablished in 1961 through his successful campaign for the U.S. Senate in 1986, argued precisely this point. The weakness of a tax equity perspective in the General Assembly is demonstrated by the fact that only once, in 1975, did repeal of the food tax receive serious debate. Democratic legislators, even most of those with a citizen-action outlook on other labor/

consumer issues, accept the modernizer consensus that the food tax brings in too much revenue to be altered. Although Jim Hunt, as lieutenant governor, had gone on record in favor of food tax repeal, he expended no political capital in that area during his two terms as governor.

In 1985, while granting tax relief primarily to business and those with large inheritances, the Democrats undertook two token measures to benefit lower-income citizens. First, they provided a $15 to $25 tax credit to those whose taxable income was less than $15,000. This benefit was insignificant when compared to the real out-of-pocket annual cost of the 5 percent food tax: $208 for a family spending $80 each week on groceries. Further, in a state with one of the nation's highest illiteracy rates, the General Assembly's requirement for another income tax form ensured that many eligible citizens would not receive the credit. The second token benefit, the repeal of the sales tax on groceries purchased with food stamps, provided no financial aid to the bulk of less affluent Tar Heels, who were not eligible for food stamps. Moreover, state legislators were well aware that this help for the very poor had already been mandated by federal legislation to take effect in a year.

The reluctance of those Democratic legislators sympathetic to citizen power to advocate progressive tax reform as a Democratic campaign issue illustrates the hegemony of modernizer ideology. The party's continued preference after 1984 for consumer taxes gave the taxation issue to Governor Martin and other Republicans.

Building Infrastructure: The Public Schools

Support for public education was a hallmark of the progressive ideology that guided North Carolina into the civil rights era. Although the schools were racially segregated and black schools were underfunded, the General Assembly recognized the importance of elementary and secondary education during the 1930s when it reshaped its tax structure in order to assume primary responsibility for school funding.

But commitment to public school funding, in contrast to that for the state's university system, has lagged over the years. In 1985, North Carolina's funding for higher education exceeded the national average by 20 percent, while public education expenditures were 14 percent below the national norm. The state ranked fortieth in per capita public education spending and thirty-second in teacher pay (National Education Association Datasearch 1987, 54, 19). The quality of education was also an issue. The General Assembly ensured a minimum standard for all school children, but individual school systems were allowed to raise additional funds through the local property tax. Not surprisingly, wealthier school districts with a larger tax base were more likely than poorer districts to use the local supplement. The risk of a widening gap in public school quality between, for example, metro Piedmont counties and rural Coastal Plain or Mountain counties was real.

In the 1970s and early 1980s, the school finance issue had not caught the attention of either governors or legislators. Instead, the General Assembly funded specific programs, such as the establishment of public kindergartens in every school district, reading skills development in the primary grades, and a major increase in the level of pupil testing as a means to determine quality and identify problem students.

In 1983, the General Assembly funded a thirty-three-member policy committee, the Public Education Policy Council (PEPC), to examine school finance, governance, and personnel issues and to make recommendations for future legislative sessions. At the same time, Governor Hunt convened a major study commission, with prominent corporate representatives, to examine the relationship between public school quality and economic development. This group, a business-government-educator alliance known as the North Carolina Commission on Education for Economic Growth (CEEG), underscored the commitment of modernizer ideology to both education and growth. Indeed, the CEEG justified its spending recommendations as a cost-effective way to provide acceptable jobs for future generations in North Carolina. It advocated improved teacher training and salaries, an expanded curriculum, and the hiring of more teachers, the effect of which would be to reduce class size.

The CEEG recommendations were not significantly different from those of the PEPC. What distinguished them was that they affirmed the self-interest of business in a better public school system. Specific improvements such as more computers and secondary school textbooks were approved in 1984. More importantly, the CEEG established a business-backed political environment for substantial increases in public school expenditures.

The 1985 General Assembly adopted an education improvement package that included recommendations from the CEEG, the PEPC, and a ten-member legislative committee convened in 1982 as the Select Committee. Labeled the Basic Education Plan (BEP), it promised a 34 percent increase in state funds for public education, to be phased in between 1987 and 1996. The money would be used to provide more teachers and support personnel like librarians and social workers, reduce class size, upgrade summer school and vocational education, and other enhancements.

The BEP was a classic example of modernizer policy-making, for it overlooked the question of equity. Did some school districts need state help more than others? The BEP, because it distributed funds on a per pupil basis, would raise the minimum standards for each of North Carolina's 143 school districts. But it lacked an equalization formula to compensate poorer counties and allow them to undertake capital improvements that they could otherwise not afford.

In 1987, the equity debate resurfaced in a three-way discussion among house Democrats, the lieutenant governor, and the governor on how best to finance the construction of more school facilities. Governor Martin proposed a $1.5 billion bond issue, with funds available to all school districts. Certainly in part because it was Martin's proposal, house Democrats wanted nothing to do with it. Their own idea, to raise the sales tax a penny, no doubt delighted Martin as it gave him another campaign issue against the Democrats, but Lieutenant Governor Jordan refused to go along with the sales tax hike. After much public feuding among the Democrats, Jordan and House Speaker Ramsey developed a ten-year, $800 million funding package that avoided a sales tax increase. Their plan put the burden on profitable corporations by raising the business income tax 1 percent, but sweetened that increase by abolishing the business inventory tax. Business had opposed the inventory tax for years; however, because local governments received the tax dollars, the Association of County Commissioners and League of Municipalities had prevailed. When the inventory tax repeal became law in 1987, the General Assembly agreed to reimburse local governments from the state treasury.

The bill's most unusual feature received little notice: that is, 20 percent of the $800 million package would be earmarked for school districts with critical construction needs. Thus, for the first time, the state was attempting to remedy inequities between the poorer and the wealthier counties. For modernizer Democrats, this was a tacit admission that the premise of the Basic Education Plan—equal funding for all districts— would not address the problems of poor school districts. Without special funding, many of these districts could not build facilities to house the teachers who would come to the district under the BEP. Lieutenant Governor Jordan initiated the critical needs provision. It was unclear whether Jordan had been permanently won over to equity funding for public school districts, or whether this was a one-time concession. Undoubtedly, his thinking was influenced by two organizations supported by the philanthropic voice of the Democratic modernizer establishment, the Z. Smith Reynolds Foundation of Winston-Salem.

The Z. Smith Reynolds Foundation had created the Public School Forum in 1985 to fill a void created by the dissolution of Governor Hunt's Commission on Education for Economic Growth in 1984. Like the CEEG, the Public School Forum brought together key Democratic politicians, corporate executives, and educators to address long-term needs, including the recruitment of future generations of teachers. One of its first projects was a scholarship program to encourage both black and white teenagers to consider careers in the public schools. In 1987, the forum considered the issue of equity and developed a consensus in its membership that school construction needs, including catch-up funds, were critical if North Carolina hoped to generate economic development in the poorer Mountain and Coastal Plain counties.

Interestingly, the Public School Forum relied on research prepared by the Atlantic Committee for Research in Education (ACRE), a Durham-based advocacy group also funded by the Z. Smith Reynolds Foundation. Beginning in 1983, ACRE monitored the various study commissions with a special focus on financial equity. Its reports criticized legislative funding proposals for ignoring the monetary differences among the 143 school districts and thus the inability of some counties to finance school construction. It pointed out that poorer counties had a higher tax rate, not a lower rate, than the wealthier counties. The issue was not willingness, but ability, to invest in the future of children.

The major difference between the Public School Forum and ACRE was the political influence of the forum's membership on education policy. In 1987, the forum, using arguments first made by ACRE, persuaded leading modernizer Democrats in the General Assembly to provide some funds toward equalization. Whether modernizer Democrats would continue to move in the direction of educational equity remained an open question. But modernizer business people and politicians were willing to do so during a crisis, much as the General Assembly of the 1930s established a progressive personal income tax.

For modernizers, a crisis constitutes a short-term, immediate problem for which equity solutions may be temporarily appropriate. The severity of the education crisis was underscored by the 1986 findings of the North Carolina Commission on Jobs and Economic Growth, a study group of business people and educators funded by the 1985 legislature to develop a Democratic economic development plan separate from that of Governor Martin. Every one of the commission's fourteen recommendations focused on public education and job training. Several of the commission's legislative proposals became law in 1987. The modernizer alliance of business, government, and education was hard at work in the late 1980s. Putting aside partisan politics, leading Democrats were worried about the state's educational and economic future.

Building Infrastructure: Transportation Policy

The General Assembly raised the tax on gasoline both in 1981 and 1986 to provide additional monies for the Highway Fund. Although advocates say it is fair because only highway users pay, the gasoline tax is problematic for three reasons. First, it is in fact a regressive tax, since poor and rich gas purchasers pay the same amount. Second, the lack of adequate public transit in North Carolina forces less affluent citizens to spend limited resources on automobiles and related expenses. Finally, the poor are most likely to drive "gas guzzlers" because they cannot afford the newer, more fuel-efficient models. Nevertheless, it fit modernizer ideology both to stand firmly committed to highway construction and to enact a regressive tax.

In 1981, Governor Hunt's proposal to increase the gasoline tax received feisty criticism from the National Congressional Club, which argued, from a traditionalist perspective, that existing funds would be adequate by simply eliminating political corruption and featherbedding from the state Department of Transportation (*News and Observer* 1981b, 1981a). At the time, one leading Democrat, state senator Russell Walker, suggested that the club-produced TV ads attacking Hunt's position were best viewed as the opening salvo in Jesse Helms's war against Jim Hunt (*News and Observer* 1981c). The club's criticism turned the gasoline tax increase into a partisan political issue, prompting Democratic leaders in the legislature to demand party loyalty on the vote.

In 1986, when the Republican governor proposed to raise the gasoline tax again, the Congressional Club did not campaign against it, although club leaders disagreed with Martin's plan. This time, Lieutenant Governor Jordan, in a move that irked his more partisan Democratic friends, reached agreement with Governor Martin on the specifics of a bipartisan gasoline tax bill. As the owner of a lumber company in

Mount Gilead in the eastern Piedmont, Bob Jordan shared modernizer business people's commitment to transportation infrastructure. House Democrats joined Jordan and his senate colleagues in supporting Martin's regressive tax plan. Even though Democratic legislators believed that they should do nothing to legitimize Republican leadership in Raleigh, their cooperation with Martin in this instance did just that.

One of North Carolina's most regressive taxes is the motor vehicle sales tax, because it has a cap that exempts the owners of high-priced vehicles from paying any tax above a certain level. Many years ago the auto dealers' lobby convinced legislators both to establish the cap and to set the sales tax at 2 percent instead of the current 5 percent. It is indicative of the weakness of a tax-fairness ideology that no legislators sought to revise this law when the need for highway revenues arose. In 1983, as part of a variety of increased consumer taxes, Democrats did raise the vehicle cap from $6,000 to $15,000. But by maintaining the cap at $15,000 when the average new car price exceeded $10,000, this revision in fact taxed the middle-class car buyer more than it did the wealthy. In the same spirit of gaining revenue primarily from the low-to-middle income Tar Heel, the General Assembly extended the 2 percent sales tax to used car sales. When the gasoline tax rose in 1986, no legislator discussed removing the $15,000 cap.

Transportation policy funded by the gasoline tax also shows a lack of equity. Unlike states with major metropolitan areas, North Carolina spends virtually no money on public transit. The assumption has been that traffic congestion can be solved by more road construction. The notion of the affluent commuter riding public transit has been alien in the General Assembly, and the transit needs of the car-less poor, whether urban or rural, have been ignored. While the cost of urban highway construction over the past decade has ranged from a minimum of $3 million per mile to $35 million per mile to build roads such as Durham's East-West Expressway extension near Duke University Medical Center and Interstate 277 in downtown Charlotte, legislators in 1985 were unwilling to appropriate the $1 million annual subsidy for daily intercity rail service between Charlotte and Raleigh.

By the late 1980s, traffic congestion in the modernizer Piedmont counties was so bad at rush hour that some politicians and business people began to explore auto alternatives for the area's commuters. These explorations did not address the concerns of the poor, although they might benefit from improved commuter transit established for the car-owning public. Nevertheless, the desire to build roads was so strong among urban politicians that rural Democrats worried that the urban areas would grab up all the highway dollars.

In response to the tendency of more affluent city governments, especially in the booming Piedmont counties, to subsidize state highway projects with local funds in order to speed up the construction timetable, rural Democrats in 1987 unified. Led by Robert Hunter, a Mountain Democrat, they argued persuasively that urban subsidies were inducing the Department of Transportation to build city thoroughfares more quickly than rural highways. A Coastal Plain Democrat, Joe Mavretic, spoke a modernizing language that linked highways to jobs, and hinted at rural resentment of urban success: "There's only so much money to go around and now it's the turn of other parts of this state to have interstate-quality roads, which in today's society are the prerequisite to development" (*Durham Morning Herald* 1987a).

The highway bill of 1987 was noteworthy in two respects. Even though it placed restrictions on highway planning for cities and was therefore hardly in their self-interest, urban Democrats overwhelmingly followed the party line in supporting the bill. Only one metro Piedmont Democrat voted against it.

More importantly, this bill illustrated the continuing power of rural Democrats in the General Assembly. But as a result of the relatively slow population growth in the rural counties of North Carolina during the 1980s, it is likely that redistricting after the 1990 census will tilt seats toward the urban growth areas. Legislation like Hunter's may represent a last hurrah for rural Democrats.

Traditionalism in the General Assembly: The Noneconomic Agenda

Traditionalist Democratic legislators disproportionately represent rural, small-town North Carolina, while modernizers usually represent the larger, more cosmopolitan cities. The Democrats' internal conflict focuses on how much the party should commit itself to a more secular definition of appropriate social relations. Traditionalist ideology of the late 1980s remained rooted in a fundamentalist-Protestant value system.

In particular, traditionalists believe in the importance of a patriarchal family. This leads to political disagreement in the General Assembly around such issues as comparable worth for women employees, abortion rights, or corporal punishment in the schools.

Comparable worth is the notion that women's jobs need reclassification to higher pay scales because traditionally jobs of comparable skill levels were assigned a lower income if the jobholders were primarily women. The General Assembly in 1984 voted to study the question of comparable worth in state government. In the 1985 legislative session, however, a coalition of traditionalist business and noneconomic opponents argued successfully against the implementation of the study. From a free enterprise perspective, traditionalist business opposed any infringements on the marketplace, even if women did make less money. Social traditionalists opposed the implication that women should be primary breadwinners. A strong social traditionalist from the Coastal Plain, Democrat Richard Wright, led the 92–21 vote against further study.

Two aspects of the comparable worth vote highlight the traditionalist-modernizer debate. First, all but four of the twenty-one prostudy votes were cast by legislators from North Carolina cities, indicating the strength of citizen-power and modernizer ideologies in the urban areas. Second, the Republican delegation was not monolithic on comparable worth. Three of the thirty-six-member GOP delegation voted for the study, indicating the existence of a small Republican modernizer perspective.

One indication that the women's delegation in the General Assembly is not strongly feminist was the decision of three of the seven Democratic women legislators to oppose the study. Four of five Republican women also voted against the study. By contrast, no one from the thirteen-member black delegation opposed the study.

North Carolina has been one of only nine states that provide funding for low-income women who could not otherwise afford an abortion. Over the years, this legislative provision, first proposed during the Hunt administration, has survived for several reasons. First, the Democratic leadership endorsed the bill. Second, modernizer ideology supports women's right to choose.

In the mid-1980s, as the right-to-life movement gained momentum with the support of the Congressional Club and Senator Helms as well as the backing of Governor Martin, traditionalist legislators faced greater pressure to oppose the abortion fund. In 1985, the state senate reached a tie vote on whether to continue the fund, forcing Lieutenant Governor Jordan to show his modernizer colors by voting yes on funding. All twelve Republican senators opposed the bill, while twelve of thirty-eight Democrats voted no. None of these antiabortion Democrats came from the metro Piedmont and all but one represented rural areas. The three black senators and the four women senators, all of whom were Democrats, supported the abortion fund.

Traditionalists in 1987 continued to make inroads in the General Assembly. By a vote of 70 to 30, the house passed a bill denying minors the right to an abortion without parental consent. Twenty-seven of the thirty nay votes came from urban and/or black legislators. Only two of the thirteen Democratic women legislators favored the bill, compared to four of six Republican women who supported it. Not surprisingly, traditionalist women of either party were more likely to represent small-town districts.

A further issue reflecting traditionalist strength is the continued right of public school personnel to use corporal punishment against pupils. In addition, modernizer legislators have not succeeded in winning a local-option provision, so that urban school districts where ideological sentiment against corporal punishment is strong could prohibit it locally. Indeed, in 1987, traditionalists rallied against a bill seeking to regulate corporal punishment more formally and, in effect, discourage its use. One urban Democrat sympathetic to social traditionalism weakened the senate version of the bill so that spanking could still be a "first-line punishment" in North Carolina schools (*Durham Morning Herald* 1987b). This urban Democrat's support of such a bill was an exception. In both the house and the senate, Republicans and rural Democrats constituted the core vote in favor of corporal punishment.

In accord with racial traditionalism, Governor Martin objected to a 1987 Democratic proposal for a paid state holiday honoring Dr. Martin Luther King. Martin's opposition, coupled with the high priority that black Democrats assigned the bill, ensured that Speaker Ramsey would identify the issue as a party-line vote. It passed in the house, for example, by 77 to 34. Only four Democrats, three from the Coastal Plain and one from the western Piedmont, voted no. Two Republicans from the metro Piedmont voted yes.

Speaker Ramsey and Lieutenant Governor Jordan allowed Democratic legislators to support a traditionalist *noneconomic* agenda as long as it gave no advantage to Republicans. Because the King holiday had provided good political mileage for Republicans in 1984, including Martin and Helms, the Democratic leadership in 1987 turned the vote into a party loyalty issue. When many traditionalist Democrats wanted to vote against the abortion fund altogether, the Democratic leadership simply hid the provision inside another bill so that the abortion fund would survive without traditionalist Democrats having to cast a politically risky vote.

Analysis of legislative politics reveals the relative power of Republicans and Democrats, as well as the strength of traditionalists and modernizers and of rural and urban legislators. As the two-party system becomes more institutionalized in North Carolina during the 1990s, the Republican delegation in the General Assembly may well increase. In part, this depends on how well the Democratic party at the local level responds to the Republican challenge.

North Carolina's changes in population between 1980 and 1990 will require a redrawing of district lines in 1991, in accord with the 1990 U.S. Census. Whatever the political party mix may be in the 1990s, changes in the state's demographic and economic structure will unquestionably result in fewer seats for rural legislators. It will probably mean a greater decline in the power of Democratic traditionalists. If Democrats can hold their own in the metro Piedmont and other urban counties like New Hanover (Wilmington) and Buncombe (Asheville), the General Assembly of the 1990s will probably consist of more modernizer Democrats and perhaps even additional Democrats sympathetic to citizen-action ideology. If Republican gains should occur in these areas, the new GOP legislators will more likely represent the modernizer-traditionalist blend of the party's mainstream rather than the traditionalist ideology of the Congressional Club.

The changes in population and economy that result in a more urban North Carolina contribute to an overall decline in the political power of traditionalism in both the Democratic and Republican parties. The next chapter presents an overview of the recent social-economic change in the Tar Heel state that underlies political change.

4

A Social-Economic Portrait of North Carolina

The politics of North Carolina reflect, as demonstrated in earlier chapters, the relative strength of conflicting political parties, interest groups, and ideologies. But political battles do not occur in a vacuum. Rather, they emerge in part from the demographic and economic structure that undergirds society. This chapter examines changes in North Carolina's population and economy, especially since 1970, and suggests that these changes have reshaped the state's politics. It also compares the differing economic circumstances of the state's three major regions.

For most of the twentieth century, North Carolina has ranked tenth in population among the fifty states. The official U.S. Census count was 5.9 million in 1980, and by 1987 it had increased to 6.4 million, a growth rate slightly higher than the national rate and about average for the South. Demographers expected similar levels into the 1990s, and predicted a population of 6.6 million in 1990 (OSBM 1987a, 1987b, and 1988). North Carolina remains the third largest southern state after Florida and Texas.

During the 1980s parts of North Carolina enjoyed unprecedented growth, while a handful of counties actually lost residents. The Tar Heel state has become a mix of economic boom and stagnation. Its population growth mostly reflects in-migration from other states. Indeed, North Carolina's birth rate in 1985 was the ninth lowest in the nation, while its in-migration level was the sixth highest (Calhoun 1988, 4). This population increase is concentrated in counties with three kinds of characteristics: either an emerging high-tech economy, in which research and development (R&D) and related services predominate; growing settlements of affluent retirees; or an economic boom at the beach along the Atlantic coast. Numerous counties illustrate these trends. Between 1980 and 1987, one-third of the state's in-migration occurred in Wake (Raleigh) and Mecklenburg (Charlotte) counties, the two largest centers of high-tech economic development. Retirees increasingly moved to Mountain counties such as Henderson (Hendersonville) and Watauga (Boone), a golfing area like Moore County (Southern Pines), or northern Chatham and southern Orange counties (the Chapel Hill area). Beach counties like Brunswick (between Wilmington and Myrtle Beach, South Carolina) and Dare (Nags Head) grew by 40 percent between 1980 and 1987 (OSBM 1987a).

Geographically, North Carolina is both large and diverse. The distance from Nags Head on the northeastern coast to Murphy in extreme southwestern North Carolina is five hundred miles, farther than from Nags Head to New York City. Murphy lies much closer to Georgia's state capital, Atlanta, than to its own capital city of Raleigh. Schoolchildren learn to divide North Carolina into three regions: the Mountains, the Piedmont, and the Coastal Plain. Relying on topography, which does not coincide precisely with county lines, geographers usually place the state's twenty-three most western counties in the Mountains (see map) and the forty-one most eastern counties in the Coastal Plain. The remaining thirty-six counties constitute the Piedmont. This book follows those distinctions. In 1987, 14 percent of Tar Heels lived in the Mountains and 31 percent on the Coastal Plain, while the majority lived in the Piedmont. Analysis of Tar Heel politics requires further refinement of the Piedmont region into three areas: metro, western, and eastern Piedmont.

The notion of a metro Piedmont reflects the cultural power that emanates from the six counties along Interstate 85 that are not even geographically contiguous: Mecklenburg, Forsyth, Guilford, Orange, Durham, and Wake (see map). The essence of modernizer values—that economic prosperity requires an activist state government prepared to invest in transportation, education, and the like—permeates the thinking of political and economic leaders in these counties. North Carolina's most influential daily newspapers are published here; these newspapers circulate, of course, in less metropolitan counties whose leaders are less sympathetic to a big-budget government. The metro Piedmont is also the home of the state's most prestigious research and liberal arts colleges and universities. Thus, although only 30 percent of all Tar Heels live in this area, its influence on state politics is disproportionately high. Growth-oriented corporations, such as banking, insurance,

The Regions of North Carolina

Note: The counties in the Metro Piedmont are, from east to west, Wake, Durham, Orange, Guilford, Forsyth, and Mecklenburg.

the media, and high-technology firms, have joined with academics and state government leaders in efforts to modernize North Carolina's economy.

The western and eastern Piedmont areas share cultural support for traditionalist values. Leaders of these counties are skeptical of change, especially if it is engineered or mandated by big government—for example, racial equality or abortion rights. The small-town, rural values of the western and eastern Piedmont also pervade the less urban counties of the Mountains and Coastal Plain. In fact, the modernizer values of the metro Piedmont often stand in sharp contrast to the small-town culture that remains strong across most of the state's one hundred counties.

The distinction between the western and the eastern Piedmont derives from the relative importance of agriculture and the level of black population. The black percentage is below the state average of 22 percent in all eighteen western Piedmont counties, and at or above 22 percent in all but one of the twelve eastern Piedmont counties. Similarly, agricultural employment in most western Piedmont counties is below the state average of 3.4 percent, but agricultural work in most eastern Piedmont counties exceeds 5 percent.

Historically, race has mattered in North Carolina. Blacks and native Americans have received less education and lower incomes, and they have suffered more unemployment and health problems. Twenty-two percent of Tar Heels are black, the eighth highest proportion in the country. One percent are native American, the thirteenth highest total. The concentration of the state's black population reflects the historical dependency of plantation owners on slave labor. After the Civil War, blacks generally remained in the same areas where they had been forced to live as slaves. Consequently, few blacks live in the western part of the state where small independent farmers were the norm. For example, just 5 percent of the Mountain population and 13 percent of the western Piedmont are black. By contrast, eastern Piedmont counties are 34 percent black and the Coastal Plain is 32 percent black. On the Coastal Plain, the black population is small in the counties along the Atlantic Ocean, which have relied over the years on fishing (and today, tourism) rather than agriculture for their livelihood. Poor blacks have moved from rural counties to the metro Piedmont in search of greater economic opportunity. More recently, black professionals have begun migrating to North Carolina, especially to the metro Piedmont counties. Currently, one-fourth of the metro Piedmont's population is black.

The North Carolina Economy: The Manufacturing Sector

North Carolina, like the forty-nine other states, is in transition away from manufacturing and agriculture and toward service employment. Throughout the twentieth century, North Carolina has ranked as the most industrial southern state. In 1920, 53 percent of the state's labor force worked on farms and 24 percent was employed in manufacturing (Hobbs 1930, 65). In the following quarter century until after World War II, employment patterns changed little. In 1947, for example, 42 percent of North Carolinians worked in agriculture, compared to 28 percent in manufacturing (Hammer and Company Associates 1961, 12).

The massive shift in North Carolina's economy occurred between the late 1940s and the 1970s. Between 1947 and 1970, the percentage of Tar Heels employed in agriculture dropped from 42 percent to 8 percent, while those in manufacturing rose from 28 percent to 40 percent. Between 1966 and 1976, only two states, Texas and California, exceeded North Carolina in the number of additional manufacturing jobs (Mahaffey and Doty 1979, 6). During the 1960s and 1970s, these new jobs fell into two categories. The first included the traditional labor-intensive and low-wage industries—textiles, apparel, and furniture; employment in this category tended to increase, especially in counties where agricultural unemployment was high (Wood 1986, chap. 3). A second category of new industries was more capital-intensive and paid higher wages—among them, fabricated metals, paper and rubber production, and machinery (Luebke, Peters, and Wilson 1985, 317). Such firms were more likely to settle in nonagricultural, industrial counties, especially in the metro and western Piedmont.

Between 1970 and 1987 both agricultural and manufacturing employment declined as a percentage of total jobs across the state. As elsewhere, employment gains in North Carolina have occurred in the tertiary sector, where the distribution of goods and services prevails. The percentage of Tar Heels employed full-time in farming dropped from 8 percent to 3 percent. Among nonagricultural workers, the number in manufacturing decreased from 40 percent in 1970 to 30 percent in 1987 (U.S. Department of Labor 1987, 1970).

During this seventeen-year period, the state's labor force expanded by 60 percent to nearly 3 million persons. Eighty percent of the new jobs were outside manufacturing. But North Carolina's continued gains in manufacturing, compared to many other states which lost manufacturing jobs, led to its present ranking as the nation's most industrial state. What has changed significantly since 1970 is North Carolina's industrial mix. First, developments in its historic industries—the manufacture of textiles, apparel, furniture, and tobacco products—are noteworthy because the patterns of change have not been uniform. Second, the new industries attracted to North Carolina since 1970 have tended to be part of the core rather than the periphery of the national economy.

Core industries are noted for capital intensity, high productivity, a high degree of monopoly, high profits, high wages, and high levels of unionization (Tolbert, Horan, and Beck 1980). In the terminology of this book, core business people are usually modernizers. Peripheral industries are noted for labor intensity, low productivity, national and international market competition, low profits, low wages, and lack of unionization. Peripheral industrialists are usually traditionalists. Core industries include construction, utilities, finance, and most forms of manufacturing, among them machinery, transportation equipment, rubber and paper products, and metal fabrication. North Carolina's mainstay industries of textiles, apparel, and furniture are examples of the peripheral sector. Between 1970 and the late 1980s, the structure of North Carolina's economy shifted from a dependency on peripheral industries to a greater balance between core and periphery (Luebke, Peters, and Wilson 1985, 316–17).

In 1970, 39 percent of all Tar Heel manufacturing jobs were in the textile industry, compared to just 25 percent in 1987 (U.S. Department of Labor 1970, 1987). But even in the 1980s, textiles employed twice as many North Carolinians as any other manufacturing industry. In the United States, textiles are a low-wage industry, and its continued dominance in North Carolina seems likely to ensure that the state will retain the dubious honor of appearing last or close-to-last in national industrial wage rankings.

As a peripheral industry, textiles have been extremely vulnerable to competition from foreign and U.S.-owned corporations paying far lower wages in the Third World, primarily in Latin America and Asia. Wage competition and dusty, antiquated machinery were two major reasons textile employment declined after 1970. In the late 1970s and early 1980s, as textile workers and the federal government demanded cleaner factories and import competition required greater productivity, the industry responded with major investments in new machinery. Contrary to popular perception of North Carolina's textile industry as near death, textile corporations accounted for one-sixth of the state's total manufacturing investment during the 1980s. In 1987, textile investment was almost one-quarter of the total manufacturing investment (NCDOC 1988, 32). But this new machinery required fewer employees to operate it.

The apparel and furniture industries share with textiles a labor-intensive production process and low wages. But unlike textiles, these industries have been less vulnerable to imports. Since 1970, the number of both apparel and furniture workers has increased, although the industries' share of the total labor force has declined. While the textile industry has become increasingly capital-intensive, thus producing fewer jobs, the apparel and furniture sectors have expanded jobs with a relatively low capital investment. For example, during 1987 each additional job in apparel required a $9,000 investment and an additional job in the furniture industry averaged $19,000, while in textiles each additional job required an $82,000 investment (NCDOC 1988, 32). The value added per employee remains far less in apparel and furniture than in most other Tar Heel industries, and they consequently are even lower-wage sectors than textiles. They remain a steady component of North Carolina's manufacturing base. In both 1970 and 1987, apparel and furniture each provided about 10 percent of the state's manufacturing employment.

The manufacture of tobacco products, primarily cigarettes, has been declining in North Carolina. Cigarette manufacturing is often mistakenly viewed, even by North Carolinians, as a major part of the state's economy. In fact, just 4 percent of industrial workers in 1970, and 3 percent in 1987, produced cigarettes. The confusion occurs because tobacco farming remains a key component of North Carolina's agricultural economy. Cigarette production today is located in the five cities where major manufacturers have plants: the Winston-Salem area; Reidsville, northeast of Greensboro; Greensboro itself; Concord, northeast of Charlotte; and Durham. Although tobacco products constitute a small part of the statewide manufacturing total, this core industry pays North Carolina's highest manufacturing wages (Sampson 1986, 282–83). One clear indicator of the industry's decline is that in 1987 24,000 Tar Heels worked in tobacco manufacturing, compared to 29,000 in 1970.

The long-range trend in the North Carolina manufacturing mix is toward core industries whose investments in the state have primarily occurred since 1970. Two excellent examples are machinery and transportation equipment, contrasted with cigarette production. In 1970, the tobacco and machinery sectors each employed 29,000 workers, while the transportation equipment industry, mainly bus and truck production, employed 8,000. By 1987, 57,000 workers were employed in machinery and 25,000 in transportation equipment, whereas tobacco manufacturing employment, as noted above, had dropped to 24,000. Although neither of these newer industries pays as well as cigarette production, both pay more than the state's average wage and well above the wage rates in textiles, apparel, and furniture (Hughes 1982, 32–34).

The North Carolina Economy: The Tertiary Sector

The tertiary sector is the formal term for all nonagricultural (primary sector) and nonmanufacturing (secondary sector) employment in an economy. In popular parlance, it is called the service sector. Because service employment is also a specific category within this larger non-agricultural and nonmanufacturing sector (copy centers and dry clean-ers are examples of a more precisely defined service industry), this book uses the term "tertiary sector" to avoid confusion.

Eighty percent of North Carolina's employment growth between 1970 and 1987 took place in the tertiary sector. Seven of ten Tar Heels outside agriculture worked in the tertiary sector in 1987, compared to six of ten in 1970. While nonmanufacturing work is less physically taxing and less dangerous than manufacturing employment, its disadvantage is that wage rates are often comparable to the low incomes in peripheral manufacturing and are usually lower than wages in core manufactur-ing. Consequently, for most North Carolinians, the economy's shift to the tertiary sector has not necessarily meant a rise in living standards. Retail trade, the state's largest single employment category in 1987, grew from 18 percent of the labor force in 1970 to 27 percent in 1987. Its average weekly wage was also the state's lowest (Employment Security Commission 1987, 10–14). Whether as cause or effect, such low retail trade wages explain why the median income of Tar Heel women re-mains far below that of men.

The other major growth area within the tertiary sector has been the service industry, which expanded from 12 percent to 17 percent of the labor force between 1970 and 1987. Jobs in government, finance and real estate, and transportation and utilities increased in absolute terms between 1970 and 1987, but their share of total state employment did not grow. Overall, employment expansion in the tertiary sector both responds to existing economic growth and can itself be a source of growth. In North Carolina, tertiary sector employment has increased primarily in metro Piedmont counties and other urban centers like Asheville, Fayetteville, and Wilmington. It has expanded secondarily in smaller cities. The establishment of shopping malls across the state since the early 1970s is a good example of low-wage tertiary sector employment.

The North Carolina Economy: The Agricultural Sector

Until the quarter century after World War II, farming was North Carolina's leading occupation. In 1925, although tenth in population nationally, North Carolina ranked second in the number of farms (Hobbs 1930, 89). It was then and has remained a state of small farms. Between 1945 and 1970, thousands of white and black Tar Heels migrated from the land either to the North or to North Carolina's cities. But many discouraged farmers also remained in rural areas to work in factories, many of which first came to North Carolina in these postwar years. Consequently, the state's rural population, the nation's sixth highest, has a higher percentage at work in nonagricultural jobs than is the case in most states. Indeed, in 1986 North Carolina ranked first in the "rural nonfarm" employment category but twelfth in the number of farms (73,000) (NCDOA 1986, 6). Farms continued to be small; the average size of 142 acres in 1980 ranked forty-fourth in the nation and, after Tennessee, was the smallest of the eleven southern states (ibid.).

The issues of farmer indebtedness and prices for farm commodities have contributed to economic uncertainty in agriculture. Total farm income for crops, livestock, dairy, and poultry products fluctuated slightly between 1982 and 1985 but, most importantly, did not increase. Although tobacco remains North Carolina's leading cash crop, and although North Carolina leads the nation in tobacco production, tobacco's percentage of total farm income in the Tar Heel state fell from 30 percent in 1982 to 23 percent in 1985. The other top cash crops in 1985 were broilers (13 percent), hogs (9 percent), turkeys (7 percent), and corn (7 percent) (NCDOA 1986, 7).

In the early 1980s, about 35 percent of North Carolina's farm labor force was directly working in tobacco. These farmers produced nearly 37 percent of all U.S.-grown tobacco in 1985. But the state's farm economy also produced leaders and contenders in several other categories: it ranked first in sweet potatoes, farm forest products, and turkeys raised; second in cucumbers for pickles; third in peanuts; fourth in broilers; and seventh in hogs (NCDOA 1986, 6).

Agriculture is not evenly distributed across North Carolina. Indeed, in 1984 eastern North Carolina, with 27 percent of the state's labor force, was home to exactly half of its farmers. The ten top-ranking counties, in terms of farm income, were all on the Coastal Plain. The continued importance of tobacco as a cash crop is suggested by the following: eight of these ten leading farm income counties also were among the top ten tobacco-producing counties (NCDOA 1986, 6, 21). Agriculture is least important in the metro Piedmont and western Piedmont areas.

Regional Differences: Occupations, Unemployment, and Income

North Carolina's per capita income ranked thirty-seventh of the fifty states in 1985. Primarily two factors account for the difference between the state's moderately low ranking in per capita income compared to its nearly rock-bottom standing in average manufacturing wages. First, some of North Carolina's jobs, especially professional work, pay salaries close to the national norm. Second, a higher percentage of Tar Heel adults participate in the labor force than in most states, and the state unemployment rate is substantially lower than the national rate (4.5 percent versus 6.2 percent in 1987) (Calhoun 1988, 16).

The statewide and national data leave an impression that North Carolina's lower income is compensated for by a lower unemployment rate. But a breakdown of the state's economy by region indicates that this is not the case. The incidence of well-paying jobs and low unemployment correlates positively. During the 1980s, for example, the Research Triangle area consistently enjoyed one of the lowest unemployment rates in the United States, often second only to the Stamford, Connecticut, area outside New York City. Meanwhile, per capita income in Wake (Raleigh) and Durham counties ranked among the state's highest, comparable to that of other metro Piedmont areas. Less than fifty miles to the north, however, eastern Piedmont counties like Person (Roxboro), Vance (Henderson), or Warren (Warrenton) had three times as much unemployment and only two-thirds of Raleigh-Durham's per capita income.

Manufacturing employment is one example of the uneven distribution of jobs in North Carolina. Statewide, 31 percent of Tar Heels held manufacturing jobs in 1984. But in the western Piedmont, the state's industrial heartland, 45 percent of the labor force worked in manufacturing. That area relies on textiles, apparel, and furniture, but also benefits from a more recent influx of higher-paying jobs from the core industrial sector. In 1983, per capita income in the western Piedmont ($9,600) was 11 percent above the state average, and 1984 unemployment (6.7 percent) was normal for the state. Although the area has been hit by plant closings, out-of-state employers find it attractive because of its centrality in the state and its location along interstates 85 and 40. For policymakers, the western Piedmont is not in crisis.

The Mountain counties, by contrast, are a problem region. Unemployment (7.6 percent in 1984) has remained above average and per capita income ($8,150 in 1983) has been below average. Although 37 percent of the labor force was in manufacturing, a disproportionate number of employees worked in low-wage industries. When a Democratic-backed bill to provide tax credits for employers who established new jobs in poor counties became law in 1987, eight of the region's twenty-three counties were eligible.

The eastern Piedmont shares many of the economic problems of the Coastal Plain. They are North Carolina's most agricultural regions, the heartland of flue-cured tobacco. But agriculture employs few persons full-time (5 percent in the eastern Piedmont and 6 percent on the Coastal Plain). The eastern Piedmont has a larger manufacturing base than the Coastal Plain, but both rely on low-wage industries like food products, textiles, and apparel. Unemployment (8.5 percent in 1984) has been highest in the state in these regions, and per capita income ($8,200 in 1983) has remained below the state average. In 1987, three of the twelve eastern Piedmont counties and nine of the forty-one Coastal Plain counties became eligible for employer tax credits.

The metro Piedmont is the center of the state's expanding economy. Based heavily on the provision of services and information, this area is leading North Carolina's transition away from manufacturing employment. Agriculture is barely visible in the six-county area. Its manufacturing level is comparable to the Coastal Plain's, but the kinds of non-manufacturing jobs are vastly different. The large number of professional jobs in the metro Piedmont, compared to the rest of the state, has led to a huge difference in per capita income ($12,150 versus $8,700 in 1983). The unemployment rate in 1984 was 4.4 percent, compared to the state rate of 6.8 percent. During the 1980s, the Research Triangle counties around Raleigh, Durham, and Chapel Hill as well as Mecklenburg County (Charlotte) have prospered more than the Triad counties of Forsyth and Guilford (Winston-Salem, Greensboro, and High Point).

Educational Levels

The dilemma facing North Carolina policymakers is linked to manufacturing and nonmanufacturing employers' increasing preference for a better-educated labor force. For potential employers, this correlates with larger cities offering good roads, airports, and a variety of cultural activities. Consequently, North Carolina increasingly resembles a dual economy, in which economic prosperity seems predictable in the metro Piedmont but much of the rest of the state is left behind. To be sure, within the other regions, urban centers with skilled labor forces, transportation, and an active cultural life are more likely to prosper than nearby rural counties. Examples include Buncombe County (Asheville) in the Mountains, and New Hanover (Wilmington) and Cumberland (Fayetteville) counties in the east.

Nevertheless, the regional educational differences are striking. Whereas less than 10 percent of western and eastern Piedmont residents were college graduates in 1980, 22 percent of adults living in the metro Piedmont had college degrees. Forty-eight percent in the western Piedmont and 47 percent in the eastern Piedmont were high school graduates, compared to 67 percent in the metro Piedmont. Statewide in 1980, 13 percent of the residents were college graduates and 55 percent were high school graduates.

By the late 1980s, policymakers recognized that many of the state's poorer counties, measured by income as well as educational levels, were not attractive to most potential out-of-state investors. This represented a shift from earlier decades, when both lower-wage peripheral and higher-wage industrialization took place. The politics of economic development, from the 1950s when Governor Luther Hodges established the theme of economic diversification to the 1980s, is considered in the next chapter.

5

The Politics of Economic Development

For three decades, from the 1950s into the 1980s, North Carolina governors pursued an economic development strategy based on recruitment of out-of-state employers. The premise of this strategy was the state's economic dependency on the low-wage textile, apparel, and furniture sectors. Economic diversification would benefit North Carolina, so the argument went, because virtually all such companies paid higher wages than North Carolina's core industries. Individual communities, however, could not afford to be choosy about wage levels, and many rural counties, especially in the Mountains and on the Coastal Plain, became home to low-wage companies. In effect, even firms paying at or near the minimum wage, including textile, apparel, and furniture plants, were welcome in North Carolina.

In the 1980s, the flow of new industry to North Carolina slowed considerably. In 1985, only one-sixth of new job announcements came from out-of-state firms. By contrast, less than a decade before, better than one-half of new jobs had been the result of corporate in-migration (Friedlein 1986, 48). This shift in Tar Heel job creation reflected a national trend away from a reliance on major corporations as a source of new manufacturing employment. Yet the principal financial commitment of North Carolina's government in the 1980s was for the recruitment of a particular out-of-state sector, the microelectronics industry.

Much lip service was paid to nonmicroelectronic issues, including the problems of the state's traditional industries (textiles, apparel, and furniture), especially after Jim Martin became governor in 1985. Both Governor Martin and Lieutenant Governor Bob Jordan focused on the economic concerns of the state's less prosperous rural counties. But in fact, funding for the Microelectronics Center of North Carolina (MCNC), established in the Research Triangle Park in 1980, far exceeded any other budget item in North Carolina's economic development program despite the rhetoric devoted to other areas. In dollar terms, micro-electronics had become the "de facto flagship economic policy" for North Carolina (Sternlicht and Finger 1986, 25).

From the 1950s to the 1970s

The decline of North Carolina's agricultural economy in the 1950s provided industrial employers with a ready supply of labor, workers who expected wages far less than what Northerners were demanding. Unemployment, and thus available labor, was greatest in the rural counties of east and west. Because many farm owners and workers migrated into cities, labor was also available in the urban areas (Mahaffey and Doty, 1979; Mahaffey and Doty 1981, 228; Wood 1986).

A major advantage of North Carolina over other southern states was its commitment early in the twentieth century to an active governmental role in the provision of infrastructure. For example, the state assumed fiscal responsibility for highways in 1921 and accepted primary responsibility for public school funding in 1931 (Wood 1986, 125–28). Prospective investors found a state government eager to cooperate to ensure a profitable venture. Further, the state adopted an unfriendly stance toward unions. In 1947, North Carolina was among the first southern states to pass right-to-work legislation, which outlawed mandatory worker membership in unions even if a union was the legally recognized collective bargaining agent with management.

In the 1950s, Governor Luther Hodges typified the state's simultaneous antiunionism and prodiversification strategies. He worked with private developers beginning in 1955 to establish a research and development park in the area between the cities of Durham and Raleigh, whose lure would be the research links to the University of North Carolina at Chapel Hill, Duke University in Durham, and North Carolina State University in Raleigh. When the project appeared near collapse in 1958, Hodges endorsed the proposal of Wachovia banker Robert Hanes to establish a nonprofit corporation to buy out the original investors. Fellow Wachovia banker and state senator Archie Davis undertook the task of raising the money, which he found surprisingly easy. The connections between growth-oriented business and a supportive state government, coupled with ties to universities, were attractive to public-spirited and affluent North Carolinians. Today, the highly successful Research Triangle Park rivals any R&D center in the world.

But at the time, the good name of Governor Hodges was key to legiti-mizing the idea (Vogel and Larson 1985, 243–48; Hodges 1962, chap. 9).

After the 1960 election, in which Terry Sanford had been the only southern candidate for statewide office who had been willing to tie his campaign openly to John F. Kennedy's, Kennedy selected Hodges as his secretary of commerce. He repaid his political debt to Sanford, who became governor at the same time as Kennedy assumed the presidency, by agreeing to locate the National Institute for Environmental Health Sciences in the Research Triangle Park. That federal decision and IBM's selection of the Research Triangle Park in 1965 for a large corporate expansion were watershed events in the park's success (Vogel and Larson 1985, 254–55).

Simultaneous with his commitment to a new economic development plan for North Carolina, Governor Hodges in 1958 sided with tradition-alists in a bitter labor dispute at Harriet-Henderson Yarns, located in the eastern Piedmont town of Henderson. The textile mill sought to break its fourteen-year-old labor contract with the Textile Workers Union of America (TWUA), and TWUA went on strike. Hodges sent the National Guard and the Highway Patrol to Henderson, who allowed strikebreak-ers to cross a weakened picket line (Hodges 1962, chap. 10; Frankel 1986). Further, the State Bureau of Investigation paid an informer who claimed that union leader Boyd Payton and others were conspiring to bomb a textile mill. State courts ruled consistently that union members, not strikebreakers, had violated the law. Both directly and indirectly, Hodges sent a message that North Carolina opposed unions (Payton 1970; Wood 1986).

The antiunionism coupled with low wages and few strikes to make North Carolina a low-cost production location. The state enhanced its attractiveness to business in the late 1950s with the establishment of customized industrial training. One of the first states to develop made-to-order job training in 1957, North Carolina over the years has main-tained one of the nation's largest budgets to meet employer requests for trained workers. Customized industrial training constitutes a direct subsidy to industry, in which the state's community college system pays instructors to provide specific job training for prospective employ-ees of a new firm. The training service is available for any firm that provides at least twelve new jobs (NCDOC 1986–87).

The message from the 1950s on was clear. North Carolina promised relatively low wages, few unions, and few strikes. Moreover, it was willing to subsidize employer costs through on-site training. Wanting to keep jobs in the nonmetropolitan areas, the state's industrial recruiters emphasized the virtues of decentralized manufacturing (Mahaffey and Doty 1981, 228). A 1957 *New York Times* advertising supplement on North Carolina was headlined "Labor Ready, Willing and Able." Governor Hodges stressed the stability of the rural labor force and its accessibility due to the state's highway network. According to Hodges, industry could "locate away from congestion and at the same time . . . draw upon a large and industrious labor supply that is mostly rural." As Hodges's successor in the early 1960s, Governor Sanford spoke of Tar Heel workers' willingness to provide a "full day's work for a full day's pay" (quotations from Wood 1986, 163, 242).

Until the 1970s, the state's recruitment program to bring industry both to urban and rural North Carolina was successful. Both urban and rural North Carolina won new jobs, and core industries such as machinery or bus production paying higher wages than the state average were more likely than ever before to locate in the state (Doty and Mahaffey 1979, 7–9). The labor-intensive industries that settled primarily in rural counties required little skill from workers. Industrialists in these areas did not worry about residents' educational attainment levels, literacy rates, or quality public schools (Rosenfeld 1983, 2).

As long as the wages of prospective firms were competitive with prevailing wages, no local conflict emerged. In the 1970s, however, the question of whether communities should welcome firms paying above the local average erupted into numerous debates across North Carolina. In general, traditionalists said "no" and modernizers said "yes." How the business community divided itself—into traditionalist and modernizer perspectives—provides insight into the ideological conflict surrounding North Carolina's economic development.

The Economic Bases of Development Ideology

Until the 1970s, the issue of wages did not loom as a major source of conflict among North Carolina business people. But after a vigorous debate among academicians during 1975 as to why North Carolina's manufacturing wage rates were fiftieth in the nation (Malizia, Crow, et al. 1975; Morse 1978; Stuart 1981, 248–49), gubernatorial candidate Jim Hunt decided in 1976 to make the raising of industrial wages an explicit plank in his campaign platform. Hunt introduced an issue that had previously not been seriously discussed in North Carolina political campaigns, even though higher wages, like apple pie, was hardly a matter that politicians wanted to oppose publicly.

Who were Hunt's major financial supporters? Would they be likely to resist higher wages in North Carolina? The presumption behind campaign contributions is that donors gain access to candidates, and that candidates' political programs bear some resemblance to the political values of financial supporters. If this is true, then Jim Hunt the modernizer politician should be backed by modernizer business people. Similarly, traditionalist business people should contribute disproportionately to a traditionalist politician like Jesse Helms.

The clearest indication of the financial supporters of Hunt and Helms emerges from campaign reports of their respective elections during the 1970s and of their race for the U.S. Senate in 1984. The first elections from the 1970s indicate support for Helms and Hunt at a time when neither candidate was regularly in the national political limelight. By contrast, the 1984 contributions are from the $26 million campaign that was at the time the most expensive in U.S. Senate history. Both analyses examine in-state contributors only, and, significantly, both data sets suggest similar patterns in business support.

Modernizer businesses have a self-interest in economic growth and change. Traditionalist businesses fear the competition that might result from widespread economic growth. Construction, transportation, and real estate firms are typical modernizers. Textile, apparel, and furniture firms, which rely on lower wages and lower levels of capitalization, are typical traditionalists. If these businesses indeed follow their self-interests, modernizer firms should back Hunt more strongly and traditionalists should support Helms.

A comparison of Helms's contributors in his first two Senate races (1972 and 1978) with Hunt's supporters in his campaigns for lieutenant governor in 1972 and governor in 1976 shows a striking difference in economic base. Forty percent of Helms's dollars came from the textile and furniture industries, while just 5 percent of Hunt's came from those industries. Twenty percent of Hunt's money came from the construction and transportation industries, compared to 3 percent for Helms (Luebke, Peters, and Wilson 1985).

The 1984 data, focusing on $1,000 contributors during 1983 and 1984, reveal clear contrasts among three business areas: manufacturing, construction, and real estate. Helms received 60 percent more funding from manufacturers than did Hunt. But in the change-oriented fields of construction and real estate, Hunt received two and one-half times the amount of money raised by Helms (B. Hall 1985a).

The causality of the relationship between business sector support and candidate ideology is not clear. But the campaign contributions indicate that Hunt and Helms had differing business constituencies. Hunt's call for higher industrial wages did not threaten his business supporters. In effect, "growth machine" business people backed Hunt; they were not threatened by a booming economy. By contrast, the textile and apparel industrialists who were more likely to support Helms had reason to fear economic development, because a labor shortage that resulted from a job surplus could force them to raise their local wages. Unlike the realtors or contractors who were more sympathetic to Hunt, textile and apparel leaders were sometimes competing with labor markets in extremely low-wage Third World societies.

Modernizers versus Traditionalists in the 1970s

Hunt's industrial recruitment division in the North Carolina Department of Commerce held onto the middle ground between traditionalists on the one hand and Hunt's "left-wing" supporters—the prounion liberals and populists—on the other. Modernizers did not seek to overturn North Carolina's long-standing reputation as an antiunion, low-wage, and probusiness state. But they did wish to welcome all new firms, regardless of their wages or collective bargaining arrangements with unions. Like other industrial recruitment offices, North Carolina's sought to match counties with industry needs. Beginning in the early 1970s under Governor Bob Scott, state officials encouraged counties, towns, and cities to develop a local recruitment office that cooperated with the state Department of Commerce (Friedlein 1986, 48).

In 1977, two incidents demonstrated the power of traditionalist business in North Carolina's less urban counties. Brockway Glass, a Pennsylvania corporation with unionized plants, sought to build a new factory in Roxboro, thirty miles north of Durham. When the local economic development commission learned that Brockway's unionized wages were 30 percent above the county's prevailing wage, it passed a resolution "disinviting" Brockway (*News and Observer* 1977a). For the commission majority, it was better to pass up several hundred jobs than risk the disruption of social and economic relations (Luebke, McMahon, and Risberg 1979). A local banker declared that the only problem with the Brockway episode was that it had become public. The state recruiters expressed a desire to avoid such conflicts in the future by redlining those counties whose business and political leaders did not want higher-wage industry (Wood 1986, 167–68).

A similar incident occurred in December 1977 in Cabarrus County, northeast of Charlotte, where Philip Morris had selected a site to build a cigarette-manufacturing factory. When it became known that the to-bacco firm intended to pay unionized wages high above the county average, the management of Cannon Mills, located in the nearby com-pany town of Kannapolis, objected to the new plant, fearing wage competition (*News and Observer* 1977c). But public opinion in Cabarrus County had been mobilized in favor of the new jobs. In a small-town traditionalist county where political demonstrations are rare, four thou-sand citizens turned out for a profactory rally. In this case, Cannon was unable to muster sufficient support on the economic development com-mission to overturn the majority endorsement of the Philip Morris investment. Symbolically, Jim Hunt made a much-publicized phone call to Philip Morris's chairman to urge the company not to withdraw from the county (Luebke, McMahon, and Risberg 1979; Wood 1986).

Hunt differed with traditionalist business people in both the Brock-way and Philip Morris cases. Yet he sought to maintain good relations with them by expressing willingness in 1978 to seek alternatives to the manufacturers' inventory tax. As a modernizer Democrat, Hunt was caught in the middle between wanting an activist state that could re-cruit new, higher-wage industry, and not wanting to alienate the tradi-tionalist wing of the state's business community (cf. *News and Observer* 1977b).

The essence of traditionalist fears of unions became apparent when business people in and around Roxboro were interviewed in 1979 about the prospect of unionization in their individual counties. Universally, the local elite felt that unions, often labeled "militant labor organiza-tions," were a disadvantage to the community. In one businessman's view, unions represented an outside power base that would give the county a bad reputation in future recruitment efforts. The belief that unions might challenge the status quo was key. The local elite ignored the probability that unionized jobs would increase workers' wages and, through a multiplier effect, benefit the county economy and even pro-duce additional jobs. The emphasis on social stability rather than social change is common to traditionalist ideology (Mahaffey and Doty 1979, 80–82). Highlighting this issue, a Charlotte-based antiunion consultant told a university audience that allowing unions in a plant was like letting the fox guard the chicken coop (Dowd 1976). In most cases such raw antiunionism is restricted to rural counties. Raleigh, the fast-grow-ing state capital, constituted an exception in the late 1970s when its chamber of commerce resolved to oppose any firm that did not agree to resist unionization (Wood 1986, 166).

Overall, Governor Hunt's economic modernization strategy faced a rocky road from traditionalists. In his second term, beginning in 1981, Hunt focused on the more glamorous goal of high-tech economic development—in particular, the microelectronics industry. Traditionalists did not view microelectronics any more favorably than they viewed other new sectors. But, because of its futuristic appeal, microelectronics proved hard to oppose politically, even though it became an expensive state-supported program.

Modernizers and Microelectronics

Changing economic conditions in North Carolina certainly established the possibility of a high-tech industry like microelectronics coming to North Carolina. But conscious political action intervened to make that form of economic development more likely. The commitment of Governor Jim Hunt and that of his business backers to modernizer ideology made Hunt sympathetic to the microelectronics industry as a major problem solver for North Carolina's economy. Hunt called microelectronics North Carolina's chance, "perhaps the only chance that will come along in our lifetime," for a "dramatic breakthrough" to increase wages and per capita income (Hunt 1981).

Hunt's plan to commit state government resources to the microelectronics industry was a textbook case in gubernatorial power. It resembled Luther Hodges's role in the organization of the Research Triangle Park during the late 1950s, except that the park was launched with virtually no state funding (Budget 1959). In spring 1980, Governor Hunt formed a blue-ribbon panel composed of representatives of the University of North Carolina at Chapel Hill, Duke University, North Carolina State University, and the community colleges to explore the possibility of attracting a high-technology boom such as existed in Silicon Valley. The panel's answer, provided within six weeks, was that the state should establish a nonprofit R&D center that would be linked to universities and serve as a magnet for private investment. The proposed organization of the Microelectronics Center of North Carolina was modeled after the Research Triangle Institute. But the panel recommended that MCNC be given independent status to ensure its political visibility both inside and outside the state (Whittington 1986, 13).

Hunt founded the center in June 1980 with $1 million from the state's contingency fund. Two months later, General Electric (GE) announced its decision to establish a major microelectronics research center at the Research Triangle Park, citing Hunt's actions as a major factor. Subsequently, Hunt invited Don Beilman, who directed GE's microelectronics division, to become head of MCNC.

Following Hunt's election to a second term in November 1980, he made a much-publicized trip to the Silicon Valley, urging high-technology firms to locate in North Carolina. After his return, he asked the Democratic-dominated General Assembly for a first-year appropriation in 1981 of $24 million to implement the development plan for MCNC. Hunt argued that his prior commitment of $1 million, his trip to California, and General Electric's investment made further funding mandatory. The General Assembly approved Hunt's request without even scheduling a public hearing (Whittington 1986, 15).

The MCNC board of directors includes six citizens as well as the chancellors of the five constituent universities (the University of North Carolina at Chapel Hill, Duke, North Carolina State University, North Carolina Agricultural and Technical State University in Greensboro, and the University of North Carolina at Charlotte), a legislator, and the presidents of MCNC and the Research Triangle Institute. The six citizens whom Jim Hunt selected for the MCNC board were prime examples of corporate modernizers. His appointees included a vice-president of the North Carolina National Bank and the chief executive officers of Carolina Power and Light and R. J. Reynolds Industries. In addition, Hunt appointed a black college president from Charlotte, a close friend in a powerful Raleigh law firm, and, from his home political base, the president of a small eastern North Carolina firm. No woman served on Hunt's board. The selection of a black professional along with white corporate executives reflects the typical choices of Democratic modernizers like Hunt who, compared to Republicans, are more likely to include blacks in their list of politically desirable appointees.

Martin's six citizen appointees in fiscal year 1986 were all white male corporate executives. They reflected Martin's modernizer side: the same utility executive and banker appointed by Hunt; corporate officers from General Electric, IBM, and Northern Telecom; and the state budget officer, C. C. Cameron, formerly chief executive officer of First Union Bank in Charlotte.

The Microelectronics Center received $51 million in state funding during the Hunt administration, ending in fiscal year 1985. Although Jim Martin demonstrated far less public enthusiasm for MCNC than Hunt, his budget recommendations paralleled those of his predecessor, totaling more than $15 million annually (MCNC 1985). MCNC works cooperatively with affiliated corporations on research, but the corporate share of its budget, including research contracts, is less than one-third. This contrasts with the Microelectronics and Computer Technology Corporation in Austin, Texas, which is a consortium of private corporations. The initiative in North Carolina reflected Hunt's view that only by making a major government investment could the state hope to benefit from the microelectronics industry. As a research center heavily funded by the legislature, MCNC actively promoted North Carolina as a corporate investment site.

MCNC received some criticism during the Hunt years from traditionalist Republicans who represented the concerns of textile manufacturers. These manufacturers worried that too much money was being spent on a new industry whose net effect might well be to force historically low-wage Tar Heel factories to raise wages (Luebke, Peters, and Wilson 1985, 312). But Martin's decision to recommend MCNC funding, coupled with the continuing willingness of Democratic legislators to support the center, ensured political survival for microelectronics. By fiscal year 1988, more than $80 million had been directly committed to MCNC, and the General Assembly seemed likely to continue annual appropriations in excess of $10 million.

Nevertheless, the heady assumptions of the Hunt administration were flawed in several respects. First, the number of high-paying jobs in the microelectronics industry was limited to scientists, engineers, and associated technicians. Many high-tech companies hired these employees from out of state. Further, companies selected sites in the metro Piedmont counties (the Triangle, the Triad, and Charlotte) and urban Buncombe County (Asheville), counties with the fewest economic problems. Indeed, rather than helping unemployment, the urban locations of some of the wafer production facilities had the potential to cause local labor shortages (Sampson 1986, 287, 289).

Besides its placement in the "wrong" counties, the microelectronics process that many academicians and corporate officials believed would come to North Carolina—wafer production—was in fact a "mid-wage" or "low-wage" manufacturing operation. Hunt's hope that General Electric's research facility would lead to the relocation of numerous other firms from either the Silicon Valley or the Route 128 area near Boston proved illusory. Rather, microelectronics officials decided to maintain R&D centers near corporate headquarters in California or Massachusetts (Sampson 1986, 288, 291).

Both the Microelectronics Center and the state-funded (although to a far lesser amount) North Carolina Biotechnology Center have the indirect effect of conveying the state's modernizer image to national and international firms (NCDOC 1986–87). How much this might influence the future location decisions of corporations, high-technology or otherwise, is unknown. But certainly Jim Hunt's high hopes that microelectronics could play a major role in solving North Carolina's economic problems, especially in the rural counties distant from urban centers, proved to be unrealistic.

Rural Economic Development: What Role for State Government?

The recruitment of out-of-state firms was long viewed as a solution to North Carolina's economic problems. But during the 1980s, across the country, national and multinational corporations were investing less in individual states than had been the case in the 1960s and 1970s. This forced Tar Heel policymakers to reexamine the state's economic development strategies. One critical insight was the growing economic gap between the generally prosperous six counties of the metro Piedmont and North Carolina's rural counties, especially on the Coastal Plain and in the Mountains.

The kinds of low-skill, low-wage factory jobs that manufacturers once gladly brought to rural counties were becoming scarce. Now employers could pay far lower wages in Latin American or Asian countries. Further, when factories remained open, fewer jobs were available because of automation. Increasingly in the 1980s, even firms with relatively low-skill requirements preferred North Carolina's urban areas, closer to airports, interstates, and universities (MDC 1986, 7). Gradually, it became clear to policymakers that any benefits of the microelectronics investment would disproportionately remain in the metro Piedmont counties. For North Carolina politicians of both parties in the mid-to-late 1980s, rural economic development joined microelectronics as a catchy issue.

In addressing rural economic issues, political partisanship won out over bipartisan cooperation. Governor Martin's Republican administration, through the state Department of Commerce, issued its report in September 1986. Secretary of Commerce Howard Haworth, whose background as a furniture executive symbolized Martin's commitment to traditionalist values, drafted the Republican report, known as "North Carolina's Blueprint for Economic Development." Lieutenant Governor Jordan, in effect speaking for the state's Democrats, established a Commission on Jobs and Economic Growth whose work paralleled that of the Commerce Department. Chaired by Jim Melvin, a modernizer Democrat, banker, and former mayor of Greensboro, Jordan's commission released a second, more comprehensive analysis, full of specific legislative proposals, in November 1986. Because the Democrats dominated the General Assembly, Jordan's rather than Martin's proposals became law in 1987.

The two reports shared a common understanding of the economic problems facing the state's rural areas. Further, they both emphasized investment in education, transportation, and water resources as the key to economic development of these areas (O'Connor 1987b). The reports differed in what role the state should play in such an effort. The Democrats recommended the creation of a North Carolina Rural Economic Development Center, to be funded by the General Assembly, which would seek to shepherd economic growth in rural North Carolina. The Democrats also proposed a tax credit for businesses that located jobs in any of the state's twenty neediest counties. The eligible list would vary from year to year, but would be based on unemployment rates and average wage rates. For 1987, the eligible counties were disproportionately on the Coastal Plain and in the Mountains.

Reflecting a greater commitment than Jordan to traditionalist "free enterprise" ideology, Martin's recommendations did not call for either a new state agency or specific tax credits. Rather, they emphasized traditionalism's antitax philosophy by seeking abolition of the inventory and intangible taxes. Labeling these two taxes on business and the wealthy "intrinsically counterproductive," the Republicans argued that economic development would result from a less restrictive tax environment. Finally, the Republican report placed more emphasis on local initiatives and less on state action (NCDOC 1986, 1, 10).

Both Democratic proposals became law during the 1987 session. In supporting the recommendations of Jordan's commission, the General Assembly merely followed party lines. In fact, policymakers disagreed on whether the greater state action promoted by the Democrats would provide better results than the Republican plan (Luger 1986, 214). But the two reports do reflect the difference between the application of Democratic modernizer ideology and the blend of modernism and traditionalism that has characterized the mainstream Republicanism of the Martin administration.

The Business of Subsidies

Since the administration of Luther Hodges in the 1950s, North Carolina has prided itself on its unwillingness to offer special tax subsidies to businesses in order to attract them to the state. But while North Carolina has avoided such obvious tax breaks as ten-year tax abatements, which frequently have been provided in states like Mississippi and South Carolina, and increasingly are offered in northern and midwestern states which fear the loss of industry, it is wrong to suggest that economic recruitment in North Carolina avoids subsidies.

Rather, North Carolina's subsidies have been indirect. Customized job training by community colleges has meant that the Tar Heel taxpayer, not incoming corporations, has paid for workers' on-the-job skill building. Second, industrial revenue bonds, first authorized by the General Assembly in 1977, allow localities to float industrial bonds for business investment. This enables the corporation to pay lower interest rates via the tax-free locality than if the corporation tried to sell the bonds directly. Third, corporations often directly benefit from water/sewer lines, an access road, or even an interstate highway interchange that local or state government is willing to build in order to attract the would-be investor.

A fourth kind of subsidy emerged for the first time from the 1987 General Assembly. High-visibility companies considering relocation in North Carolina were able to receive specific legislative appropriations as inducements to settle in the state. Ironically, only one of the three appropriations, a $750,000 electrical generator to entice Sara Lee bakeries to Tarboro, the seat of Edgecombe County in eastern North Carolina, was made to a high-unemployment area. The community college system received a $1.5 million appropriation for customized training of workers at American Airlines' new reservation center near the Research Triangle Park, while $6.5 million was granted to help Verbatim, a Kodak subsidiary, expand its facilities at Charlotte's University Park R&D center. Not only were unemployment rates low in Raleigh-Durham and Charlotte, but beginning wages at the American Airlines reservation center were set at $5.25 per hour. The annual income for a single parent with two children who worked at that starting rate when the reservation center opened in 1988 would have been under the federal poverty line.

These legislative appropriations reflected effective lobbying by the corporations, which often threatened to locate the jobs outside of North

Carolina without the subsidy (*Greensboro News and Record* 1987b). One lobbyist for American Airlines, for example, was former Governor Jim Hunt. But these General Assembly appropriations hardly reflect careful spending priorities. Indeed, the three subsidies described above totaled twice as much as the General Assembly appropriated in 1987 for all activities of the Rural Economic Development Center, the centerpiece of Jordan's job commission proposal.

Dollars Speak Louder than Words

The General Assembly's direct intervention in 1987 to subsidize economic development in the metro Piedmont shows that North Carolina's economic development goals were not what they seemed. Large, direct grants to aid high-tech economic recruitment in the metro Piedmont say more about priorities than the rhetoric of concern for the economically distressed rural areas of the state.

Some rural areas would benefit from the 1987 education funding earmarked for poorer counties that need new school facilities. The highway legislation that restricted urban counties' ability to fund roads jointly with the state would indirectly improve the chances of rural areas to win new construction dollars.

But the $80 million spent on the Microelectronics Center between 1980 and 1987, the $8 million to recruit American Airlines and Verbatim, as well as direct legislative appropriations in excess of $10 million to woo, unsuccessfully in both cases, the research and development programs of the Sematech Corporation and the federal Energy Department's Supercollider project indicate clearly that General Assembly funding priorities remained in the high-tech sector. Because high-technology employers would most likely stay in the metro Piedmont, North Carolina's economic development policy, in a backhanded way, was supporting those counties that, it could be argued, needed the least help. Republican and Democratic rural-oriented proposals notwithstanding, dollars were allocated to high-visibility projects that helped the haves, not the have-not counties.

A further problem lay with the beneficiaries of such investment within the larger urban counties. Affluent counties still have citizens, many of them black, who lack the job skills, transportation, and/or child care to participate in the high-technology economy. Thus, within the metro Piedmont, substantial numbers of workers are as unlikely to benefit from the high-technology investments as workers in the rural areas. Uneven development occurs not only between urban and rural counties, but within urban counties as well.

Why have these economic development strategies not become political issues in North Carolina? First, the policy bias toward urban high-tech is difficult to detect, given both parties' stated concern about rural development. The bias has emerged from the dominant position of modernizers in the Democratic party. Traditionalists from rural North Carolina, if Democrats, have a difficult time making their case against their party's modernizer interest in metro Piedmont growth. Republican traditionalists, a small minority in the General Assembly, have simply not been taken seriously by Democrats. Both Democratic and Republican traditionalists, although they usually dislike the high-technology bias of economic development policy, have themselves failed to develop policy alternatives.

Republicans like Governor Martin have agreed with Democrats' support of microelectronics. Modernizers have preferred major high-technology, urban-oriented development projects, and continued microelectronics investment supported that interest. For state politicians, the probability of successful high-technology urban development is higher than rural development, since investors are more inclined toward urban locations in the first place (MDC 1986; Rosenfeld 1983, 3). In any case, these determinations are largely taken outside the public eye. Citizens learn of budgetary appropriations only after a handful of legislators have made decisions, devoid of public input.

Perhaps over time, educational improvements will lead to a better-skilled labor force in rural North Carolina. Further, other infrastructural investments like highways or sewer lines might make rural counties more attractive to investors. But in the short run, the hidden bias of economic development policy toward the metro Piedmont counties in effect undermines Democratic and Republican attempts to promote economic growth in North Carolina's rural areas (Luger 1986, 215).

6

Organized Labor on the Defensive

When state government officials in North Carolina undertake long-range planning, the business community is automatically included as a planning partner. But this is not so for labor. Whether under Democratic or Republican governors, modernizer or traditionalist ideology, organized labor has not succeeded in winning a regular seat at the table. In the Hunt years, a token labor representative would sometimes be included on commissions otherwise dominated by corporation executives, politicians, university professors, and other politically active upper middle-class citizens. The denial of equal status to North Carolina unions contrasts sharply with other major states outside the South. Even though unions nationwide lost members in the 1980s (*Durham Morning Herald* 1988), planning at the federal level or in states such as Massachusetts, Illinois, or California maintains the pattern established in the heyday of organized labor following World War II (Goldman and Luebke 1985). There the policy players are business, government, and labor. In North Carolina, the third seat is usually assigned to the state's major universities.

Labor's status as outsider also became evident in the 1984 Helms-Hunt U.S. Senate race. When Jesse Helms sought to prove that Jim Hunt was a "closet liberal," one of his most effective media spots simply scrolled across the TV screen the names and amounts of labor union contributions to the Hunt campaign. Borrowing from a prounion advertising campaign of the International Ladies Garment Workers Union, the Helms piece ended with the line, "Look for the union label."

These two political events—quiet planning meetings in a state office building and high-stakes negative campaign advertising—have more in common than meets the eye. Both presume that organized labor has no place in state politics. Unlike regions of the United States where union power is institutionalized, and where indeed unions are sometimes viewed as part of a power elite that opposes political change, North Carolina is guided by the belief that unions are an unnecessary disruption of the routine affairs of business and government.

Traditionalist business people, still a key force in the state's textile, apparel, and furniture industries, question whether unions have ever served a useful purpose in American or North Carolina history. Their emphasis on individualism leads to the conclusion that unionism constitutes inappropriate interference in the employer-employee relationship. Free enterprise flourishes best when unfettered by a third party (Judkins 1986, 164–66). Traditionalists feel strongly that unions should stay weak in North Carolina.

Modernizer business people in the Tar Heel state disproportionately represent capital-intensive (and usually high-profit) industries such as cigarette production or paper products, as well as nonmanufacturing growth sectors such as banking. These modernizers, like traditionalists, draw negative conclusions about unions, but their logic follows a different route. They see unions as anachronistic in today's era of enlightened management. Further, in the 1980s modernizers recognized an opportunity to fight off unions in North Carolina because of labor's weakened position nationwide. However, unlike traditionalists, modernizers have developed a pragmatic attitude toward unions in the workplace. If workers insist on union representation, modernizers accept the union as a necessary part of doing business (Goldman and Luebke 1985).

Traditionalists, by contrast, try to avoid the implementation of a union contract even if unions have won an election. J. P. Stevens, one of the nation's largest textile corporations, constitutes an excellent example of traditionalist ideology. Stevens stalled for six years, between 1974 and 1980, before signing a contract affecting its plants in Roanoke Rapids, a small town in eastern North Carolina just south of the Virginia line (Mullins and Luebke 1982).

This traditionalist-modernizer accord on labor's illegitimacy has helped to keep unions weak in North Carolina. Throughout the 1980s, North Carolina ranked among the lowest of the fifty states in the level of unionization among blue-collar workers. In 1982, the latest year for which official data are available, 9 percent of Tar Heels belonged to unions, compared to 22 percent nationwide (Troy and Shaeflin 1985). North Carolina ranked forty-ninth, ahead of only South Carolina; even Mississippi had a somewhat higher percentage of unionized workers than North Carolina.

The strength of unions is concentrated in large corporations that have branch plants in North Carolina. The leaders of these companies tend to be modernizers rather than traditionalists. For example, utilities (Bell South), breweries (Miller), paper mills (Georgia Pacific), cigarette manufacturers (Lorillard), trucking companies (Roadway Express), and grocery chains (Kroger) are the most heavily organized sectors of the North Carolina economy. While executives of such firms may not like unions, they are, in most cases, accustomed to labor-management agreements in other states.

Unionized firms are disproportionately located in larger cities. In many rural counties of North Carolina, not a single business is unionized. Two factors help to explain the urban concentration. First, the types of large firms least hostile to unions are more likely to locate in metropolitan rather than rural areas because they wish to be close to population centers (for example, utility companies or supermarkets) or because they desire easy access to airports, interstate highways, and railroad trunk lines. Second, in metropolitan areas, employers have less direct social control over their workers. The argument that a union will damage a local economy irrevocably by raising wages or by ruining a town's reputation for harmonious labor relations is simply less persuasive to workers who live in the city (Wood 1986, 164).

By the late 1980s, union membership had stabilized in North Carolina. Few new firms were organized, but neither were employers able to remove unions from previously organized workplaces. In its major industrial recruitment report of 1986–87 entitled "Business Climate," the state Department of Commerce informed potential employers of unions' weakness: "North Carolina's labor force is one of the most productive in the nation. . . . Labor-management relations are harmonious, and work stoppages are rare" (NCDOC 1986–87, 6, 8).

Out-of-state corporations have heard the message clearly. When Alexander Grant and Company in 1985 asked a national sample of corporate leaders to rank North Carolina's business climate, the state came in eighth among the fifty states. The study listed low wages and low level of unionization as North Carolina's chief attractions (*Greensboro News and Record* 1985).

Within the state, organized labor has so little public clout that decision makers do not appear to give much thought to union and wage questions. According to a 1985 study of state political and business leaders, a majority was unaware that North Carolina's average industrial wage had stood close to fiftieth, near that of Mississippi and South Carolina, for almost a decade. Similarly, most did not know that North

Carolina ranked last among the fifty states in level of unionization (Baker 1986).

Both traditionalist and modernizer business people as well as state politicians take it for granted that North Carolina will not repeal its right-to-work law. This law, passed in 1947 shortly after the Congress authorized such state-based labor legislation, allows workers not to pay union dues even if their workplace is covered by a union contract. One major consequence of the right-to-work law is to deny unions the financial resources that accrue when a union contract and mandatory union membership go hand in hand.

A further indicator of Tar Heel antiunionism has been the difficulty that workers have had, compared to other states, in receiving compensation for either unemployment or injuries in the workplace. A specific problem with workers' compensation developed in the textile industry during the 1970s. Thousands of textile workers who had contracted brown lung disease from inhaling cotton dust in the mill over the years were initially declared ineligible for compensation because they only belatedly—past the statute of limitations—realized that their breathing problems stemmed from the workplace. They received adequate compensation only as a result of a well-organized occupational health movement in the late 1970s (Judkins 1986).

On occasion, reports surface that question North Carolina's desirability as an industrial site. In 1975, a storm erupted in government, business, and university circles when a study, conducted by the Department of City and Regional Planning at the University of North Carolina (UNC) at Chapel Hill, concluded that North Carolina's "wage gap" existed because the state was excessively hostile to unionization (Malizia, Crow, et al. 1975; Stuart 1981, 248–49). The campus's School of Business Administration conducted a symposium that also laid out counterarguments, in particular the human capital argument that Tar Heel workers, having relatively low levels of formal education, were being compensated fairly for their labor (Morse 1978). Thus, the views of free-market-oriented academicians were consistent with traditionalist ideology: that unionization would only artificially and improperly raise industrialists' cost of doing business. It is unclear whether or not the planning school study, named the Malizia Report after lead investigator Emil Malizia, provided a definitive argument that low levels of unionization cause low-wage levels. But the reaction to the very publication of the Malizia Report demonstrated the sensitivity of many corporate and political decision makers to any criticism of North Carolina's labor relations.

Similarly, in early 1987 a Washington-based research group singled out North Carolina for its allegedly bad industrial climate (Corporation for Enterprise Development 1987). Governor Jim Martin took the lead among the state's politicians in criticizing the report, noting that North Carolina received low marks because the report assumed that unionization improved a state's economic climate. Sounding like a traditionalist ideologue, Martin noted during the March 1987 annual luncheon of the North Carolina Citizens for Business and Industry—in effect, the state chamber of commerce—that, with increased unionization, North Carolina could "lose the confidence of business decision-makers" by creating an "anti-business climate." He argued that low marks were welcome if it affirmed the state's nonunion orientation.

The Rise and Fall of the Labor Education Center: A Vignette

In 1976, modernizer Democratic gubernatorial candidate Jim Hunt, seeking to strengthen his ties to the citizen-action wing of the party, sought the endorsement of the state AFL-CIO. The AFL-CIO did endorse Hunt, both in the crucial first primary, when he needed an absolute majority to avoid a runoff election, and in the November general election, when he faced weak Republican opposition. In exchange, Hunt agreed to encourage UNC President William Friday to find a home on one of the university system's sixteen campuses for a labor education and research center, modeled after similar centers in two dozen other states, including six southern states (Adams 1981).

By April 1977, Chancellor Albert Whiting of historically black North Carolina Central University had agreed to house the center at his campus in Durham. The curriculum, designed like those in other states to help especially unionized workers, was to include courses in collective bargaining, grievance procedures, labor history, and occupational health and safety. Governor Hunt's office approved temporary staff with federal funds available under the Comprehensive Education and Training Act (CETA). The expectation was that regular funding would follow after routine approval from the UNC Board of Governors.

Institutionalizing a union-oriented program into the UNC system was, however, hardly a routine activity. The Board of Governors consisted primarily of business people and professionals, both traditionalists and modernizers, who had little sympathy for unions or other manifestations of citizen power. Modernizers differed from traditionalists in their willingness to listen to a pro–Labor Center presentation from President Friday. He argued that such a center followed precedents in other southern states and provided services appropriate for a state university, comparable to applied programs in law, medicine, banking, business, public education, agriculture, and the arts.

Traditionalists lost an early round in October 1977 when the board's planning committee approved the Labor Center proposal, but traditionalists pressured UNC board members in November to reexamine their support. Their arguments centered on their belief that North Carolina's prosperity depended on antiunionism. They harped on a private AFL-CIO eight-year organizing plan, accidentally left by a union official in a Raleigh motel room, which showed the Labor Center as part of a larger union plan to increase its power in North Carolina (Adams 1981, 362–63). The traditionalist opposition was led by board members from the textile and furniture industries who feared that an active labor movement would endanger their low-wage businesses. Board member and textile company president Daniel Gunter spearheaded the fight against the AFL-CIO's right to appoint a majority of the Labor Center's board. Although this provision was dropped from later drafts, planning committee member and furniture industrialist Harley Shuford argued candidly: "I am opposed [to the center] because I think it would strengthen the cause of organized labor in our state. I feel organized labor is detrimental to both the quality of life and economic development in our state" (*Durham Morning Herald*, February 19, 1978, quoted in Goldman and Luebke 1985, 26). Republican businessman-legislator Cass Ballenger, who was subsequently elected (1986) to Congress from a western North Carolina district, had these blunt words in the heat of the battle: "The first thought of most industries moving out of the North is the antiunion attitude of the workers in the state of North Carolina. It's an attraction. So why is the state going to try to change the attitude of the workers?" (*Charlotte Observer*, December 31, 1977, quoted in Goldman and Luebke 1985, 26). In fact, Tar Heel workers' attitudes toward unions are far more favorable, if complicated, than Ballenger believed. But in the Labor Center debate, the traditionalist arguments were taking root. As one Charlotte-based antiunion consultant put it, at still another university seminar on labor-management relations, legitimating unions' role as partners in political and economic decision making "would be a disastrous inviting the fox-into-the-hen-house approach" (Dowd 1976, 87; Goldman and Luebke 1985, 26).

Significantly, on the UNC board itself, no member spoke strongly for the proposal. Friday and other UNC staff, as well as editorial writers of the state's major daily newspapers, were the only advocates. The UNC administration argued the case on technical grounds. Only the newspapers made the case that, inasmuch as unions appeared to be a permanent structure in North Carolina, labor-management relations would be more stable if union members could benefit from university course work. But the one modernizer politician who could have turned the day for the Labor Center, Jim Hunt, chose not to act. The AFL-CIO itself appeared to acquiesce in defeat, deciding that to try to mobilize its members to pressure either the governor or UNC board members would only encourage traditionalists to fight harder. The Democratic party's "black and (white) liberal" wing is usually credited with influencing at least 30 percent of a primary vote and 25 percent in a general election. But in the Labor Center case, these various constituencies, including blacks and campus groups, hardly raised a protest.

Governor Hunt's moves as a modernizer politician were completely predictable. Modernizer ideology can tolerate unions if necessary. In the Labor Center case, a firestorm of protest came from traditionalist business people, while from the citizen-action wing of the party hardly a murmur was raised. It taught Jim Hunt and other modernizer politicians of the day that the AFL-CIO and its citizen-action friends may be reliable for some votes on Election Day, but, in a direct confrontation with traditionalists, antiunionism wins hands down. When Hunt ran for reelection in 1980 and for the U.S. Senate in 1984, he sought to avoid the label of a prolabor politician. The lesson was clear: labor remained illegitimate in North Carolina politics.

Hard-Line and Genteel Antiunionism: Politicians at Work

As part of his defense of free enterprise, Jesse Helms has made unions a favorite whipping boy in his efforts to strengthen the traditionalist political agenda for North Carolina. His staunch antiunionism has been adopted by the state Republican party and remains a strong component of many Democratic politicians' ideology as well. The key elements of Helms's critique are communism and corruption.

This traditionalist stance builds on both fact and fiction. It is a fact that a Communist-oriented union sought to organize workers at the Loray Mill in Gastonia in 1929, but it is fiction to suggest that North Carolina textile industrialists would have accepted the union had it lacked leftist ties. Indeed, when the non-Communist United Textile Workers organized workers in Marion several years later, it too faced massive resistance from the elite. The reality of some Communist influence in many CIO unions of the 1930s and 1940s, including the food and tobacco workers' local at R. J. Reynolds during and after World War II, provided traditionalism with a favorite point of attack. If unions could be labeled socialist, then they could be criticized both as anticapitalist and anti-Christian. The fact that leftist influence was minimal was beside the point (Marshall 1967; Luebke 1989).

Similarly, the corruption unearthed in national unions during the 1950s, associated especially with the Teamsters, constituted another building block in traditionalist antiunionism. Within North Carolina, the 1982 conviction of former AFL-CIO chief Wilbur Hobby for misuse of CETA funds confirmed the traditionalists' view of unions as inherently corrupt.

A kind of antiunionism by omission permeates some of North Carolina's social institutions. Schoolteachers in Detroit are unionized and recognize the United Automobile Workers (UAW) as a part of the Michigan landscape; in other words, union membership is normal. In North Carolina, teachers are far more likely never to bring up unions. Similarly, unions as important organizations of working people are rarely mentioned in the North Carolina media, in contrast to Michigan coverage of union Fourth of July picnics, Labor Day solidarity parades, or UAW participation in United Way fund-raising. News coverage in North Carolina is usually restricted to the conflict surrounding a strike or a union election. In their contrasting behavior, teachers and editors in Michigan and in North Carolina can help shape the long-term probability of unions' winning representation elections several decades into the future.

Perhaps more significant than the blatant antiunionism of traditionalist ideology has been the subtle opposition to unions within modernizer ideology. The actions of Terry Sanford illustrate this genteel antiunionism. In his 1986 Senate race, candidate Sanford accepted contributions from union political action committees. As governor in the early 1960s, he commuted the sentence of a textile union organizer who had been convicted in a state court of conspiracy charges on very dubious grounds. But as president of Duke University in the late 1970s, Sanford agreed to the hiring of an antiunion consulting firm that helped the Duke University Medical Center defeat a vigorous organizing drive by the American Federation of State, Municipal, and County Employees (AFSMCE).

Sanford's predecessor as governor, Luther Hodges, Sr., similarly opposed unions while seeking to modernize the state's economy. In the same years that Hodges endorsed the concept of the Research Triangle Park, he called out the National Guard to police a textile workers' strike in Henderson, the effect of which was to weaken and ultimately defeat the union's efforts at Harriet-Henderson Yarns. It was also during Hodges's administration that the State Bureau of Investigation built a conspiracy case against union members, the same case in which Sanford would intervene several years later. Hodges entered politics after many years as a manager at Fieldcrest Mills, a unionized textile firm, but that experience did not convince him of the benefits of collective bargaining between workers and management. Rather, his interest in the modernization of North Carolina's economy, especially to reduce its reliance on textile manufacturing, went hand-in-hand with a preference to decrease, not increase, collective bargaining (Billings 1979, 227–28). Yet Hodges avoided blatant antiunion statements. Like Sanford, he demonstrated the substance of genteel antiunionism, evidenced less by strong words and more by deliberate action.

Jim Hunt's tenure as governor, especially in his first term, provides another example of genteel antiunionism. The case of the North Carolina Labor Center illustrated Hunt's unwillingness to take a major political risk on unions' behalf. Equally importantly, Hunt's industrial recruitment efforts, organized in the state Department of Commerce, maintained a formal neutrality on the question of whether North Carolina welcomed corporations that were committed to unionization of their employees. But while officially neutral, the state, in ads appearing in business magazines across the United States, used code words like "competitive wage rates" and "low level of work stoppages" to indicate that North Carolina possessed two major attractions: low wages and few strikes. Although more subtle in his rhetoric, Hunt sent a message through his Department of Commerce that he would certainly tolerate a low-wage, nonunion environment. In practice, the difference between Hunt and his Republican successor, Jim Martin, is not clear. When faced during 1977 with two industrial recruitment battles over the high-wage question, Hunt took differing positions.

The conflict arose when corporations offering higher wages were challenged by local leaders who did not wish to see wages rise in their areas. State Department of Commerce officials often yielded to the desires of local elites who were threatened by higher-wage and especially unionized firms. One such case occurred in Roxboro in 1977 when the local economic development commission, appointed by the Person County Commission and heavily weighted toward business, discouraged the unionized Brockway Glass Co. of Pennsylvania from building a southern branch plant in the county (see Chapter 5). Although workers in the county sought to counter that opposition with a pro-Brockway petition drive, the firm chose instead to settle a few miles to the north in Danville, Virginia. After the fact, state officials indicated that they preferred to know ahead of time whether to steer companies away from certain counties. In working with local elites, the Hunt administration may have strengthened the governor's political alliances with traditionalist business, but as a consequence local workers faced more restricted job and income opportunities (Luebke, McMahon, and Risberg 1979; Wood 1986).

A short time later in 1977, a similar fight erupted in Cabarrus County, when Cannon Mills feared that the high wages and unionization of a Philip Morris cigarette-manufacturing factory could hurt the stability of its work force (see Chapter 5). In this much-publicized case, the county's economic development committee had first endorsed the new plant and then had second thoughts. This time Hunt chose to intervene on behalf of the new plant, making an early-morning phone call to Philip Morris's president. The governor emphasized the importance of higher wages and his commitment to new industry. Since Philip Morris had a national understanding with unions in both cigarette manufacturing and its Miller Brewery subsidiary, Hunt, in accord with modernizer ideology, did not object to unionism. This stand enhanced his reputation as an advocate of higher wages (News and Observer 1977b). But the conflicting responses in the Brockway and Philip Morris cases indicated that Democratic modernizers like Hunt had a less-than-total commitment to higher pay for North Carolina workers.

When Philip Morris's subsidiary, Miller Brewery, selected Eden, home of Fieldcrest Mills, as the site for a high-wage brewery, Fieldcrest initially objected because of wage competition. But after county citizens overwhelmingly passed a water referendum, Fieldcrest recognized the reality of a two-tiered manufacturing wage market. Miller would pay as much for unskilled labor as Fieldcrest would for skilled labor, but just so many workers could "get on" at Miller. Although within the textile industry, Fieldcrest, founded by Marshall Field of Chicago, is better characterized as a modernizer firm because of its long-standing collective bargaining agreement with the Textile Workers Union. Fieldcrest's behavior in this case, adapting to economic change rather than continuing a never-ending ideological war against high-paying firms like Miller, illustrates the importance of pragmatism in modernizer strategy.

A final manifestation of genteel antiunionism lies with many national corporations themselves, which have unionized plants in other parts of the country but choose to fight the union when they build new plants in North Carolina. Oftentimes, the suggestion to resist unionization comes from traditionalist business people, who do not want to give unions a foothold in the community. One example is Dana Corporation, organized by the UAW elsewhere in the country, but which defeated the union at a 1982 representation election in Gastonia (*News and Observer* 1981d; Mullins and Luebke 1984, 26). Similarly, Firestone has fought off union attempts in recent years, both at a large new plant in Wilson and at the still-operating Loray plant—famous because of the 1929 strike—in Gastonia. Elsewhere in the country, Firestone has collective bargaining agreements with the United Rubber Workers.

The North Carolina General Assembly constitutes a mix of both hardline and genteel antiunionism. But, as in the case of the ill-fated Labor Center, the traditionalists' hard line holds sway. One of the clearest indications of antiunion sentiment is the prohibition of collective bargaining for state and local employees. While state employees and teacher groups certainly lobby the legislature for benefits, no public employee group can bargain for a union contract with a government employer. Once again, a traditionalist-modernizer alliance affirms the illegitimacy of unionism.

Why Unions Lose Elections: The Culture of Antiunionism

Throughout the 1980s, unions in North Carolina won only about one-third of the nearly three hundred representation elections that have been held at private-sector workplaces subject to the jurisdiction of the National Labor Relations Board (NLRB). One reason for this relatively low success rate is national. In the 1980s, the decline of the manufacturing sector, increased competition within that sector, especially from overseas, and a less-cordial attitude toward unions under President Ronald Reagan (epitomized by the ill-fated 1981 air controllers' strike) contributed to an environment unfriendly to union advances. Throughout the country, American workers worried about losing their jobs are less likely to go on strike or, if unorganized, less likely to support a union drive.

But North Carolina's reputation as last in unions has roots in additional factors. The most important is the strength of institutional opposition to labor. As illustrated above, both traditionalist and modernizer ideologies within government and business are unsympathetic to unions. This lack of sympathy carries over into other institutions as well. Public school teachers are prohibited from collective bargaining, so that they rarely debate the case for unionism. No newspaper or radio-television station in North Carolina is organized, so that unions are perforce presented in the media as somebody else's issue. Judges generally respond favorably to corporations' requests to limit the number of picketing strikers to a handful. Baptists, North Carolina's predominant Protestant denomination, have no tradition of support for organized labor. In short, the Tar Heel state lacks any strong institutional base for a positive presentation of unionism. On the contrary, the dominant institutional message, as illustrated throughout this chapter, is that unions are at best superfluous and at worst evil. It is no surprise that unions win few elections.

Some observers argue that unions' defeats are linked less to institutional opposition than to the strong tradition of rugged individualism that permeates the state's culture. But, contrary to popular thought, surveys of North Carolina workers have found support for trade unions (Leiter 1986; *Greensboro Record* 1979). Attitudes toward unions depend on employees' perception of the "fairness" of their working conditions. Union support is highest among those who feel that their pay and work situation are unsatisfactory. Younger, lower-income, and black workers are most likely to support unions, and gender makes no difference (Leiter 1986; Zingraff and Schulman 1984). The traditionalist view that unions disrupt the proper deferential relationship between worker and employer has not been supported in recent research (Leiter 1983; Schneider 1986). Many workers, especially blacks, seek greater power on the job (Goldman and Luebke 1985; Zingraff and Schulman 1984). Why, then, do unions not win more representation elections? The answer lies in the complex web of factors that intervene between workers' response to a survey and their actual vote in a union election.

Some of these factors are practically constants. For example, workers who express prounion attitudes to researchers have usually not been confronted by the counterarguments that elite institutions raise when an actual union organizing drive is underway. In a normal North Carolina setting, politicians, business people, and newspaper editors are likely to raise the issues of lengthy strikes and thus loss of pay, violence, and the possibility of a plant shutdown to avoid higher labor costs and union grievance systems. Workers typically are asked if they know how their union dues will be spent, and why they think their grievances cannot be met with direct appeals to management (*News and Observer* 1977c).

Unions also lose elections if their organizing team is weaker than the consultants who virtually every firm today will hire during an organizing drive. Although companies may well have retained an out-of-state antiunion consultant, they will no doubt hit unions with the "outsider" charge. Further, unions that have not solidified a strong interracial team of in-plant workers will find companies sowing seeds of dissatisfaction among either black or white workers. At Cannon Mills' main plants in Kannapolis, for example, many black workers unexpectedly opposed the Amalgamated Clothing and Textile Workers Union (ACTWU) in an October 1985 election. Several local black ministers argued, on the company's behalf, that the union would threaten recent gains by black workers.

These specific company strategies, undertaken against the backdrop of North Carolina's antiunion culture, put the burden on the union to convince workers that they should undertake *the risk* of a prounion vote. However bad pay, benefits, or working conditions might be, workers in North Carolina have few positive precedents to lead them to conclude that the benefits of a prounion vote outweigh the risks.

Win the Election, Lose the Contract

Once North Carolina companies have lost a union representation election, they do not automatically move to sign a contract. Rather, given labor's weakness in the state at large, firms often adopt a wait-them-out attitude, stalling during contract negotiations in hopes that workers will become dissatisfied with the union. The best example of beating the union after an election occurred in the late 1970s in the area around Winston-Salem. In a flurry of activity, a Teamsters' local won five representation elections within a short time, benefiting from unusually extensive and sympathetic news coverage—perhaps because the lead organizer, an attractive twenty-six-year-old woman, broke the stereotype of crusty unionist (*News and Observer* 1978b). After three years, having encountered opposition from virtually every workplace, the Teamsters had negotiated only two contracts (Botsch 1980, 205). The Winston-Salem police and sanitation workers, whom they had organized, were prevented by state law from gaining a contract (*Greensboro Daily News* 1978); both groups lost interest when a new city manager improved policies. In most places, the failure to win contracts not only demoralized employees who had won their elections, but also sent a message of futility to other workers in the Winston-Salem area.

An ACTWU campaign against J. P. Stevens took seven years to negotiate a contract, from an August 1974 election to an October 1980 settlement. In this case, involving primarily workers at Roanoke Rapids plants, the union was required to appear incessantly before the NLRB, and attempted a consumer boycott of Stevens products. ACTWU finally forced Stevens's hand only after outside Stevens directors, because of citizen pressure on their own companies, insisted that Stevens management sign a contract (Mullins and Luebke 1984, 1982). Although ACTWU won a major victory with J. P. Stevens, it was unable with this contract to achieve any domino effect at other North Carolina textile plants. Its major 1985 campaign against Cannon Mills resulted in a sound defeat, as Cannon management raised the familiar issues—listed above—against the union.

The Brown Lung Association:
A Successful Occupational Health Movement

As long ago as 1942, Britain identified cotton dust as an occupational health hazard, but well into the 1970s the American Textile Manufacturers' Institute continued to maintain that no such risk existed in the United States. A movement of North Carolina textile workers, most of them retired and in poor health, assisted by a bevy of energetic community organizers, forced textile companies in the late 1970s to begin providing compensation (Conway 1979). In addition, effective lobbying of Governor Hunt and the General Assembly led in 1982 to the state's elimination of certain regulations that restricted mill workers' eligibility for workers' compensation.

The Carolina Brown Lung Association (CBLA) is one of the few instances where workers defeated corporations in the halls of the General Assembly. The movement succeeded both because it marshaled significant resources within a short period, and because the workers—home-grown Tar Heels, white, sickly, elderly, and nonunion—constituted a difficult target for textile companies to discredit. The CBLA's victory instructs because of the contrasts with union organizing attempts. First, in the early 1970s, federally funded researchers had identified cotton dust as a probable source of occupational disease. Ralph Nader had publicized the problem as brown lung, a spin-off term from the black lung disease that coal miners contracted from coal dust. Second, the Occupational Safety and Health Administration (OSHA), in response to the research findings, was developing a cotton dust standard that would force textile manufacturers to reduce the amount of cotton dust inside a mill. Third, various liberal foundations were willing to fund CBLA staff to go into mill villages in Greensboro, Erwin, and Roanoke Rapids, for example, to organize brown lung victims into an active community force. Fourth, the workers themselves, prototypes of the employees who constituted the backbone of the state's cotton-textile economy for decades, were sympathetic figures, especially for television and newspaper reporters. How could one deny that these ailing workers were entitled to compensation?

The CBLA had to fight for compensation because of state laws requiring workers to file a claim within a short period after leaving employment. The workers argued that, inasmuch as their employers denied that their respiratory ailments had anything to do with cotton dust, how could workers possibly know they could file? All of these factors led to a public perception that greatly favored the CBLA: an organization of low-income and sick retired mill workers in a David-Goliath battle against the insurance companies of some of the country's major textile firms, such as Cone Mills, Burlington Industries, and J. P. Stevens. Over an eight-year period, from 1974 when the CBLA was founded until 1982 when the General Assembly eased the regulations for workers' compensation, the CBLA successfully captured the positive symbols of a *sympathetic* underdog. Brown lung victims, after all, had played by the rules of traditionalist North Carolina, working hard for the free enterprise system, and now the textile companies, holding to the letter of the law, sought to deny these workers decent compensation in the last years of their lives.

CBLA's victory for ailing cotton-mill workers also demonstrates the difficulties of union organizing. Unionism's dominant symbols in this state are negative, in sharp contrast to the appeals of the CBLA. At a minimum, modernizers see unions as a bureaucratic layer that is no longer needed in these days of enlightened management and, more fundamentally, traditionalists oppose unions as a leftist-influenced and corrupt interference in the prerogatives of management. In contrast to their support for the brown lung movement, the federal government is not a sympathetic ally of union organizers and liberal foundations are not underwriting union drives. In short, healthy workers pushing for unions may simply be viewed as selfish.

Making the Best of a Bad Situation

After the Republican victories in 1984, it became apparent that even the token recognition that modernizers like Jim Hunt granted organized labor would be missing during the term of Jim Martin. For the state AFL-CIO, the question was how to respond to the increasingly negative situation. To state president Christopher Scott, an English literature Ph.D. candidate turned labor politician, the answer was clear. Scott and other labor lobbyists at the General Assembly moved toward building behind-the-scenes coalitions of friendly representatives and senators. Their goal was to promote prolabor legislation without trying to claim public credit for their activities.

One such effort succeeded in 1985, when the General Assembly passed a right-to-know bill that gave workers and communities the right to information concerning hazardous chemicals in the workplace. The law was modeled on legislation passed in other states. Several incidents in the early 1980s had demonstrated that dangerous chemicals were in abundance in North Carolina. In particular, an explosion at a chemical storage plant in East Durham in 1983 prompted a Durham citizens' coalition to demand the removal of the plant and, more generally, a local right-to-know ordinance.

The AFL-CIO joined with the Sierra Club and the North Carolina Occupational Safety and Health Project (NCOSH), a Durham-based statewide organization of union members and health professionals, to lobby for right-to-know in the General Assembly. Harry Payne, a Wilmington Democrat sympathetic to these citizen-power organizations, introduced the bill in the house. Payne, other supportive legislators, and the lobbyists promoted the bill as a public health measure rather than as a labor issue. Although so labeled, the bill was vigorously opposed by various business lobbies. Business argued that the bill would require firms to divulge trade secrets and that these companies should be trusted to care responsibly for their chemicals. Although the legislation was weaker in terms of citizens rights than Durham's local ordinance and the new law preempted the Durham statute, the 1985 right-to-know statute nevertheless constituted a significant victory for the labor-environmentalist coalition.

In 1987, labor continued its policy of quiet worker advocacy. Workers' compensation laws (see Chapter 3) were liberalized, maximum unemployment compensation was increased, and the state minimum wage was coupled with the federal wage so that both would increase simultaneously (AFL-CIO Legislative Report 1987). In all three cases, the AFL-CIO lobbied privately but never sought to take public credit for the new legislation.

Labor was less successful with proconsumer legislation from which union members, among others, would benefit. For example, despite labor's opposition to expansion of the food tax, the General Assembly raised the local-option sales tax by one-half cent in 1983 and again in 1986. In 1987, two bills to set limits on electric utility rates failed to win support in the House Public Utilities Committee.

Labor's recent gains in the General Assembly have been real. But they have been achieved only by maintaining a low profile, by playing by the rules of North Carolina's political game. In that game, labor cannot be a visible public player. Ironically, even as the AFL-CIO joins a small group of like-minded lobbyists and legislators in promoting economic populist legislation, unions remain illegitimate in the eyes of both the modernizer and the traditionalist elite. Labor illegitimacy is promoted by government and business alike, conveying the message publicly both in-state and nationally that North Carolina prospers in part because unions are so weak.

Only a handful of legislative insiders knows that the AFL-CIO lobby is a small but constant force in the General Assembly. For any citizen relying on the daily press, the probable conclusion is that unions play no role in state politics. Unfortunately for the AFL-CIO, the perception of unions as both insignificant and illegitimate perpetuates a view that unions serve no useful purpose in today's North Carolina. Like other lobbies promoting citizen power, the AFL-CIO remains an outsider. But more so than either civil rights or environmentalism, union association remains a stigma. Even prolabor legislators fear being labeled pro-union.

Because prolabor politicians are so outnumbered in the General Assembly, they find it safer to hide behind the cloak of modernizer ideology. In short, both citizen-power lobbies and the legislators who agree with their political priorities pretend publicly that they are less sympathetic to labor and more centrist than they really are. The blurring of differences between North Carolina's prolabor legislators and corporate modernizers like Terry Sanford, Jim Hunt, or Bob Jordan makes political survival easier for those legislators. But it also confirms the dominance of modernizer ideology in the North Carolina Democratic party. The weakness in state politics of labor unions and, more generally, of citizen power constitutes a major difference between North Carolina and most other industrial states outside the South.

7

Racial Politics: The Quest for Black Political Power

North Carolina through most of the twentieth century maintained its reputation as the southern model of moderate race relations. The Tar Heel state stood, from a national perspective, in welcome contrast to the extreme racial politics characteristic of Deep South states like Mississippi and Alabama. More recently, with the political ascendancy of Jesse Helms and the 1979 killings of Communists by Nazi and Ku Klux Klan members in Greensboro, that reputation became tarnished.

From the perspective of black North Carolinians, however, the state's racial moderation was always problematic. To be sure, compared to the Deep South setting, black Tar Heels had less to fear from lynching and other racial violence. But the moderate path that the white elite chose nevertheless institutionalized and legitimated a segregated society in which blacks could not expect either political or economic equality. The reality was that blacks had little voting strength and even less political power, especially in the state's small towns and rural counties.

After the U.S. Supreme Court's 1954 declaration, in *Brown v. Topeka Board of Education*, that segregated public schools were inherently unequal and must be eliminated "with all deliberate speed," North Carolina's white leaders faced a dilemma. The progressive ideology that had guided Tar Heel governors and business leaders over the decades promoted economic change without encouraging substantive changes in the system of racial segregation known as Jim Crow. Yet the federal courts were demanding immediate reforms. The North Carolina solution was to strike a middle ground between the Supreme Court's ruling and the policies of some other southern states (mostly in the Deep South but also including neighboring Virginia) whose politicians had decided on hard-core resistance.

102

In 1956, when Luther Hodges served as governor, the General Assembly approved the Pearsall Plan, named after a Rocky Mount legislator and Hodges ally. Architects of the Pearsall Plan, including Hodges, began with the premise that the North Carolina NAACP and other black advocates of desegregation were illegitimately agitating for political change. As a progressive elite, this group of white politicians believed that they should determine the speed of school desegregation. Tar Heel progressives felt the Supreme Court decision had been wrong in the first place; their job was to steer a middle course between the NAACP and the Ku Klux Klan. The flaw in this argument, as historian William Chafe points out, was the assumption that white Tar Heels would not accept school desegregation. In fact, a sociological survey of the Greensboro area in 1956 found that most whites would not actively oppose desegregation if it were implemented. Chafe argues that the progressive elite blamed "rednecks" for requiring a slowing down of desegregation through the Pearsall Plan, when it was Hodges and other progressives who themselves wanted to maintain the segregated status quo (Chafe 1981, 59).

The Pearsall Plan allowed any North Carolina school district to close all or some of its schools if desegregation occurred, and provided state tuition grants for white students to attend segregated private schools (Chafe 1981, 53). While the Pearsall Plan did not prevent local school districts from establishing a process for desegregation, the entire burden of petitioning for desegregation fell upon black children and their parents. The plan nonetheless gave North Carolina the appearance of complying, albeit slowly, with the Supreme Court's ruling. Token desegregation occurred in Greensboro, Winston-Salem, and several other Piedmont cities. North Carolina progressives claimed they had moved the state as fast they could. From the perspective of black parents seeking educational equality, however, the Pearsall Plan illustrated the reality that "North Carolina progressivism consisted primarily of its shrewdness in opposing racial change." An Arkansas school official summarized Tar Heel school desegregation policy as "one of the cleverest techniques of perpetuating segregation that we have seen" (quotations from Chafe 1981, 70).

Two decades after the Brown decision, the evolving modernism ideology in North Carolina accepted the value of racial equality as a necessary societal goal. The strength of the national civil rights movement and resultant federal legislation meant that, by the early 1970s, the old Tar Heel progressive ideology, which promoted economic and educa-

tional change while sustaining Jim Crow segregation, could not survive. Modernism's importance as a New South ideology lies in its continued commitment to an activist state government and its recognition
that blacks must be offered a minimal level of participation in this
activist government. White Democrats as well as Republicans have
become modernizers, or at least have shown some commitment to
modernism. But blacks have a different relationship to white Democratic and Republican modernizers.

In North Carolina, almost all politicized blacks are Democrats. In
1988, for example, more than 95 percent of black voters were registered
Democrats. This means that most blacks expect little from Republicans.
A Republican governor's appointment of a handful of black Republicans to boards or patronage jobs serves two functions. First, it provides
a practical reason for upwardly mobile middle-class blacks to gravitate
to the GOP. And second, it suggests that Republicans are indeed committed to racial equality. (Jesse Helms's selection of a black press secretary for his 1984 U.S. Senate race, when Jim Hunt's campaign had no
blacks in visible positions, provided him with a public relations coup,
even though few blacks voted for Helms on Election Day.)

Black Democratic leaders can deliver an overwhelming straight-ticket
vote for Democratic candidates. Consequently, they expect white
Democratic modernizers to respond to black demands. This generates
conflict between white modernizers and blacks because the white modernizers tend to view themselves as representing black interests well.
Similar to Luther Hodges's progressivism in the 1950s, which sought a
middle road between racial equality and hard-line segregation, most
white modernizers of the 1970s and 1980s believed that their political
decisions benefited blacks without pushing too many white Democrats
into the Republican column. On racial issues, however, this frequently
meant that blacks felt unrepresented. Tar Heel black leaders often perceived that white modernizers only cared about them shortly before
Election Day, at a time when white candidates needed straight-Demo-
cratic-ticket endorsements from local black organizations around the
state. Feeling taken for granted, black leaders did not work as hard as
they might have for the all-white statewide Democratic ticket, and
turnout was lower among blacks, especially poor blacks, than it might
have been. The controversy over how well, if at all, white modernizer
Democrats represented black interests lay at the heart of blacks' conflicts with the white-modernizer-dominated state Democratic party.

Racial Conflict in Greensboro: A Matter of Perspective

When, on February 1, 1960, four college students from North Carolina Agricultural and Technical State University (A&T) sat down in the whites-only section of Woolworth's lunch counter in Greensboro, the city's progressive business and political leaders believed that such direct action was a mistake. Twenty years later, white modernizer leaders had, of course, a different evaluation. In retrospect, they viewed the sit-ins as forcing long-overdue changes. City fathers even dedicated a historic marker in downtown Greensboro on that twentieth anniversary.

In celebrating desegregation, the ceremony obscured the fact that racial change in Greensboro and elsewhere in North Carolina did not come easily. In the first place, the 1960 sit-ins, after months of negotiations, led to only token desegregation of public facilities in the city. In spring 1963, A&T students demonstrated in much larger numbers in the streets of downtown Greensboro, forcing mass arrests by the police department. White leaders again regarded the sit-ins as disruptive and criticized A&T student leaders, including student body president Jesse Jackson, for making excessive demands. Blacks countered that the white elite should not dictate the pace of desegregation, but black-white negotiations stalled. In fact, despite Greensboro's reputation for moderation, widespread desegregation of public facilities occurred only after the 1964 federal civil rights law required it.

The reluctance of Greensboro's political and economic elite to initiate desegregation even after extensive organized protests from blacks highlights a component of modernizer ideology. Modernizers recognize in theory the legitimacy of racial equality, but hesitate to take the necessary steps to achieve it unless they see no alternative. But they differ from traditionalists in listening more closely to black demands, even if they do not gladly share power.

The official praise accorded the four A&T demonstrators in February 1980, two decades after the fact, came ironically just three months after a widely publicized event that badly tarnished Greensboro's reputation. This event was the killing of four whites and one black by members of the Ku Klux Klan and the Nazi party in a black public housing project on November 3, 1979. A small Communist party known as the Workers Viewpoint Organization had scheduled a "Death to the Klan" rally in the low-income neighborhood to try to gain support among black workers. According to Elizabeth Wheaton, despite much publicity about the rally and advance information that Klansmen and Nazi party members from outside Greensboro planned to attend, no Greensboro police were present when these individuals drove into the housing project (Wheaton 1987, 165). The Klan-Nazi members emerged from their cars in front of the demonstration and, after a brief shoving match, began shooting at the crowd. Eighty-eight seconds later, five persons—all Communists or sympathetic to the party—were dead (ibid., 135–51). The national publicity surrounding the killings was negative for both Greensboro and North Carolina. City and state modernizer leaders responded that the criticism was unfair, because it implied that segregationist whites were dominant in Greensboro and North Carolina. The leaders had a point. Modernizers, not racial traditionalists, held key positions of power in Greensboro. But how much did the city's white leaders share power with blacks?

One indicator came in May 1980, six months after the killings. Blacks and white liberals, allied as the Citizens for Representative Government (CRG), had developed a ward system for city government, the effect of which, if implemented through a voter referendum, would redistribute power among black and white neighborhoods and increase the number of black representatives from one to at least two. The proposal called for six city council members to be elected only by ward residents, plus three members and a mayor elected citywide (the 6–3–1 proposal). The existing city council, composed of six members and a mayor, was elected every two years in an at-large election. Except for one black, the council year-in, year-out consisted of well-to-do whites from the city's affluent Northwest quadrant. In 1968, 1969, and 1975, the proward referendum lost by sizable margins (*Greensboro Daily News* 1980, May 4). But in 1980, the CRG believed that sentiment was turning against the established system. Greensboro's white modernizers were divided on the plan. The chamber of commerce supported the 6–3–1 proposal, believing blacks needed to be better incorporated into government decision making. But a prominent Greensboro insurance firm, the Jefferson-Pilot Corporation, usually eager to modernize Greensboro's image, disagreed that the at-large system was flawed. Indeed, Jefferson-Pilot and several other firms resigned from the chamber of commerce in protest because they philosophically favored at-large systems (*Greensboro Daily News* 1980, May 7). Combining the votes of modernizers who did not think the at-large system unfairly burdened blacks and those of traditionalists who opposed more black political power outright, an antireform coalition called "Save Our City" defeated the ward system proposal by 314 votes out of 22,000 cast. More than 70 percent of white affluent Northwest Greensboro voted to maintain the status quo, while 90 percent of black Southeast Greensboro supported the ward system.

In November 1980, an all-white jury in Greensboro found the Klan-Nazi defendants not guilty of all charges. Although Greensboro's white leaders correctly argued that they could not affect the trial outcome, the acquittals sent a symbolic message about the Klan through the black community.

The following October, a well-organized black voter turnout in the city council primary election raised the possibility that black candidates could win two or even three of the six seats that were at stake in the November general election. Although blacks at that time constituted a third of the city's population, they had never elected more than one black to the six at-large seats. Indeed, this was why black leaders had long advocated reform of the city electoral system.

But blacks found that even trying to win under the existing system evoked white opposition. Many white leaders took the traditionalist view that expanded black political power, under any system, was a threat to Greensboro's future. They hastily organized opposition groups under the ethnocentric rallying cries of "Stand Up for Greensboro" and "the Committee to Keep Greensboro Greensboro." One full-page ad in the *Greensboro Daily News* appealed to white residents with the argument: "The way you vote will affect your home life, your family life, and your job life" (Lavelle 1981, 4–5). With extensive newspaper and radio advertising and a heavy turnout from affluent white wards, the 1981 election had a shocking result: an all-white city council was elected. Greensboro's progressive reputation was once again under challenge.

The embarrassment of the racial overtones during the campaign and the all-white outcome forced white modernizer political and business leaders to act. In February 1982 they established a biracial elite commission, the Greensboro Dialogue Task Force Committee, which recommended a compromise ward system. Instead of the 6–3–1 plan advocated by the CRG in 1980, the task force called for a 5–3–1 electoral structure. The task force demonstrated the ability of the Greensboro modernizer elite to implement change when it concluded that change was necessary.

By November 1982, the modernizer elite had convinced leaders of the 1981 all-white political campaigns to support the compromise district system. The stated reason was a consensus among white modernizers that "Greensboro's black community feels alienated from the all-white City Council" (*Greensboro Daily News* 1982, November 16). But black political alienation from white political power had certainly not begun in November 1981. An equally plausible reason for the white elite's newly found interest in a ward system was a decision of the U.S. Justice Department that prohibited city annexation of affluent white suburbs. In the light of election results in Greensboro in 1980 and 1981, the Justice Department ruled that further annexation of whites would make it more difficult for blacks to win political representation on the city council (*Greensboro Daily News* 1982, June 24).

An obvious remedy was the implementation of the ward system. To avoid further public divisiveness in a referendum, the Greensboro task force recommended that the city council redistrict by ordinance. This request tested the task force's influence, because each of the council members had promised during the 1981 campaign to change to a district system only by referendum. Recognizing the need to establish a new political consensus that included blacks, the all-white city council acted unanimously in December 1982 (*Greensboro Daily News* 1982, December 17). Beginning with the November 1983 election, blacks held two of the nine council seats.

Can blacks count on whites to represent them well? The Greensboro case suggests that, without blacks in official positions of power, the possibility of their becoming an invisible minority is real. Despite Greensboro's excellent public reputation for caring about race relations, the demonstrations of the early 1960s, the 1979 Klan-Nazi killings and subsequent acquittals, and the 1980 and 1981 elections indicate at a minimum that blacks had little power to shape the city's future. From a black perspective, the goodwill of whites helped very little. Only after the results of the 1980 and 1981 elections led the Justice Department to block city annexation policies, did the white modernizer elite take decisive action to change the city's electoral system. Now blacks have more local political power than ever before. This brief story of Greensboro explains why, across North Carolina, changing the electoral system became during the 1980s the primary political goal of black North Carolinians.

The Impact of Racial Traditionalism

Hard-core segregationists never attained a dominant position in North Carolina politics during the 1950s and 1960s. But the traditionalist ideology nevertheless had great appeal for many white North Carolinians, especially in the rural eastern counties where blacks made up sizable minorities or even absolute majorities. By the 1980s, the modernizer value of racial tolerance had become an obligatory position for any aspiring politician, forcing racial traditionalists to use code words to indicate their stand vis-à-vis blacks. Just two decades earlier, however, open opposition was common.

Two prominent traditionalist personalities of the 1960s were I. Beverly Lake, Sr., a Harvard-trained lawyer who twice ran in the Democratic gubernatorial primary and was subsequently appointed to the state supreme court, and TV editorialist Jesse Helms. Lake and Helms shared an outspoken style, stating publicly what many whites would not say aloud. Their favorite whipping boy was the NAACP. After the Brown decision in 1954, Lake criticized the Pearsall Plan for not resisting desegregation more strongly and urged Tar Heel communities to develop whites-only private schools if necessary. Lake ran in the 1960 Democratic primary as a staunch segregationist, denying the legitimacy of the Brown decision and blaming the NAACP for North Carolina's racial problems. On the nightly news, Helms reminded viewers which politicians were supported by blacks, or the so-called "Negro bloc vote." According to Helms, any politician whom blacks endorsed, whatever his public position on segregation, was untrustworthy. He also condemned black leaders for insisting on rapid racial change.

The impact of traditional racism on the state's political debate during that period was formidable. Terry Sanford, for example, while running for governor in 1960 against Lake and two other major primary opponents, adopted segregationist positions (Black 1976, 217–19). At the time, no advocate of racial desegregation could have won a statewide election. Sanford demonstrated allegiance to the national Democratic party by supporting John Kennedy for president, but he covered his racial bases by campaigning as a segregationist. This typified North Carolina's progressive ideology—that is, supporting economic change while defending the racial status quo. Sanford's supporters in eastern North Carolina implied that staunch segregationists could count on him, even if his language differed from Lake's (Spence 1968, 11). In a bitter runoff, Sanford defeated Lake by a 60–40 margin.

During the early 1960s, the civil rights movement mushroomed in North Carolina and Sanford was forced to respond to black demands. He established Good Neighbor Councils to try to maintain racial harmony in communities racked by protest. This conciliatory position did not please Lake supporters. At the same time, Sanford angered protestors by criticizing their demonstrations against segregated public facilities (Chafe 1981, chap. 5).

In 1964, Greensboro federal judge Richardson Preyer sought to succeed Sanford as governor and thus become the symbolic leader of the Democrats' progressive wing. But Lake, who placed third in the May 1964 primary, and Helms both explicitly publicized the high level of black support for Preyer in that first election. In the runoff, Preyer's campaign tried to emphasize his opposition to the civil rights bill then before Congress, but Lake and Helms questioned the depth of Preyer's segregationist commitment. With race as a key issue, Lake threw his support to Dan K. Moore, a western North Carolina judge whose racial ideology fell between Preyer's and Lake's. Moore defeated Preyer by 62 percent to 38 percent. Moore's racial position was certainly not the only reason he won. For example, many business leaders, including executives at both Duke Power Company and Carolina Power and Light, preferred Moore's more conservative economic views. But the results suggested that many if not most white voters were fearful of racial desegregation.

The traditionalist critique of racial change centered on the federal institutions that, in response to the organized civil rights movement and related litigation, had forced new dynamics in North Carolina's race relations. With support from Democratic presidents Kennedy and Johnson, the Congress had passed two landmark bills, the Civil Rights Act of 1964 and the Voting Rights Act of 1965. The former meant that restaurants, waiting rooms, hotels, and workplaces could no longer be segregated. And the Voting Rights law, under a formula calculating the percentage of unregistered blacks in a county, placed forty of North Carolina's one hundred counties under the scrutiny of the federal Department of Justice before any local electoral laws or districts could be changed. Perhaps the greatest change for white and black Tar Heels, however, came in 1971, when the U.S. Supreme Court unanimously ruled in *Swann v. Charlotte-Mecklenburg County* that busing was an appropriate remedy to end public school segregation that occurred because of segregated housing patterns. Thus, the era of busing for racial balance began as a result of a black North Carolinian's complaint that the Charlotte-area school board was still resisting genuine desegregation. Once again, the federal government—this time, the courts—could be viewed, from a traditionalist perspective, as interfering with race relations that had worked fine for decades.

Certainly candidate Lake and journalist Helms pushed the parameters of the political debate to the right, so that racial equality, into the 1970s, was viewed with suspicion by a significant percentage of white North Carolinians. Of the two, Helms's words took on greater significance because they were heard everyday, not just during the campaigns of 1960 and 1964. Lake and Helms both bolstered the cause of resistance as political opponents of desegregation, but Helms also served as a cultural symbol of opposition. His WRAL editorials continually wove the themes of traditionalism: the God-fearing people of North Carolina, and its government and economy, were doing fine until the outside agitators from the North, supported by the liberals in the Congress, the White House, and the Supreme Court, stirred up black Tar Heels and forced unwelcome and unnecessary changes in race relations. As the civil rights movement gained strength and some change appeared inevitable, Helms assailed not so much the goal of equality but the methods that blacks and their allies had allegedly adopted. His television commentary from April 1965, shortly after the Selma-to-Montgomery voting rights march, brought together much of Helms's racial ideology in one place: "The Negroes of America, regardless of the merits of some of their complaints, have recourse through exceedingly sympathetic courts to settle their grievances. They have a president whose ear is constantly cocked to the frequent reminder by civil-rights leaders that he received 95 percent of the Negro vote in 1964. They have a Congress which would tomorrow morning enact Webster's Dictionary into law if someone accidentally threw it into the hopper with a civil rights label on it. And the Supreme Court would stand in applause" (Nordhoff 1984, 41).

Helms effectively summarized the sentiments of states' rights advocates in North Carolina and across the South. Since the federal government actively worked against traditionalist racial values, state legislatures and the courts should do what they could to stop change. This antichange perspective manifested itself in North Carolina in various ways, even while state leaders espoused racial moderation. For example, until 1977, a huge Ku Klux Klan billboard along U.S. 70 greeted visitors to Smithfield, a county seat twenty-five miles east of Raleigh. Its message said simply to "fight communism and intergration [sic]" by joining the Klan. The sign's existence did not suggest, of course, that all of Smithfield's citizens were Klan sympathizers. Indeed, the twice-weekly *Smithfield Herald* was a leading voice for racial modernism, continually urging residents to reject violent resistance to desegregation.

But the fact that the sign remained until the late 1970s suggests the strength of racial traditionalism in eastern North Carolina.

After the Brown decision, the General Assembly sought to keep itself lily-white, even while key state leaders, with the prominent exception of Beverly Lake, avoided the rhetoric of resistance. Because most legislative districts had more than one member, legislators were concerned that blacks might concentrate their votes on one black candidate, who could be elected if whites spread their votes around various white candidates. This process, known as "single-shooting" or "bullet-voting," has historically been the major method that a black must choose to win an election if whites are unwilling to support a black candidate (Luebke 1979). First in 1955 with an anti–single-shot law, and later in 1967 with a numbered-seat plan that also precluded single-shooting, the all-white legislature took two concrete steps to keep blacks from holding seats. These civil-rights-era laws were in addition to literacy tests, a mechanism stemming from the turn of the century to keep blacks from even being registered to vote.

In 1982, black Greensboro attorney Henry Frye would become the first black to serve on the North Carolina Supreme Court. In 1956, however, as a college graduate and veteran returning to his small eastern Piedmont hometown of Ellerbe, he was denied the right to vote by a local registrar who claimed Frye failed the literacy test. Just twelve years later, Frye would be the first black to be seated in the General Assembly in the twentieth century. He was elected from Greensboro, where a coalition of blacks and white modernizers provided the necessary votes. Frye overcame the legislative obstacles to black victories and was for many a sign of hope. But in 1969 he remained the sole black legislator out of 170 representatives and senators, even though more than one-fifth of the state's residents were black.

Also highlighting North Carolina's resistance to racial change was a nationally publicized trial following conflict in Wilmington in early 1971 over school desegregation. Ben Chavis, a United Church of Christ (UCC) minister and employee of the UCC's Commission for Racial Justice, went to Wilmington after white-instigated violence sought to undermine court-ordered school desegregation. A Wilmington UCC minister asked Chavis to help black high school students negotiate their differences with the all-white school board. After the school board proved recalcitrant Chavis helped organize a nonviolent student boycott, which was met by white vigilante actions. Throughout this period, city government refused Chavis's request for a curfew to curb the violence. Several firebombings occurred, including one at a small grocery named Mike's.

One year later, in March 1972, Chavis, seven black male teenagers, a twenty-one-year-old black man, and a thirty-four-year-old white woman were arrested for the firebombing. The "Wilmington Ten," as they became known, were found guilty of arson in November 1972 and sentenced to a total of 282 years in prison. Chavis's 29–34–year term was the longest imposed for arson in North Carolina history. The prosecuting attorney urged that the ten defendants receive maximum sentences, describing them in courtroom arguments as "dangerous animals who should be put away for the rest of their lives" (Pinsky 1977, 754; Myerson 1978, 188–89; Fox 1982).

In retrospect, the Wilmington Ten prosecution appears to be a prime example of racial traditionalism. The three major witnesses for the prosecution, two of them convicted felons, recanted their testimony in 1976 and early 1977 after a five-year campaign by defense attorneys and political support groups (Pinsky 1977, 755). Nevertheless, the Wilmington Ten's state and federal appeals were exhausted before the witnesses' recantations became public.

Following recognition of the Wilmington Ten by Amnesty International, the Congressional Black Caucus, and CBS's "60 Minutes," as well as criticism of the state's case from dailies such as the *Charlotte Observer* and the *News and Observer*, Governor Jim Hunt in January 1978 felt pressure to act (*News and Observer* 1978a). Black leaders wanted the governor to issue a pardon, but he merely reduced the sentences so that the defendants could be eligible for parole. Hunt's move was consistent with the moderate actions that are central to modernizer ideology. In refusing to pardon the Wilmington Ten, he acknowledged that the case was hurting North Carolina's reputation. Yet he declined to take sides between the prosecution and the defense (*News and Observer* 1978a; King 1978).

The Klan billboard in Smithfield, anti–single-shot legislation, and the Wilmington Ten case all demonstrated the strength of North Carolina's racial traditionalism behind a facade of racial modernism. Politically active black Tar Heels in the 1970s had few illusions about the reality of racial politics in North Carolina. Blacks' low voter registration and little electoral success statewide also became evident late in the decade. This lack of success led to a historic voting rights case by black plaintiffs against the Democratic-dominated government of North Carolina. It focused the argument of whether black Democrats should seek political power without relying on an alliance with white Democrats.

Documenting Voting Discrimination: *Gingles v. Edmisten*

In 1960, nearly 40 percent of all eligible blacks were registered to vote in North Carolina, by far the highest percentage in the South. In 1980, North Carolina fell to last place in that category, although the number of registered blacks actually increased to 49 percent. In the six other southern states covered by the 1965 Voting Rights Act, federal intervention to prevent harassment of black voters by white registrars sparked major voter registration drives. The most dramatic change occurred in Mississippi, where the percentage of eligible blacks registered to vote jumped from 5 percent in 1960 to 72 percent in 1980.

In North Carolina, however, the presence of racial modernizers in the state's political leadership had the apparent effect of reducing the amount of local civil rights activism by blacks. Black leaders acknowledged that North Carolina's moderate reputation influenced blacks' own perceptions of the necessity of political organizing. As NAACP state president Kelly Alexander, Jr., said, "Everybody looked at North Carolina as a liberal state. It [the discrimination] was more sophisticated. A lot of blacks themselves had been propagandized into believing North Carolina wasn't Mississippi or South Carolina. . . . We've had to fight a feeling of apathy, complacency" (*News and Observer* 1981e).

But political success was constrained by more than black complacency. The major barrier lay in the presence of multi-member voting districts. Because of housing segregation, blacks usually lived in a particular part of a county. If electoral districts had only one representative, blacks' chances of election from a majority-black district were enhanced. Multi-member districts tended to dilute black voting strength.

The problem of vote dilution became clear in the November 1980 election. In the three metropolitan counties that surround the cities of Charlotte, Greensboro, and Winston-Salem, where blacks constituted more than 20 percent of the registered voters, four blacks (two in Charlotte) had captured the Democratic nomination for the state house. Yet none of the four black Democrats won a seat even though most of the white Democrats in these counties were successful. Had each of these blacks campaigned in a single-member district (similar to a ward seat in a city council election), all would have been elected. Electoral analysis showed that many whites in the three counties were unwilling to vote for a black Democrat (Luebke and Feeney 1981).

As a consequence of the multi-member district and racially polarized voting by whites, only 4 out of 170 seats in the General Assembly were occupied by blacks. Twelve years after Henry Frye's precedent-setting election to the legislature, progress had been minimal. For blacks to win a General Assembly seat, it appeared that several factors were necessary. First, a substantial minority of whites in a multi-member district had to find the black candidate attractive. In Greensboro in 1980, state senate candidate Frye, after six terms in the North Carolina House of Representatives, was popular enough with white voters to defeat the opposition. But fellow black William Martin, a political unknown in white Guilford County, could not garner enough white votes and a white Republican was elected instead.

Second, for blacks to win representation, the Republican party had to be weak. If the party was strong, as in Charlotte, Greensboro, and Winston-Salem, whites who did not want to support a black Democrat had a viable option in the white Republican candidate. That explains William Martin's loss in 1980 even though Frye had won from the same senate district in 1978. But the metro Piedmont counties around Durham and Raleigh produced a different political story in 1980. All Republicans in Wake County (Raleigh) ran far behind the black Democrat from Raleigh, and the black was elected. In Durham, the Republicans failed to field a candidate. In both counties, the black Democratic candidates won but by fewer votes than the successful white Democrats.

A third factor that helped blacks was single-shooting. A 1971 federal court ruling had thrown out both General Assembly laws that restricted single-shooting. But in Charlotte, Greensboro, and Winston-Salem in 1980, black political organizations urged support of the entire Democratic ticket. Therefore, when white Democrats failed to support blacks while black Democrats voted for whites, the blacks lost (Luebke and Feeney 1981).

This constellation of factors led blacks to undertake two challenges of the multi-member approach. First, and most importantly, four black plaintiffs in September 1981 filed suit in federal court against the state of North Carolina on the grounds that the multi-member electoral system violated the constitutional rights of all black Tar Heels. This action become known as *Gingles v. Edmisten*, named after the first black plaintiff, Ralph Gingles, and the state attorney general, Rufus Edmisten, who was formally responsible for defending the state of North Carolina. Second, in February 1982, when the Democrat-dominated General Assembly considered redistricting in accord with the 1980 census, blacks urged the creation of single-member districts both in the urban Piedmont and in the heavily black counties of eastern North Carolina. White Democrats balked at the idea, both for philosophical and practical reasons.

Philosophically, modernizer Democrats believed that the party was and should be color-blind. To build majority-black single districts that assured the election of black representatives, in the view of white modernizers, accentuated race consciousness which might otherwise disappear gradually. Traditionalist Democrats, with less sympathy for black concerns, saw no reason to give blacks what appeared to them to be a guaranteed legislative seat.

White Democrats, modernizer and traditionalist alike, also opposed majority-black districts for a practical reason. In the metropolitan counties where Republicans were strong, the loss of black Democrats' votes would almost assuredly lead to some GOP legislative victories. Despite a strong argument from blacks, the General Assembly drew majority-black single-member districts only in those counties whose election laws were subject to U.S. Justice Department approval because they fell under the provisions of the Voting Rights Act. A state senate seat and a state house seat were carved from Guilford County (Greensboro), three state house seats were drawn in Fayetteville and in the Rocky Mount area, and a state senate seat was constructed in a half-dozen heavily black counties in eastern North Carolina.

The redistricting decision disappointed blacks, even though they gained 4 additional seats in the house in the fall 1982 election—bringing their total to 8 out of 170 seats. But blacks still believed North Carolina's redistricting plan discriminated against them in many parts of the state that were not subject to the Voting Rights Act.

The stage was set for the *Gingles* case, led by Leslie Winner, a white female attorney from the biracial law firm of Julius Chambers and James Ferguson in Charlotte, the black lawyers who had previously argued the *Swann v. Charlotte-Mecklenburg* school desegregation case and defended the Wilmington Ten. The state remained confident that the suit would be rejected, particularly because the 1982 election results doubled the number of black seats in the General Assembly. The state's argument was rooted in the modernizers' premise that race relations were improving gradually and the federal courts should not interfere with this political process. The state hired a Washington-based firm that specialized in voting rights cases to coordinate a defense with lawyers from the attorney general's office. The North Carolina Republican party joined the suit in support of the black plaintiffs. Republicans correctly presumed that, if the courts forced single-member districts on the state's metro Piedmont counties, some Republican legislators could be elected from majority-white suburban areas.

A three-judge federal panel heard the evidence in summer 1983 and ruled in the plaintiffs' favor in January 1984, thereby forcing seven single-member districts to be created in the state house and two in the state senate. The U.S. Supreme Court in June 1986 upheld all but one of the seats. In retrospect, it is clear that the strong 1982 revision of the 1965 Voting Rights Act provided the basis for the plaintiffs' victory. Yet when Gingles and others filed their suit in 1981, no one knew what would be the content of the new act.

The 1982 act focused on the "totality of circumstances" that might result in a situation where "a racial minority has less opportunity than other members of the electorate to participate in the political process and elect representatives of their choice" (the Voting Rights Act of 1965, as amended June 29, 1982, quoted in Roach 1984). The Congress construed these circumstances very broadly, accepting the sociological argument that the total social forces that influence racial politics must be considered. For example, according to the law, one of the seven factors that built a plaintiff's case was whether the socioeconomic status of blacks was lower than that of whites, a condition that was virtually a certainty in the United States. Congress accepted the scholarly insight that a lower socioeconomic status reduces the likelihood of political participation and is, for blacks, primarily a consequence of past racial discrimination. The plaintiffs in *Gingles* could easily show socioeconomic differences in just about every institutional category in North Carolina—from the absence of indoor plumbing to the small number of blacks in professional and managerial jobs.

The plaintiffs also recounted the conscious actions of the General Assembly, from 1900 through the 1960s, to reduce black political participation and thus black political power. These included poll taxes, a literacy test, and anti–single-shot legislation. Further, they argued, the Democratic runoff primary, which began in 1915 in the one-party South as a substitute for the meaningless November election, allowed whites in the post–civil rights South to gang up against a black candidate who had led white candidates in the first primary. Former Chapel Hill mayor Howard Lee's bid for lieutenant governor in 1976 and Durham state representative Mickey Michaux's campaign for Congress in 1982 were two such examples.

Another key circumstance covered in the Voting Rights Act of 1982 dealt with the absence or presence of racial appeals. Did a white candidate draw attention to a black candidate's race in order to attract white votes? The plaintiffs in *Gingles* noted that at the turn of the century the Democratic party used the specter of black political power to win key elections. In 1950, the campaign of traditionalist Democrat Willis Smith successfully used racial appeals against Smith's opponent, former University of North Carolina President Frank Graham. In 1976, traditionalist Jimmy Green ran newspaper ads in eastern North Carolina featuring a picture of his black opponent, Howard Lee. The same advertisement said that "unless the people come out and vote on September 14, the election will be decided by a relatively small segment of the population." Such language telegraphed the importance of white votes in countering black electoral participation without actually using the words "white" and "black."

Parallel racial appeals were evident in the 1982 Second Congressional District runoff election between Mickey Michaux and former state legislator Tim Valentine. Michaux, who in 1972 had become the first black to represent Durham in the state house, was a blend of citizen-power and modernizer ideologies. In the first 1982 Democratic primary, he had won 42 percent of the vote, and white traditionalist Valentine, from Nash County in the Coastal Plain section of the congressional district, had shared the remaining 58 percent with another white candidate. Shortly before the runoff primary, Valentine circulated an anti-Michaux "Dear Neighbor" flyer among white voters both in the district's rural counties and in selected white-traditionalist precincts within Durham County. The one-page sheet first identified the nonracial threat to traditionalist values, asking voters "whether you want to be represented in Congress by a big-government, free-spending liberal with close ties to the labor bosses." The flyer then closed with a racial appeal: "It's not easy to stop and take time to vote, but *you* must. Our polls indicate that the same well organized block [*sic*] vote which was so obvious and influential in the First Primary will turn out again on July 27. My opponent will again be *bussing his supporters* to the polling places in record number." References to a "block vote" and "bussing" communicated the information about a black candidate to white voters. And

Michaux, electoral analysis indicates, received almost no white votes beyond those he had already received in the first primary.

A final example of racial appeals emerged shortly before the beginning of the *Gingles* trial. In spring 1983, the Helms campaign had run a series of newspaper and radio ads that identified Governor Jim Hunt as beholden to black voters and suggested that such white-black alliances were illegitimate.

Another circumstance identified by Congress in the 1982 bill was the electoral success rate of blacks compared to their proportion of the total population. In North Carolina in 1980, blacks constituted 5 percent of the elected officials but 22 percent of the population. Thus, for each of the circumstances described above, the North Carolina evidence painted a picture of blacks handicapped by past and present discrimination.

But probably the most crucial circumstance was the level of racially polarized voting in a district. In particular, how much evidence was there that whites would support a qualified black candidate? Congress focused on whether "substantially significant" differences existed between the voting patterns of whites and blacks. In *Gingles v. Edmisten*, the plaintiffs' expert witness testified that, of the fifty-three elections that had taken place in the nine electoral districts in recent years, strong racial polarization prevailed fifty-one times.

The federal court concluded that, given the "totality of circumstances," "the creation of each of the multi-member districts challenged in this action results in the black registered voters being submerged as a voting minority." Such submerging of the black vote, according to the court, was precisely what Congress sought to prohibit under the 1982 Voting Rights Act. Consequently, the court unanimously ordered redistricting in all of the affected districts.

Primarily as a result of the *Gingles* decision, blacks in November 1984 won a record number of 14 seats in the General Assembly. And over time the decision's impact was felt in city councils, county commissions, and school boards across North Carolina. In most cases, after *Gingles* was upheld by the U.S. Supreme Court in 1986, local governments reached out-of-court settlements with black plaintiffs, providing for single-member districts that gave blacks an excellent chance of electoral victories roughly proportional to their percentage in the population. Primarily as a result of these voting rights suits, the number of black elected officials at the municipal level jumped more than 30 percent between 1985 and 1987, from 144 to 194 seats. Prior to the *Gingles* decision, between 1980 and 1985, the number of local officials increased by just 6 percent, from 136 to 144 seats (JCPS 1980, 1985, and 1987).

But white Democrats' fears of Republican victories were realized. In cities like Charlotte and Winston-Salem, majority-white districts supported Republicans in both 1984 and 1986. To white Democratic modernizers, this showed the error of blacks' thinking, as it allowed Republicans with less sympathy for black concerns to win legislative seats. For blacks, however, two points remained salient. First, white Democrats needed to develop a political program that appealed to white voters, and they must not rely on the party loyalty of blacks to win seats in the strongly two-party sections of the state. Second, blacks believed in their right to elect candidates of their own choosing. Before the *Gingles* case, blacks could be elected in multi-member districts with creditable Republican opposition only if their views were acceptable to a substantial minority of whites. Blacks supported the thrust of the revised Voting Rights Act, that the candidate need only be the choice of blacks. In the view of both Congress and most politicized blacks in North Carolina, the history of institutional racism made it likely that black and white citizens might not have the same political values and priorities.

The Future of Black Politics in North Carolina

Black Tar Heels face the political dilemma of few electoral choices. The strong traditionalist component of the state Republican party has little appeal for blacks. Most blacks vote Democratic, not simply out of habit but also because the Democrats' modernizer programs come closer to fitting a black agenda. Blacks, in fact, constitute the largest political interest group in North Carolina that would prefer economic populism as an alternative to either modernism or traditionalism. But the white Democratic elite has shown little desire for such populism. The most visible case for an economic justice program was made in the 1988 campaign speeches of Jesse Jackson. During the brief time Jackson spent in the state, his message focused on the centrality of economic rather than racial conflict. In Jackson's view, the important conflict is between workers and the wealthy, and not any conflicts that may exist between white and black workers. This open discussion of economic populism was most unusual for North Carolina.

But few black Tar Heel Democrats have put energy into developing a state political agenda parallel to Jackson's national economic issues. The tension emerges between white Democrats, who claim that the black agenda—including the Martin Luther King holiday and the abolition of the runoff primary—runs a high risk of alienating white voters, and black Democrats, who insist that the white Democrats provide something to black Tar Heels in exchange for their overwhelmingly pro-Democratic black vote. Neither group has examined the economic issues that might appeal to both black and white lower-income voters.

It is not just white Democratic leaders who question the value of a biracial economic populist agenda, however. While most black legislators in the General Assembly are inclined to favor such an economic program, some black Tar Heel politicians are more content with the trickle-down economics of white modernizer ideology. Several examples illustrate this political debate. First, in 1987 former black state representative Kenneth Spaulding of Durham established a pro-developer political action committee, and supported some candidates for the Durham City Council who were not endorsed by either the Durham Committee on the Affairs of Black People or the committee's white political allies. In 1988, as a Dukakis delegate to the Democratic National Convention, Spaulding spoke during the platform debate against the Jackson minority plank to restore federal income taxes on large corporations and "the very richest Americans" to their pre-Reagan levels (Minority Report to the 1988 Democratic Platform, 2). Almost the entire North Carolina Jackson delegation booed Spaulding during his speech (Yeoman 1988b).

Second, when a coalition of blacks and whites elected Democrat Harvey Gantt, a black city council member and architect, mayor of Charlotte in 1983, many of Gantt's supporters expected him to pursue a citizen-power agenda that would increase government sensitivity to the needs of lower- and middle-income neighborhoods and place more restrictions on suburban-oriented developers. However, under great pressure from Charlotte's modernizer business people, representing such firms as North Carolina National Bank, First Union Bank, and Duke Power, Gantt permitted the city to engage in unlimited economic growth. Although Gantt won reelection in 1985, he was defeated in 1987 over the issue of unsolved suburban traffic jams; his opponent, a white Republican woman, convinced the voters that she would be a better road builder. Gantt's pro-development stance led some Charlotte blacks to conclude that he had forgotten his political base in low- and middle-income black neighborhoods. Nevertheless, election analysis indicates that black turnout, compared to earlier elections, remained high for Gantt. Gantt lost because too many whites rejected his attempted blend of citizen and modernizer politics in favor of a modernizer Republican (*Charlotte Observer* 1987).

A third example of a black candidate's ideological fuzziness occurred in 1976, when Howard Lee, former black mayor of Chapel Hill, ran against white traditionalist Jimmy Green for the Democratic nomination for lieutenant governor. Lee's economic program sounded more modernizer than populist, even to the point of supporting repeal of the food tax, a tax that is especially burdensome to black Tar Heels because of their disproportionately low income, "only if the revenue picture allows it." In 1972, when Lee ran for Congress in the heavily black Second Congressional District, he had campaigned openly as an economic populist. Lee explained in a post-1976 interview that leading Democrats close to Jim Hunt and Terry Sanford persuaded him to soften his economic views in preparation for the 1976 campaign (Luebke 1979).

Lee's promises about economic development were virtually indistinguishable from the campaign literature of traditionalist Jimmy Green. Not surprisingly, as noted earlier in this chapter, Green relied on racial appeals to white voters in his second primary victory over Lee. The consequence of Lee's adoption of modernizer ideology was minimal among black voters, who supported him anyway for reasons of racial solidarity. But among less affluent whites, Lee's equivocation made him just another mainstream Democratic candidate, albeit a black one. Jesse Jackson's presidential campaign of 1988, which explicitly urged white lower-income voters to respond to economic-populist rather than racial appeals, provides a significant contrast to the economic agendas of Spaulding, Gantt, and Lee.

Without open discussion of an interracial economic program to benefit less affluent Tar Heels, white and black Democrats will likely spar over racial issues and reach an uneasy accommodation on the substantive content preferred by modernizer Democrats. As the North Carolinians with the greatest economic, educational, and health needs, blacks could help themselves by developing a nonracial legislative program comparable to the agenda of the Congressional Black Caucus or candidate Jackson. The failure to do so keeps black Democrats dependent on the modernizer agenda of white Democrats, which generally has demonstrated relatively little commitment to solving the problems facing the poorer citizens of the state.

The inability of blacks and their few white allies (Durham is one of the few places in North Carolina where a local black-white coalition committed to citizen power has enjoyed some success) to develop an economic populist alternative to the modernizer agenda in the General Assembly ensures that North Carolina's political debate will be fought out between the center and the right. That there is substantial public opinion among most blacks and some whites in favor of a more egalitarian political program does not matter if such an alternative receives no serious discussion. The absence of such debate in the General Assembly demonstrates the continued success of modernizers and traditionalists of both political parties in keeping issues of economic equity out of the political limelight.

8

Jesse Helms and the
National Congressional Club

Jesse Helms is perhaps North Carolina's most controversial politician of the twentieth century. He became a household word among Tar Heels during the 1960s, when his editorials blasting black and antiwar protestors aired daily on a Raleigh television station and on statewide radio. Among those who care about North Carolina politics, few are neutral about Helms. To his partisans, his years in the U.S. Senate have represented a major counterattack against liberal domestic and international policies. To his detractors, Helms tarnishes North Carolina's long-held national reputation as the progressive pacesetter in the New South.

Both nationally and in North Carolina, no one represents social and economic traditionalism better than Jesse Helms. But it is not his traditionalist views that make him unusual; indeed, traditionalists, especially in the Republican party, abound in North Carolina and many other southern states. Rather, Helms makes his mark because of his personality. From 1973, when he entered the Senate, through the Reagan years, Helms pulled the political agenda to the right. He opened discussion on issues that national Democrats and modernizer Democrats in North Carolina had considered beyond debate. Anti-abortion, prayer in the public schools, elimination of food stamps, and no accommodation with Communist societies are just a sampling of Helms's unwavering priorities.

Significantly, Helms has won election to the Senate three times with a coalition of Republicans and Democrats, many of whom disagree with some of his strong traditionalist beliefs. Poll data show clearly that Helms's views are not typical of those of most North Carolinians. Like

124

Ronald Reagan, Helms has a charismatic personality that attracts voters who do not share many of his opinions.

Nevertheless, in national political terms, Helms stands as the leader of a successful countermovement, the New Right, that arose in response to the egalitarian movements of the 1960s (cf. Lo 1982). Within North Carolina, it has remained questionable whether the senator's electoral victories would ever translate into political power for other traditionalist Republicans.

The National Congressional Club

The major organization that has sought to promote Helms's New Right in national and state politics is the National Congressional Club, founded in 1973 by his political confidante, Tom Ellis, to retire the $350,000 debt incurred during Helms's first successful race for the Senate. Over the years, the club has became one of the nation's leading fund-raisers among political action committees, generating more than $30 million between 1980 and 1988. Even in 1987, when the club was reeling from political defeats at the hands of North Carolina mainstream Republicans, it raised $2 million. (Fahy and Reid 1986; *News and Observer* 1988a). Its contributors live across the United States, and checks commonly range in size from $25 to $200. The club lists 118,000 persons as members, and has millions of names on its direct-mail solicitation lists (Reid 1986; Peters 1986).

Beyond its financial success, the Congressional Club stands out in national and state politics for two reasons: the fervor of its political beliefs, and its technical skill at promoting those beliefs or attacking political opponents. Like Helms himself, the club has a missionary dedication to traditionalist ideology, to what its leaders call "the conservative cause." Beliefs are more important than party label, and occasionally the club even supports a Democrat. Club chairman Tom Ellis told an interviewer in 1986 that "the reason the Congressional Club exists is to do everything it can to further the conservative cause. That's what it's all about—we have to save this country" (Peters 1986, C6). Unlike many Tar Heel traditionalists who seem resigned to the changes in American society promoted by liberal and modernizer Democrats during the 1960s and 1970s, Ellis and Helms are determined to resist and reverse those changes. In short, the club's raison d'être has been the support of ideological candidates, primarily Helms himself and

Ronald Reagan, who, if elected, would shift the political debate to the right.

From 1973 to 1980, the club's reputation grew both because its fund-raising appeals brought in millions of dollars and because the two major candidates on whom it focused, Helms and Reagan, won key elections. The Congressional Club engineered a Reagan upset of Gerald Ford in North Carolina's 1976 Republican presidential primary, helped Helms in his 1978 reelection, defeated an incumbent North Carolina senator in 1980, and spent $4.5 million as an independent committee for Reagan, also in 1980. The club's power peaked during 1983 and 1984, when Ellis and executive director Carter Wrenn ran the multi-million-dollar advertising campaign that resulted in Helms's narrow victory over Governor Jim Hunt.

The fairness of Helms's negative attacks on Hunt will be long debated. Hunt responded at times with television ads that also were labeled unfair. But unquestionably Helms could not have been elected to his third term in 1984 had Ellis, Wrenn, and their assistants not developed the hard-hitting ads that weakened voter confidence in the governor. In the club's view, Helms was a conservative man of principle running against Hunt, a pragmatic politician whose generally liberal views changed to fit the political moment. (For details on the Helms and Hunt advertising campaigns, see Chapter 9.)

Jesse Helms's Monroe Heritage

Helms was born in 1921 in Monroe, a small county seat about forty miles southeast of Charlotte. His traditionalist values of free enterprise, racial segregation, and patriarchal family were nurtured in this small-town environment, where his father served as police chief. Fundamentalist Protestantism, in particular the Baptist denomination, provided the religious underpinnings for traditionalism in Monroe, as it did elsewhere in North Carolina and the South.

During his youth, Helms's family was not particularly interested in politics. Helms enjoyed journalism and the high school band, and won a state prize for his tuba playing. On graduating from high school in 1938, he enrolled in a nearby Baptist college only after encouragement from his high school principal, Ray House. Many years later Helms remembered House as "the greatest exponent of the free enterprise system," telling Helms that with hard work "you can make it in this country" and "you'll own your own homes and you'll have two cars and all that." Interviewed at about the same time, House recalled that in high school Helms was "a regular old boy—long-legged and bug-eyed" and always working hard on part-time jobs (quotations from Furgurson 1986, 37).

House also provided a good feel for the racial environment of Monroe in the 1930s from the standpoint of apolitical whites: "Segregation was a way of life. We couldn't have done anything. If we would have started a fight against it, somebody would have shot us. You had to live like that. But we didn't have malice" (Furgurson 1986, 38–39). Helms's analysis of race relations often sounds similar to House's. The senator's public comments during the 1970s and 1980s underscored his view that Jim Crow racial segregation was part of the times and that, therefore, the demands of blacks for immediate desegregation in the 1960s were inappropriate (Nordhoff 1984, 12, 41, 47).

In 1939, after his freshman year, Helms decided to transfer to another Baptist college, Wake Forest, at the time located just north of Raleigh in the town of the same name. The decision would change his life, because while attending Wake Forest he worked part-time as a proofreader at the *News and Observer* in Raleigh. Owing to ideological differences, his relationship with the newspaper proved tumultuous. More importantly, he met his wife-to-be, Dorothy Coble, a society reporter for the *News and Observer*. After marriage in 1942, Helms developed an interest in politics as a result of conversations with his father-in-law (Snider 1985, 23). Jacob Coble was the first to provide specifics that fleshed out the worldview Helms brought from Monroe.

Because of a hearing disability, Helms's military service was restricted to noncombat roles. He spent most of World War II writing press releases for the navy in Elizabeth City, North Carolina. Afterward, Helms decided against returning to college and worked for the *Raleigh Times* and a Roanoke Rapids radio station. Understanding the appeal of interviews in a radio newscast, he would lug a 60-pound wire recorder to press conferences and city council meetings to speak directly with politicians. In 1948, A. J. Fletcher, founder of WRAL, then a small 250-watt radio station, offered Helms a position as news director. Fletcher, a strong advocate of traditionalist ideology, liked Helms's personality and his political beliefs. Helms later said Fletcher had been "like a second father" to him (Furgurson 1986, 45). In 1976, Helms dedicated his book of essays, *When Free Men Shall Stand*, to Fletcher and Tom Ellis.

In May 1950, Helms made a crucial appeal on WRAL to Willis Smith supporters to gather at Smith's house in Raleigh and insist that Smith seek a runoff election against Frank Graham for the Democratic nomination to the U.S. Senate. Smith subsequently defeated Graham in a bitter runoff campaign highlighted by attacks on Graham for his alleged sympathies with communism and support of civil rights. More than thirty-five years later, witnesses differed as to Helms's role in Smith's negative campaign. Ernest Furgurson's 1986 biography of the senator presents conflicting accounts of his involvement. In any case, after the election Smith appointed Helms as his administrative assistant in Washington, D.C.

While in Washington, Helms served as press officer for the 1952 Democratic presidential campaign of Georgia's traditionalist U.S. senator, Richard Russell. From Russell, Helms learned how to pursue unpopular political principles with shrewd parliamentary tactics on the Senate floor. Because of his strong commitment to Jim Crow segregation, Russell placed no better than third in the three-ballot Democratic convention of 1952. But he provided a role model for Helms, who remembered that Russell "would not consent to compromise, let alone be controlled by, the political manipulators" (Furgurson 1986, 59). Twenty years later, Helms would make his own mark as a U.S. senator, seeking on-the-record votes on issues such as public school prayer or school busing in order to embarrass liberal Democratic colleagues who preferred to avoid such roll calls. One victim of Helms's parliamentary skill was Indiana Democratic Senator Birch Bayh, whose on-the-record liberal votes provided campaign ammunition in 1980 for Bayh's youthful opponent, Dan Quayle. Quayle's victory ended Bayh's eighteen-year Senate career.

Helms returned to North Carolina in 1953 as publicist for the North Carolina Bankers Association, where he remained for seven years. In the association's monthly, the *Tar Heel Banker*, Helms was given free rein to sound off on current political issues. He attacked the Supreme Court's school desegregation decision and criticized the *News and Observer* for its alleged antibanker mentality. In 1957, Helms blended his journalism career with electoral politics, winning the first of two two-year terms on the Raleigh City Council. As a council member, Helms pursued the same antitax, anti–big government themes that he would later carry to the U.S. Senate. While his city council terms helped establish his reputation as a newsmaker, his first breakthrough to a mass audience came in 1960. That year his former benefactor, A. J. Fletcher, offered him a vice-president's position at WRAL and, most importantly, a daily five-minute television editorial known as *Viewpoint*.

Fletcher and Helms agreed that *Viewpoint* should serve as a "voice of free enterprise." Over the next twelve years, *Viewpoint* would run 2,761 times, ending only when Helms resigned to run for the 1972 Republican nomination for the U.S. Senate.

The civil rights and anti–Vietnam War movements of the 1960s as well as the related hippie counterculture provided excellent grist for Helms's editorial mill. From 1960 through the early 1970s, he provided ongoing commentary on religion, economics, civil rights, and foreign policy. His editorials characterized the United States as a Christian nation whose leaders ought to uphold free enterprise, family morality, and public prayer. Public welfare and other programs of Lyndon Johnson's Great Society were depicted as liberal steps on the ladder of socialism. Communism represented both a religious and an economic threat to American society. The fundamentalist Baptist base of Helms's traditionalist ideology viewed any redistribution of economic power as un-Christian and tantamount to communism. Helms wrote in his reelection campaign biography: "The loving and provident God of the Scriptures has been pushed aside in favor of a notion that the civil government is the ultimate provider and lawgiver. There is nothing to distinguish these people fundamentally from the most committed Communists who believe that evil is the consequence, not of sin, but of private property" (Helms 1976, 119). Despite Helms's strong political doctrine, his election campaigns relied much more on his charismatic personality than on ideological specifics.

Helms on the Campaign Trail

How does Jesse Helms win elections? That is the favorite question of non–North Carolinians who have trouble reconciling Helms with the modernizing image associated with Democrats like Luther Hodges, Sr., Terry Sanford, or Jim Hunt. One of Helms's bases is Tar Heel Republicanism. Although Republicans made up less than 30 percent of the state's registered voters as late as 1984, Helms has always counted on almost 90 percent of this group supporting him and others on the Republican ticket. More interesting is how Helms, in his three elections to the U.S. Senate, has won more than 40 percent of the non-Republican white vote. Over the years, Helms has maintained his appeal to white registered Democrats, whether at the country club or at the country store.

The author attended a campaign dinner in the early stages of the

Helms-Hunt race in order to gain a better understanding of Helms's personal appeal to white registered voters. The dinner was held in September 1983 at the Henderson Holiday Inn, a standard-issue Interstate 85 motel in a tobacco/textile county forty miles north of Raleigh. The Helms campaign made no profit on this $7.50 "rubber chicken and peas" affair. Nor would the campaign make any money on the dozens of other identical Saturday night dinners scheduled before the 1984 election. The dinner in Henderson was pitched to the broad middle class; the well-to-do had been invited to an earlier fund-raising reception at the local country club. It was Helms's personal political show, an amalgam of Christianity, free-enterprise economics, anticommunism, and bravado. He would be addressing primarily Jessecrats, those registered Democrats who vote in the Democratic primary in the spring and then switch to Helms and other Republicans on the statewide ticket, like Richard Nixon in 1972 or Ronald Reagan in 1984, in the November election.

Behind the podium in the Holiday Inn's banquet hall, a larger-than-life drawing of Helms spanned the wall. Next to the drawing, six-foot letters spelled out "JESSE" in bold red. This backdrop was the campaign's only prop; the staff carried it each weekend from town to town. As guests of honor at the head table sat the editor of the *Henderson Daily Dispatch* as well as two local ministers. Helms has never forgotten the importance of either media or religion.

Master of ceremonies for the evening was Lucius Harvin III, president of the thriving Rose's Stores, a Henderson-based retail chain that competes with K-Mart in towns across North Carolina and much of the South. Harvin recognized that this "Salute to Jesse" resembled a church supper far more than a corporate board meeting. Harvin's planning committee had ensured that both strains of local Protestants—the more establishment First Congregational Church as well as the more fundamentalist Gospel Baptist Church—had places on the program. The crowd stood for the Reverend Ed Yancey's long invocation, followed by Pastor Gary Roy's rendition of the National Anthem. They remained standing for the Pledge of Allegiance.

Harvin was one of the few wealthy residents in the hall. But economic differences were not a political issue for the people gathered that night. Helms has been able to attract an economically diverse crowd of white North Carolinians on any occasion. Jessecrats respect Helms because they believe he is kindly, sincere, conservative, and Christian. They also believe he has gone to Washington, D.C., to fight for his principles, not for personal gain. Interestingly, Senate financial reports uphold that faith in Helms. In 1988, he was among the least affluent of the one hundred senators—fellow Tar Heel Terry Sanford reported four times as much wealth (*News and Observer* 1988a). In Henderson, Helms affirmed the traditionalist belief in hard work and in the legitimacy of economic differences. He introduced the straw man of liberal Democratic handouts to great applause: "What we have to do is face up to the pressure groups who are demanding more and more handouts, and say we are going to look after the truly needy, but the truly greedy, you're way down the line" (Helms 1983b).

Helms also engaged the Henderson audience by framing the 1984 Senate election as the lonely struggle of a principled conservative against the national liberal establishment: "Every pressure group known to man is converging on North Carolina, and they're forthright in saying that their number one goal is to eliminate me from the Senate." Helms went on to name some of those groups, selecting several most likely to offend his listeners: "It's the homosexuals, labor unions, those militant feminists, all of them" versus his "talking about things I've been talking about for a long time" (Helms 1983b).

Resentment toward black aspirations for increased political power has historically fueled the voting behavior of Jessecrats. In Henderson, Helms did not miss an opportunity to slap at the 1980s' most visible advocate of black power, Jesse Jackson: "The big factor in this election will be whether there will be a balance to the efforts of Jesse Jackson, who came into this state earlier this year to meet with Governor Hunt and then announced that he was going to register, I-forget-what-it-was, 200 or 300-thousand blacks for the sole purpose of defeating Jesse Helms" (Helms 1983a).

But Helms offered more than serious warnings. Lightheartedly, he made cracks at the *News and Observer* and *Washington Post* reporters who were covering his speech: "Ferrel Guillory of the *News and Observer* is here from Raleigh. Ferrel and I don't agree on anything, but he's one heck of a nice guy." As the crowd warmed to his gentle media-baiting, Helms added: "Now I don't expect you reporters to be my Chamber of Commerce, but for gosh sakes get the facts straight just one time."

Helms's down-homeness has been an important part of his Tar Heel political appeal. While northern liberals remain appalled at his political victories in Washington, most white North Carolinians are undisturbed. They see their senior senator as gentlemanly, courteous, and humorous. Style is as important as substance, and perhaps more so.

On that hot September night in Henderson, Helms ended his speech with a characteristic folksy touch: "I know you're hot as the hinges of your you-know-where. But I do appreciate your coming out for so much time. You're great friends, and I love you. God bless you. Come see me in Washington."

In his closing remarks, Lucius Harvin, the Rose's executive, added a line about Helms that has reassured many a Jessecrat: "You may not always agree with Jesse Helms, but you always know where he stands" (Harvin 1983). That slogan subsequently became a major theme of Helms's 1984 campaign.

In the Henderson audience were two brothers, Eddie and James Grissom. Both in their thirties, they worked in blue-collar jobs at Rose's headquarters and were using free tickets distributed at work. But the Grissoms insisted to an interviewer that they would have paid for the tickets if necessary, because they had admired Helms since they were teenagers watching his *Viewpoint* editorials on WRAL-TV. Although the brothers, both registered Democrats, had their minor beefs with Helms, they sounded as positive about him as did their company president. They agreed with Harvin that Helms should stand tough against communism, support free enterprise, and uphold personal morality. They placed political beliefs above party registration, and felt that Helms's Republicanism was irrelevant. James Grissom summarized it well: "I'm with Helms on most everything. And above all he's principled" (Grissom and Grissom 1983).

Eddie and James are the "little people" on which Jesse Helms has built his political career. To beat Jim Hunt, Helms needed people like the Grissoms to mobilize their neighbors—registered to vote but usually indifferent to politics—on Election Day 1984. A look at election returns for the Henderson area demonstrates the strength of Jessecrats. Although registered Democrats outnumbered Republicans in Vance County by 10 to 1, Helms won 57 percent of the vote in 1972, 58 percent in 1978, and 48 percent in 1984. His lack of a majority in 1984 appears to be a direct consequence of the 20 percent increase in black voter registration in Vance County between 1980 and 1984. But the Grissom brothers did their part for Helms. In an interview shortly before the 1984 election, they said that they planned to vote for Helms as well as for Jim Martin and Ronald Reagan.

Beyond Jesse Helms: The Congressional Club in 1976 and 1980

After retiring Helms's 1972 campaign debt, the Congressional Club waged its first political battle in March 1976, when it endorsed challenger Ronald Reagan against incumbent Gerald Ford for the Republican presidential nomination. Reagan's campaign seemed doomed, having lost to Ford during February and March in five states, including New Hampshire and Florida. Jesse Helms and Tom Ellis maintained, however, that Reagan was falling behind because he refused to advocate unequivocally a strongly traditionalist agenda. With little to lose, Reagan accepted the club's advice to buy a half hour of television time statewide to air an old-fashioned patriotic Reagan speech, with unabashed praise of free enterprise, condemnation of the liberal welfare state, and specific criticism of Ford and his foreign policy adviser, Henry Kissinger. (In the address, Reagan attacked Kissinger for "giving away the Panama Canal to the Panamanian Marxists.") Helms and Ellis also insisted that Reagan campaign heavily in North Carolina during the final week in order to highlight the distinction between Reagan principle and Ford pragmatism.

Reagan's 52 to 48 percent victory over Ford baffled both in-state and national observers, who had been busy drafting Reagan's political obituary. Helms's stature rose both with the Reagan campaign and with the press as a kingmaker, for the club's advice had saved Reagan from almost certain political death. But Reagan's victory also had internal consequences for the North Carolina Republican party, because it enabled Helms sympathizers—rather than the mainstream Republicans associated with Governor Jim Holshouser, the symbolic head of Ford's primary campaign—to gain control of the North Carolina delegation to the Republican National Convention.

In a move that would affect GOP politics for more than a decade, the Helms forces denied Governor Holshouser a place in the August 1976 convention delegation in Kansas City. To leaders in both the mainstream and Congressional Club factions, the lesson seemed obvious: if Helms's political star was climbing, mainstream Republicans would lose visibility. For example, after Helms won reelection to the Senate in 1978, he and Ellis selected traditionalist Republicans to run the state party (W. Lee Johnston, from Lamis 1984, 141).

As 1980 approached, the club took aim at two Democrats, incumbent Governor Jim Hunt and U.S. Senator Robert Morgan, each of whom intended to run for a second term. In Helms's 1978 race against Democrat John Ingram, club leaders had spent money both on conventional voter identification and mailings and on thirty-second TV ads. After reviewing in-house polling of the 1978 electorate, they concluded that hard-hitting negative advertising was a more cost-effective way to influence voters (Wrenn 1987).

Although Governor Hunt appeared unbeatable, the Congressional Club sought to damage his credibility in a brief negative ad campaign during 1979. The thirty-second TV spots linked Hunt to a political supporter, state AFL-CIO president Wilbur Hobby, who had been convicted of misappropriation of federal job training funds. They suggested that Hunt approved of Hobby's activity, showing stacks of one-hundred-dollar bills on the screen and asking rhetorically, "What does the state do with your money?" The style of thirty-second political commercials would reappear four years later when Helms began his 1984 reelection campaign against Hunt. In 1979, however, the club ads were unable to touch an apparently invulnerable Hunt. In retrospect, given Helms's successful negative campaign against Hunt during 1983 and 1984, it is probable that the ad linking Hunt to Hobby had little effect because it was not seen by enough of the public. Thirteen North Carolina television stations refused to run the ad, claiming that it was too controversial (Greenhaw 1982, 166).

In 1980, the Congressional Club did spend enough money to repeat a series of negative ads attacking incumbent Senator Robert Morgan and promoting the club's handpicked Senate candidate, John East. Morgan was a well-established, if lackluster, eastern North Carolina politician who began his career as a traditionalist Democrat. He later adopted a more modernizer philosophy when running for statewide office in the early 1970s. Morgan was elected state attorney general in 1972 and easily won election to the U.S. Senate in the aftermath of Watergate in 1974. Because he was so entrenched in Democratic politics, leading Democrats, including Morgan himself, believed East could not win. The only question was whether President Jimmy Carter would carry North Carolina against Ronald Reagan.

In fact, Reagan won North Carolina comfortably with 55 percent of the vote, and his coattails no doubt helped John East, who won just 50.1 percent, a margin of three votes per precinct statewide. East, an East Carolina University political scientist, was an intellectual advocate of traditionalist ideology who also enjoyed practical politics. In 1980, he was unopposed for the Republican nomination for the U.S. Senate, and was, at the start of the campaign, a virtual unknown among Tar Heel voters.

The club's negative campaign argued that Robert Morgan was both a domestic and a foreign policy liberal, neither of which was true. His Senate voting record was in fact moderate-conservative, similar to that of most Southern Democrats. But the club selected a few of Morgan's Senate votes, most of which had been cast along party lines, to build the image of a liberal. Club ads talked about the giveaway of the Panama Canal to "the Marxists" and of "our tax dollars" to fiscally beleaguered New York City. According to these commercials, Morgan sent "hard-earned American dollars to help Communists in Nicaragua" and opposed efforts "to strengthen our defense by voting against the B-1 bomber" (Greenhaw 1982, 167; Lamis 1984, 141).

Believing he had nothing to fear, Morgan ignored the club's advertising. But, as Democrats in North Carolina subsequently recognized, the failure to refute a negative ad immediately can leave the impression in television viewers' minds that the assertion is fact. With the foreign policy ads as a centerpiece, the club's media campaign appeared to shift voter allegiances in the last weeks of the campaign. Morgan lost even though every other North Carolina Democrat on the 1980 statewide ticket won by a comfortable margin.

Hard Times for the Congressional Club

John East's upset constituted a major victory for the National Congressional Club. Chairman Tom Ellis summarized the group's aspirations for the decade in a postelection article: "I think we know how to get conservatives elected, how to put the nuts and bolts together to go over the heads of the liberal editors and TV commentators and get the message out there to the people on TV. . . . The Congressional Club can be the most effective organization in the country when it comes down to doing the hard work it takes to win an election" (*Conservative Digest*, December 1980, quoted in Greenhaw 1982, 168). But except for Helms's victory in 1984, the club would have little to cheer about during the 1980s.

Besides supporting Helms in 1983 and 1984, the Congressional Club undertook three North Carolina campaigns in 1981, 1982, and 1986. All were unsuccessful. In 1981, the club ran a series of anti-Hunt ads similar to its 1979 attacks linking Hunt with Wilbur Hobby. This time the thirty-second TV spots depicted Hunt as a big-spending political operative who was advocating a gasoline tax increase only because he supported featherbedding at the state Department of Transportation (*News and Observer* 1981c). The Democratic majority passed the gasoline tax in 1981, largely along party lines; the club's ads probably increased the legislators' support for Hunt's bill. At the same time, because the ads tarnished Hunt's image, this campaign might also be seen as a club success, the opening salvo in a multi-year plan to reelect Jesse Helms in 1984.

After 1981, the club sought to elect its brand of Republican to federal offices. In 1982, all club-backed North Carolina Republicans running for Congress were defeated. In the 1986 U.S. Senate Republican primary, David Funderburk, the club's candidate, lost decisively to mainstream Republican congressman Jim Broyhill. (The club's declining influence within the North Carolina Republican party is discussed in Chapter 11.)

In the 1980s the evidence was mounting that Congressional Club campaigns produced electoral victories only if the candidate was Jesse Helms. Nevertheless, with its fund-raising ability intact, the club appeared likely to continue its role into the 1990s as an ideological bulwark of traditionalism. How much money it raised in a particular year related to the larger political circumstances. For example, in 1984, when both Helms and Reagan were running for reelection, the club's direct-mail letters generated more income than in 1988, when traditionalist Republicans including Carter Wrenn and Tom Ellis were forced to accept George Bush as the alternative to Michael Dukakis.

Despite the lack of enthusiasm for Bush, club officials produced anti-Dukakis ads comparable to their 1984 negative attacks on Hunt as a "Mondale liberal." In 1988, the thirty-second spots, which ran on national cable stations, identified Dukakis of Massachusetts as the spitting image of the state's well-known liberal U.S. senator, Ted Kennedy.

Parallel to its electoral efforts, the club after 1984 also sought to challenge what it perceived as liberal bias in two of American society's key knowledge centers, the mass media and the university. Although both Accuracy in Media, which gained fame primarily as a hostile buyout attempt against CBS News in 1985, and Accuracy in Academe, which encouraged the monitoring of left-of-center college instructors, did not immediately achieve their goals, the campaigns underscored the club's character as a traditionalist movement organization.

If the anti-Dukakis electoral advertising as well as the antiliberal media and antiliberal university campaigns were accurate indicators, the Congressional Club of the future, in spite of current hard times, will persevere as more than a Republican political action committee. Rather it will remain as a passionate defender of traditionalism, continuing its countermovement mission to pull national and North Carolina politics to the right.

9

Why Helms Beat Hunt

In October 1983, thirteen months before Jesse Helms narrowly defeated Jim Hunt in the renowned 1984 U.S. Senate race, a *Washington Post* writer was finishing off Helms's political obituary. "Barring an act of God," wrote Richard Whittle (1983), "Jesse Helms can't win." At the same time, Republicans at the White House, speaking off the record, reached a similar conclusion. Unfortunately for Jim Hunt, many members of his campaign team also believed that Hunt could not lose. After all, one statewide poll during summer 1983 showed Hunt twenty percentage points ahead of Helms. And in every previous political contest, Hunt had won comfortably. Granted that Helms represented formidable competition, Hunt and his staff felt the voters would remember his own solid, eight-year record of accomplishments as governor.

But all of them, from the *Post* to the White House to Tar Heel Democratic insiders, were wrong. With help from Ronald Reagan's coattails, Helms took 62 percent of the white vote (Reagan himself won 73 percent) (CBS News 1984). Despite an overwhelming black vote for Hunt, Helms squeezed out a 52 to 48 percent victory, a margin of 86,000 out of 2.2 million votes cast. The winning formula developed by the Helms organization, including the senator's close friends Tom Ellis and Carter Wrenn at the National Congressional Club, centered on a media blitz to undermine the governor's credibility and personal image. Once on the defensive, Hunt's team never could find a way to seize the initiative from Helms.

As the 1984 campaign season began taking shape, national Democrats set their sights on North Carolina's Senate race. Although Helms was already ending his second term, Democrats believed this incumbent was vulnerable because of his controversial stands on many issues. To liberal whites and blacks in Washington, D.C., Helms's relentless attacks on the food stamp program, his outspoken opposition to abortion, school busing, and the Martin Luther King holiday, and his hard-core anticommunism made him the worst right-wing menace since Senator Joe McCarthy.

Yet countless North Carolinians—bedrock Helms voters—had a totally different opinion of him. While 1984 Democratic National Committee chair Charles Manatt labeled Helms the "Prince of Darkness," Helms supporters in North Carolina viewed him as a beacon of enlightenment, fighting for free enterprise and Christian morality. The National Organization for Women (NOW) placed Helms at the top of its political enemies list. But thousands of Tar Heel families would have been honored to have Senator and Mrs. Helms come to dinner.

North Carolina Democrats wanted the 1984 race to be a referendum on the views and style of the senior senator. For committed Democrats like Jim Hunt, Helms symbolized opposition to the progress promoted by modernizer ideology. According to this view, Helms's negativism undermined North Carolina's reputation as the most forward-looking southern state; his defeat would allow North Carolina to regain its honor. But the election took place after more than a year of saturated media advertising, in which both sides sought to shape the issues and personalities around which voters should cast their ballots. The election became much more than a voter evaluation of Helms.

For Helms and his core supporters in the Congressional Club, the race had to be transformed into a referendum on Jim Hunt and modernizer ideology. White North Carolinians in particular had to change their assessment of Hunt. This would be a difficult task. In 1980 he had won reelection with 62 percent of the vote, and in 1983 polls showed that three times as many voters approved as disapproved of Jim Hunt as governor.

Helms in Washington: Legitimating the Traditionalist Agenda

Helms's goal in Washington had been to stretch the parameters of political debate to the right. He wanted to reopen issues that moderates and liberals had felt were part of a new national consensus around racial justice, reproductive rights, and detente. Helms would have no part of this consensus.

As stated in Chapter 8, hard work, free enterprise, patriarchal family, and Baptist morality were the core ideas that made Helms unalterably opposed to the egalitarian movements of the 1960s. The underlying theme of his ideology was that he represented normalcy; it was his opponents who were improperly trying to move America away from its God-fearing values. Helms's political core included both social and economic values. But his social traditionalism was far more controversial than his economic views.

Helms's first base of support was North Carolina's business community. His strong antigovernment, antitax ideology afforded him enthusiastic backing from traditionalist business as well as substantial backing from modernizers. A 1985 study of modernizer-oriented Tar Heel executives found that most had voted for Helms even though many of them disagreed with his views on race and abortion (Baker 1986). Most modernizer business people supported Helms for the Senate seat because they felt that he would be more likely than Jim Hunt to prevent new domestic spending by the federal government. The fear of national Democratic policies led these corporate modernizers to reject Hunt, even though they had previously backed him for governor in 1976 and 1980 (Luebke 1981b; Baker 1986). A preelection poll by the National Chamber of Commerce of its North Carolina members revealed that 70 percent favored Helms. In short, within the business community Helms held a lead over Hunt comparable to that of most incumbent Republicans running for Congress.

A second strong Helms base consisted of registered Republicans. Although less than 30 percent of Tar Heel voters were enrolled in the Republican party, their party loyalty was much stronger than Democrats'. Indeed, even with Republican gains, Democrats held nearly a three-to-one registration advantage. If registered Democrats were as loyal to their party on Election Day as Republicans, Democrats would never lose a statewide election.

Helms's third support base included nonbusiness whites who revered his traditional social values. As a media commentator during the 1960s, Helms had developed a strong following by attacking groups that symbolized disruption of the social order. He criticized not all blacks, but "militant Negroes," not all students, but "beatnik students" (Nordhoff 1984, 44). When he first ran for the Senate in 1972, he opposed "forced busing" for school desegregation. The composite picture drawn by Helms was of a federal government run amok by liberals (he often called them socialists or Marxists) who sympathized with radical egalitarian movements that aimed to provide easy times for the millions (for example, blacks or college students) who preferred a handout to hard work. Despite the broad ideological attack on federal programs,

Helms pragmatically held his fire regarding the federal tobacco program. Indeed, after becoming chair of the Senate Agricultural Committee in 1981, he insisted that the tobacco program would be killed if he were not in Washington to protect it (Luebke 1984b).

The economic ideology of Jesse Helms emphasized limited government, except for the tobacco and peanut programs that benefited Tar Heel farmers. Rhetorically, he favored a balanced federal budget, but he avoided any censure of President Reagan when the federal budget deficit soared in the early 1980s. In fact, his 1984 campaign speeches blamed the deficit on the Democratic liberals who had placed so many "entitlement" programs in the federal budget. Was Helms talking about cutting Social Security? When pressed, he said no. But Helms was skilled at keeping his criticism vague, winning applause from audiences who admired his antigovernment talk. He would say, for example: "I don't think anyone in any program is entitled to anything from your pockets which you worked for" (Helms 1983b). Such speechmaking confirmed the picture of a high-minded politician who was willing to stand up for "what's right" against the so-called special interests.

When the polls showed Helms trailing Jim Hunt by a huge margin in mid-1983, Helms and his Congressional Club advisers decided to promote him as a courageous, principled leader—in contrast to Hunt, whom they would portray as a pragmatic, wheeling-dealing politician with no firm beliefs. The decision to begin these early attacks on Hunt's character turned out, in retrospect, to have been crucial for Helms's uphill battle.

The Helms Strategy: Making Jim Hunt the Issue

Helms's goal was to draw public attention away from his Senate record and to the alleged liberal pragmatism of Jim Hunt. On the social side, Hunt was, according to Helms, soft on abortion, blacks, and Christianity. On economic matters, Helms viewed Hunt as a tax-and-spend liberal. The question in 1983 was whether Helms's criticism of Hunt would stick with the voters.

The first volley that year zeroed in on race; it came via the cheapest media, radio stations and small-town newspapers, especially in eastern North Carolina. Among a series of ads highlighting Helms's virtues (protector of the tobacco program, opponent of government spending, friend and supporter of Ronald Reagan) were attacks on Hunt as a prounion, problack governor. Most of the connections to Hunt were unfair. For instance, because he was politically close at that time to the North Carolina Association of Educators, one Helms ad showed a picture of black schoolteachers in Washington, D.C., on a picket line and wondered whether Hunt supported teacher strikes. In fact, he did not. These newspaper ads also hinted that Hunt had ties with black politicians like the late mayor of Chicago, Harold Washington, or Georgia state senator Julian Bond.

Probably the most damaging ad reprinted a 1982 photo from *The Carolinian*, Raleigh's black weekly, which showed Jesse Jackson visiting Hunt in the governor's office. The ad made clear that Hunt supported Jackson's goal of greater black voter registration. By identifying the Hunt-Jackson connection, the Helms campaign sent a coded message both to racist whites and whites who resented black political gains that there was a difference between Helms and Hunt. The Helms forces were genuinely worried about black voter registration, but they also saw that publicity about Hunt's support of black political activism could help Helms among certain white voters.

The U.S. Senate debate over the Martin Luther King holiday in September and October 1983 proved to be a windfall for Helms. National political observers thought he was foolish to attack the King holiday so stridently. But, in fact, the criticism Helms received from the national media hurt as much as a rabbit's confinement in a briar patch. To many white North Carolinians, it confirmed his claim as a man who dared to stand alone for a principle. What Helms stood for, in this instance, was a traditionalist view of the United States. In a speech on the Senate floor, Helms characterized King as unpatriotic and a Communist-sympathizer: "King's view of American society was thus not fundamentally different from that of CPUSA (American Communist Party) or of other Marxists. While he is generally remembered today as the pioneer of civil rights for blacks and as the architect of non-violent techniques of dissent and political agitation, his hostility to and hatred for America should be made clear" (*Congressional Record*, October 3, 1983, quoted in Nordhoff 1984, 48).

Further, Helms's opposition to the King holiday proposal and the subsequent criticism of Helms in the national media tapped a strong feeling among many traditionalist Tar Heels that blacks and their white sympathizers were pushing for another giveaway, this time a paid holiday for federal employees. The King holiday issue helped Helms in the polls, particularly in areas of eastern North Carolina where black political organization could threaten white power. Coincidentally, some of these heavily black counties overlapped with the area where Helms's editorials in earlier years could be seen on WRAL-TV. Helms appeared to gain from the King controversy because he had tapped a volatile issue and because he had reached, particularly in the WRAL viewing area, thousands of voters who had long ago come to respect his political opinions.

The King holiday issue gave Helms free publicity. He accompanied this free airtime in fall 1983 with his first extended paid foray into Tar Heel living rooms. These thirty-second TV spots had both positive and negative themes, but it was the anti-Hunt attack that reaped the most rewards. The positive ads underscored Ronald Reagan's support for the senior senator, since Reagan was more popular in North Carolina than Helms. This coattail advertising would continue until the election.

Helms's team at Jefferson Marketing, a subsidiary of the National Congressional Club, developed a twofold attack on Hunt: that he was in fact a liberal, but, as a deft, pragmatic politician, he sought publicly to be all things to all people. The message was simple: Helms the principled conservative faced Hunt the pragmatic liberal who sought to hide his true political colors. Helms researchers found what they identified as contradictory positions in Hunt's record on such issues as school prayer or tax increases, and juxtaposed these alleged differences in the same ad. They also contrasted Helms and Hunt on symbolic issues like the King holiday or the Panama Canal "giveaway," a theme that Republican John East had used to defeat Democrat Robert Morgan in the 1980 U.S. Senate race. Hunt mildly supported the King holiday and the Panama Canal treaty. The Helms advertising turned Hunt's ability to forge compromises with the majority, normally considered a political asset, into a liability, while Helms's intransigence became a virtue. The tag line on these ads—"Where Do You Stand, Jim?"—could not be forgotten by friend or foe.

The Hunt Strategy: Doing More for North Carolina

As governor, Jim Hunt gained a reputation as a hard-driving, action-oriented leader who wanted to promote countless programs through the General Assembly. Along the general lines of modernizer ideology, Hunt was leaving his mark on North Carolina. The assumption of Hunt and his associates was that he could articulate similar themes in the race against Jesse Helms. Thus, while Helms was launching his pointed negative ads against Hunt, the governor was developing his "Four E's" (economy, education, the elderly, and the environment), a vague set of issue areas that, like his plans for the governor's office, laid out Hunt's future goals for the U.S. Senate. Hunt chose the overall slogan, "He Can Do More for North Carolina," to contrast his can-do style with the right-wing posturing of Helms.

Hunt's strongest political base consisted of black North Carolinians. Blacks had voted overwhelmingly for Hunt in earlier elections, and he hoped that Helms's negative image among blacks would lead to a large turnout on Election Day. His second base, about 10 percent of the electorate, included self-identified white liberals. Like blacks, white liberals seemed to be motivated by their dislike of Helms.

Hunt's largest political base was also his least solid. These were moderate and conservative Democrats who had voted for him in 1976 and 1980. Hunt needed to convince these voters that his achievements as governor were substantial, despite Helms's claims to the contrary. With a big vote from self-identified white Democrats, Hunt could win.

Initially, the Hunt campaign did not recognize that the generalities of the Four E's made a weaker impression on voters, including Democrats, than the specific attacks of the Helms forces. What exactly was it that Hunt had achieved, or would achieve, for the economy or education? Was he maybe just promoting big government, wasting the taxpayers' money? Doing more for North Carolina could also be interpreted as the self-serving activities of a political machine. Even when Hunt and his associates began to acknowledge the skill of their opposition, they still thought the positive impression of the Hunt years would hold with the voters. Consequently, as the Helms campaign over the late fall and winter of 1983–84 maintained a heavy barrage of "Where Do You Stand, Jim?" ads, Hunt barely responded, believing that his advertising dollars should be saved for later. The governor's failure to launch a counterattack in the media proved costly, for by early 1984 the polls showed that Helms had caught up with Hunt. It was a remarkable comeback.

Once on the defensive, Hunt sought to speak directly to the charge that he was a liberal by laying out a variety of conservative positions. He told campaign audiences that he supported prayer in the public schools, the death penalty, aid to the Nicaraguan Contras, and the Reagan military buildup. He opposed a nuclear freeze and abortion, although he did as governor favor a state abortion fund for poor women. Helms himself labeled Hunt's conservatism as "Johnny-come-lately" behavior. In the spring, during a Senate debate on organized school prayer in which Helms was a vocal advocate for a constitutional amendment, Hunt announced that he too supported the school prayer amendment. Helms quipped in reply: "I am glad to share my prayer book with the governor."

But Hunt's move to the right failed to have the desired impact, and perhaps even backfired. Why should white conservatives switch allegiances when Helms held the same positions and supported them with greater fervor? White liberals, on the other hand, wondered why they should work their precincts for Hunt if he was determined to blur his differences with Helms. The effect was to engender disenchantment among Hunt's most ideological backers without winning back support from large numbers of conservative whites.

Negative Advertising in the Hunt Campaign

Except for a brief spurt in February 1984, when Hunt announced his candidacy and ran a short media campaign, he was unable to gain any ground against Helms in the polls. If Helms's ads raised doubts among political observers because of their negativism, Hunt's initial media spots were controversial because they adopted such a soft-sell approach. Playing on his Four E's themes, the ads showed a relaxed Hunt talking with workers, students, or farmers about his plans for economic growth and education programs. The criticism of Helms was muted, in contrast to Helms's direct attacks on Hunt's alleged wishy-washiness. Hunt wanted voters to feel good about him and what he promised to do for North Carolina, while Helms wanted voters to question Hunt's character.

Hunt did not run his campaign ads during March and April, partly to save money and partly to avoid the highly competitive race for the Democratic gubernatorial nomination, which involved two of his college classmates and one of his cabinet members. But internally, the Hunt campaign was debating whether to take off the gloves and go on the offensive against Helms. When a May Gallup Poll showed Helms in the lead, Hunt became convinced that the Four E's and the related soft-sell media had to go.

Hunt challenged Helms in two areas. In a series of ads first telecast in May, he charged that Helms was not a reliable protector of Social Security funds. Helms developed a rejoinder to the accusation, which prompted a second attack by Hunt. Poll data showed that Helms was vulnerable on this concrete economic issue; Social Security was one of the few themes that clearly helped Hunt.

Then in late June, the Hunt campaign pulled no punches in criticizing Helms's right-wing associations in Latin America. In particular, Hunt suggested that Helms was linked, through Salvadoran presidential candidate Roberto D'Aubuisson, to right-wing death squads in El Salvador. The most outspoken Hunt commercial opened with the rat-a-tat-tat of machine gun fire, and ended with a picture of Helms, described as D'Aubuisson's best friend in Washington. The voice-over stated that "Jesse Helms may be a crusader, but that's not what our senator should be crusading for."

Helms responded that Hunt had reached a new low in political campaigning. More significantly, the ad bothered Hunt partisans, who felt that the governor had joined Helms in the gutter. In short, the moral high ground had been lost. Hunt's staff concluded nonetheless that such advertising did put Helms on the defensive. The campaign never ran the "death squad" ad again, but during October aired a similar ad attacking the senior senator for his associations with right-wing ideologues in the United States such as Texas financier Nelson Bunker Hunt and Moral Majority leader Jerry Falwell.

A further criticism of the Hunt advertising accepts the decision to run a negative campaign but questions its focus. Surely the details of Helms's right-wing connections made little sense to the average viewer. How many North Carolinians knew anything about political actors in El Salvador or recognized Nelson Bunker Hunt as a friend of Jesse Helms rather than a cousin of Jim Hunt? By contrast, Social Security was understood by everyone, especially the elderly. To suggest that Helms was skipping his homework on such a serious economic issue unquestionably was more meaningful to most voters than his alleged foreign policy connections.

The 1984 CBS Election Day exit polls support this critique of Hunt's issue selection. Nine percent of the sample listed Social Security as the primary reason for candidate support, and Hunt won 83 percent of those votes. Further, 29 percent of the sample said the economy had the greatest influence on their vote. Despite the generally positive economic conditions (in contrast to either 1982 or 1986), Hunt and Helms were supported almost equally (49 percent versus 50 percent) by voters who focused on the economy (CBS News 1984). Yet except for the Social Security series, Hunt had virtually no advertising that critiqued Helms's shepherding of North Carolinians' economic interests. Why, for example, did Hunt not attack Helms for the loss of textile jobs since Ronald Reagan had become president? As indicated in a more detailed analysis below, Hunt received fewer votes from white factory workers than from any other white occupational group.

The CBS data show that Central America was less important to the voters than either the economy or Social Security. But for the 4 percent who named it as their primary concern, Hunt won 56 percent of the vote. This suggests that hammering away on Latin America probably helped Hunt. Poll data during the campaign revealed that, for any issue, Hunt's negative ads changed public opinion more than his soft-sell approach.

The Hunt camp was convinced that economic issues would not work to the Democrats' advantage in 1984. Ironically, in failing to develop a worker-oriented economic critique of Helms, Hunt ensured that Helms's social agenda would by default be paramount in white workers' minds. If Hunt conceded economics, then the spotlight would be placed on abortion, the King holiday, communism, or school prayer, the kinds of issues on which Helms loved to run. Helms continually reminded voters of the strong stands that were part of his traditionalist upbringing. For example, even though Hunt was a devout Presbyterian, Helms's supporters in white working-class precincts promoted Helms as the "Christian" candidate.

According to the CBS data, Helms's antiabortion message got through to fundamentalist voters. Among the 38 percent of the white electorate who considered themselves "born-again," Helms beat Hunt 71 to 29 percent.

The Hunt campaign conceded economics, and waffled throughout the summer and fall on how negative it should be. In the final week before the election, a women-oriented ad attacked Helms for allegedly wanting to prohibit birth control because he was a cosponsor of the controversial family protection bill. The ad produced a flurry of counteractivity from the Helms campaign, suggesting that younger whites, who are most likely to be pro-choice on abortion and birth control, had been influenced by Hunt's commercial.

The key Helms rejoinder showed a young working woman in front of a new car, who claimed she would not be able to afford the car if Hunt won because "the Hunt-Mondale tax plan will take $157 a month out of my family take home pay." In a reversal of usual Democratic-Republican themes, it was Helms pushing economic issues to try to save his campaign.

The Hunt organization, including David Sawyer's out-of-state group which produced the commercials, vacillated throughout the campaign on what issues to stress and how to present Hunt. By failing to answer the first "Where Do You Stand, Jim?" ads questioning his integrity, Hunt conceded the initiative to Helms and never regained it.

Once the Democrats nominated the Walter Mondale–Geraldine Ferraro ticket, the Helms campaign developed a hard-hitting negative ad series, used throughout the fall, which asserted that the Democratic National Convention had identified Hunt's true colors: he was cut from the same cloth as national Democrats like Mondale and Ferraro. The tag line on every ad, "Jim Hunt—a Mondale liberal," became as memorable as the "Where Do You Stand?" jingle. Both series succeeded in casting doubt on Hunt's character and political ideology. After a year of such ads, who could remember the middle-of-the-road, modernizer governor who carefully compromised to avoid being typed as either too much to the right or to the left? The Jim Hunt accustomed to favorable reviews in the press found himself badly damaged by the Helms spots. The attacks were, in the final month, incessant from both sides. Seventy-eight hundred ads were run in the last five weeks of the race (Peterson 1984).

Grass-roots Campaigns: Voter Registration and Election Day

Voter registration is a nonpartisan activity. But each side in an election has a base from which it hopes to mobilize large numbers of voters, and consequently focuses on those voters alone. Hunt's base was lower-income blacks, especially in the larger cities of the modernizer Piedmont and in the rural areas of eastern North Carolina. Tar Heel blacks are by far the most loyal Democratic constituency. Helms's plan was to counter Hunt by encouraging voter registration among previously uninvolved lower-income whites affiliated with fundamentalist Protestant churches. Symbolically, it was a battle of the preachers. Already in 1982, before he had become a presidential candidate, the Reverend Jesse Jackson supported black registration to aid Hunt. In July 1983, the Reverend Jerry Falwell urged "evangelical" residents to register in order to help Helms. In fact, the two preachers did not actually lead these drives, although Falwell's Moral Majority contributed $40,000 toward voter registration activities (*News and Observer*, September 6, 1983).

Between 1980 and 1984, the number of black registrants in North Carolina increased by 179,000. Virtually all of these new voters could be expected to support the Democratic ticket. Among the groups claiming credit for black voter registration was the foundation-funded North Carolinians for Effective Citizenship, whose board included representatives from the League of Women Voters, the NAACP, and the AFL-CIO. The underlying impetus behind this drive was to replace Helms's traditionalist, antigovernment program with a candidate more sympathetic to social spending for the poor.

The publicity surrounding Jesse Jackson led the Helms organization to seek a counter-registration effort. Although the Moral Majority generally received a great deal of the credit, the Helms campaign actually organized its major voter registration drives internally, relying on the network of white fundamentalist churches (Luebke 1985–86). A Helms staff member directly sought out pastors who would allow voter registration tables to be set up outside church buildings. The Helms organization viewed church members' aroused feelings about abortion and school prayer, rather than race, to be the basis for successful drives. Helms's staff encouraged people to register Republican, even though historically such working-class whites would have been registered Democrats. Any new Republican registrants would potentially help the Congressional Club in the kinds of intraparty conflict that occurred in the 1986 Republican primary for the U.S. Senate nomination between Jim Broyhill and David Funderburk.

A comparison of new Republican and black registrants between 1980 and 1984 (162,000 versus 179,000) showed, assuming that blacks were Democrats, a near standoff. It is doubtful that all new Republicans were motivated by Helms's abortion and school prayer agenda. However, two facts suggest that the Helms voter registration effort mattered. First, more than 80 percent of the new Republican registrants since the 1980 election were added to the books during 1984, the very time when the church-based voter registration drives were in high gear. Second, in the textile/Bible Belt counties of the western Piedmont, Democrats historically have outregistered Republicans by a two- or three-to-one margin. But during 1984, Republican registration equaled that of Democrats in those counties (Luebke 1985–86).

On Election Day, the Helms and Hunt campaigns differed in their get-out-the-vote approach. Right up to the end, Hunt's county organizations were polling undecided voters by telephone and urging them to support Hunt. By contrast, Helms's workers had compiled lists of both Republicans and Democrats who supported Helms; they ignored the undecideds. These lists of pro-Helms Democrats came especially from a computerized telephone interview with registered Democrats asking whether they supported Helms or Hunt. The standard computer message referred to Helms's antitax position and claimed that Hunt favored higher taxes. Democrats who told the computer they supported Helms were added to the precinct lists.

A comparison of the two special groups—white evangelicals and blacks—that Helms and Hunt sought especially to mobilize on Election Day indicates that Helms had an advantage. His strong religious agenda allowed devout fundamentalists to believe that they would be voting for "the Christian candidate" if they turned out for Helms. Campaign workers in numerous counties of the western Piedmont placed antiabortion, pro-Helms flyers on windshields of cars sitting in church parking lots during the Sunday morning service preceding Election Day. In speaking to parishioners, many fundamentalist pastors made a coded endorsement of Helms by referring to him as the Christian on the ballot, despite the fact that Jim Hunt was also a practicing Christian. In short, activists within Helms's targeted group had high motivation.

By contrast, Hunt's gradual shaping of campaign positions to minimize his differences with Helms—for example, his defensiveness about the Martin Luther King holiday or his support of the death penalty—troubled some black politicians across the state. Hunt's September decision not to halt the execution of convicted murderer Velma Barfield, a white woman, was unpopular with blacks, even though most whites supported the decision. Her execution four days before Election Day reminded black political leaders that they had major disagreements with Hunt on some issues. While the governor's positions certainly did not cause either black leaders or whites with similar citizen-power views to abandon him, their enthusiasm was dampened.

Further, some local party activists, both modernizer and citizen-power Democrats, felt that Hunt expected rather than asked for support at the precinct level. Such leaders criticized him for separating his campaign organization from the Democratic party and for omitting the word "Democrat" from his bumper stickers. It is an intangible, but important aspect of grass-roots politics that volunteer activists believe that their candidate holds to political principles worth fighting for, and does not take the volunteers' efforts for granted. Unlike Helms, Hunt left doubt in some supporters' minds on both counts. Turnout was in fact lower in Hunt's strongholds than in Helms's. Unfortunately, it is impossible to document whether the difference in enthusiasm levels mattered.

Analyzing the Results

Basking in the glory of Election Night 1984, Jesse Helms told cheering supporters at his Raleigh headquarters that his reelection was a victory for "God-fearing conservatives." Certainly the dual foci of religion and politics fit many if not most of the staff and volunteer activists across North Carolina who worked for Helms that year. But by no means was every Helms voter religiously motivated.

A less exuberant Helms knew his narrow win over Hunt was neither a New Right mandate nor a sign of Republican realignment in North Carolina. Rather, the Helms organization had crafted a patchwork of diverse voters, only some of whom were directly influenced by the religious-political concerns usually associated with "evangelicals" or the Moral Majority. While often disagreeing with each other, Helms voters on Election Day could agree that he was preferable to his Democratic opponent. The coalition ranged from the country club to the country store.

During the 1980s, Republican victories in North Carolina occurred statewide if GOP candidates received 60 percent or more of the white vote. Conversely, Democrats would win if they captured 40 percent of the white vote. According to the 1984 CBS Election Day exit polls, Helms took 62 percent of the white vote against Hunt, and Jim Martin won 65 percent in defeating Democrat Rufus Edmisten for governor (CBS News 1984). But in 1986, according to exit polls, Republican Jim Broyhill won 58 percent of white support and so lost the U.S. Senate seat to Terry Sanford (CBS News 1986).

Despite Helms's large share of the white vote in 1984, the race was close because blacks, who constituted more than one-fifth of the electorate, cast more than 90 percent of their votes for Hunt. Voter turnout as well as the occupational and regional basis of Hunt and Helms support can be examined with the help of exit poll data as well as actual county and precinct-level returns.

The normal pattern in American politics is that the higher one's socioeconomic status, the more likely one is to support Republican candidates. Poll data show that in 1984 the black vote varied little by socioeconomic status or region. By contrast, differing levels of support within the white vote proved to be significant. One clear finding is that the normal relationship between occupation and party preference among whites did not hold in the Helms-Hunt case. Hunt was most popular among professional-managerial voters (41 percent) and received the least support from blue-collar workers (32 percent). He won 37 percent from the intermediate group, white-collar employees. Similarly, Hunt ran better among white college graduates (43 percent) than among white nongraduates (34 percent) (CBS News 1984).

These results suggest that the content and style of the two campaigns brought differing benefits to the candidates. Hunt reduced Helms's margins among higher-status whites who either liked Hunt's growth-oriented campaign themes, disliked Helms's far-right positions, or both. By contrast, he won less than one out of three votes cast by factory workers. Members of the Hunt organization acknowledged that Helms outorganized them in this area. But the Hunt team's postelection analysis was fatalistic, indicating doubt that any economics-based argument could have made inroads among blue-collar whites (Luebke 1985–86).

It is ironic that a Democratic candidate would concede blue-collar votes to a Republican. In effect, Hunt felt that Helms's appeal to blue-collar voters by emphasizing the traditionalist social agenda, especially such fundamentalist-oriented issues as school prayer and abortion, was insurmountable. But if Democrats do not raise pocketbook issues among white working-class voters, how can they hope to win their support? Certainly no modernizer Democrat can hope to "out-religion" a Republican traditionalist. In retrospect, it seems plausible to ask why more election resources were not targeted on the problem of textile plant closings and the growing concern about textile imports (Luebke 1984d).

When faced with the import question during the campaign, Helms usually responded by focusing on textile goods from "Red China." In fact, during 1983 and 1984, more than twice as many textile imports came from Taiwan than from the People's Republic of China. In dollar value, the top three major textile exporters to the United States in 1983 were the non-Communist countries of Taiwan (16 percent of total), Hong Kong (16 percent), and South Korea (14 percent); China (7 percent) ranked only fifth (U.S. Department of Commerce 1986, 12). Why did Hunt let Helms off the hook so easily?

The turnout analysis indicates that the heavily blue-collar western

Piedmont region was a crucial area for Helms. While statewide turnout was 68 percent, seven of the eighteen western Piedmont counties had turnouts above 72 percent. Located south and west of Greensboro on Interstates 85 and 40, all seven of these counties (Davidson, Rowan, Cabarrus, Stanly, Davie, Iredell, and Catawba) gave 60–65 percent of their votes to Helms. The counties were all below the state average in percentage of college graduates and above-average in percentage of employment in the manufacturing sector. These results give credence to the Helms campaign organizers' claim that their Election Day turnout depended on the mobilization of large concentrations of fundamentalist blue-collar voters in certain key counties. In the three western Piedmont counties where turnout was only average, Helms won majorities but less than 60 percent. In sum, a positive correlation existed between high turnout and a high vote for Helms (B. Hall 1985b).

Although the western Piedmont was Helms's key region, additional evidence suggests that he also turned out white voters at high rates elsewhere in the state. Further, from an analysis of heavily black counties in the eastern Piedmont and on the Coastal Plain, it appears that black voters, although a major source of Hunt's votes, turned out at a relatively low level. For example, in North Carolina's four counties with a black voting majority (Northampton, Warren, Bertie, and Hertford), Hunt won 65 percent of the vote but turnout was 60 percent, a full eight percentage points below the state average. Helms's organization seemed to concentrate its eastern North Carolina efforts in counties where whites constituted about 70 percent of the voters. In Wayne and Nash counties, for example, Helms defeated Hunt by 58 to 42 percent. Significantly, turnout there exceeded 70 percent. Turnout analysis within eastern North Carolina suggests that the Helms-Hunt race would have been much closer had each side's voters participated at similar rates. But in fact, based on county voting patterns, it seems conclusive that whites committed to Helms turned out at higher rates than blacks who supported Hunt (B. Hall 1985b).

Hunt benefited from disproportionate white support in the metro Piedmont counties. He carried all three counties around the Research Triangle Park by comfortable margins, in part because in-migrating whites, even if Republican sympathizers, were opposed to Helms's traditionalist politics. The university, state government, and research and development base of the Triangle economy attracts professionals who are more likely to prefer a candidate touting microelectronics to an incumbent fighting the King holiday. This is best suggested in Orange

County, home to the University of North Carolina at Chapel Hill, where Hunt won his highest percentage (69 percent) even though blacks made up just 15 percent of the county's voters. The use of counties as an analytical unit runs the risk of overgeneralization. This assumption that all voters within a county have certain behaviors because a majority does is known as the ecological fallacy (Luebke 1979; Robinson 1950). Because Hunt's white support came disproportionately from metropolitan Piedmont counties in which Helms did not win majorities, the potential fallacy lies in ignoring Helms's support among diverse groups of whites. A better insight into that vote emerges from precinct analysis. In Durham County, for example, Helms won only 36 percent of the vote, but he received 71 percent in a semi-rural precinct with a high percentage of middle-income and fundamentalist whites. Similarly, in Guilford County (Greensboro) he ran even with Hunt, but in a white fundamentalist semi-rural area he took 66 percent of the vote.

The Limits of Hunt's Appeal

The CBS exit poll (CBS News 1984) provides further insight into the difficulties that Democrats have in winning white votes. Focusing on Hunt's results, the poll reveals:

- While 87 percent of self-identified white Republicans supported Helms, only 62 percent of whites who considered themselves Democrats voted for Hunt. This does not include the registered Democrats who identified themselves as Independents (those voters who regardless of party registration perceive themselves as unaffiliated), 42 percent of whom cast their ballot for Hunt. But the high level of defection from self-identified Democrats (38 percent to Helms) was a major source of worry for Democratic party officials.
- Hunt support among white women (39 percent) was only marginally above his vote level among white men (37 percent). The data refute the notion that modernizer Democrats like Hunt, compared to Republicans, would necessarily have a substantially higher appeal to women (the so-called gender gap).
- Although Social Security worked mostly as a Hunt issue against Helms, whites over sixty were only slightly more likely than other whites to support Hunt (40 percent). Support for Hunt did correlate positively with age, and whites under thirty were least likely to vote

for him (34 percent). This suggests that younger whites had some sympathy for Helms's free enterprise, anti–big government themes, and indicates that Helms must be viewed as having appeal across the age structure.

The Hunt-Helms results demonstrate that statewide Democratic candidates have limited appeal for whites. Hunt won more than 40 percent of the white vote only from the Mountain counties—historically, the most loyal white Democratic region—and the metropolitan Piedmont. In the rest of the state, he averaged 35 percent among white voters. The differing social bases of the parties in the two regions—more blue-collar workers in the Mountains and more professionals in the metro Piedmont—reveal two sources of the party's appeal. Of the two, the Mountain whites proved to be a less fickle source of Democratic votes. For example, Mountain whites gave 42 percent of their votes to both Jim Hunt and gubernatorial candidate Rufus Edmisten, whereas support for Edmisten among metro Piedmont whites dropped to 28 percent, compared to 41 percent for Hunt (CBS News 1984).

Metro Piedmont whites felt a less strong attachment to the Democratic party than did Mountain whites. Hunt's growth-oriented agenda won him substantial support in the metro Piedmont, but Edmisten, whose image was that of a good old boy, was passed over there in favor of the more businesslike Jim Martin. In fact, Edmisten was a modernizer Democrat who differed little from Hunt on social issues like abortion and the King holiday or on economic issues like taxation and development policy. But his symbolic appeal was far different, and apparently more significant for voters, than his positions on issues. In several professional precincts around Duke University in Durham and the University of North Carolina at Chapel Hill, Edmisten won 20 percent fewer votes than Hunt, even though Martin's voting record as a congressman was close to Helms's. This suggests that, if Democrats wish to avoid alienating the affluent urban and suburban voters in North Carolina's metropolitan areas, their candidates must adopt the symbolism of urban modernism (of Hunt or Martin), not of rural traditionalism (of Edmisten or Helms).

But the voting of Mountain whites indicates an alternative, or at least an additional model for Democrats. The relatively strong support that the Democratic party receives from Mountain whites is often overlooked. (Eastern North Carolina appears more Democratic, but is so only by virtue of a large Democratic vote from blacks. Further, the absence of a strong Republican party in the eastern Piedmont and on the Coastal Plain allows traditionalist politicians to win office as Democrats. A more active Republican party in the east might someday lead to an ideological division whereby Democrats, in the two-party setting, would be modernizer or citizen-action Democrats in a race against traditionalist Republicans.) Mountain Democratic legislators in the General Assembly are, compared to small-town Democratic representatives elsewhere in the state, more supportive of economic populist measures—for instance, the legislative proposal to limit the interest rates that banks can charge on credit card accounts. Mountain Democratic legislators, who often face strong antigovernment traditionalism from Mountain Republicans, appear to have a regional electorate that may prefer Democratic populism for the "little guy" rather than the trickle-down, pro–big business economics of Democratic modernizers.

But the argument that Democrats should make greater economic appeals to middle- and lower-income Tar Heels usually falls on deaf ears in modernizer Democrats' circles. Modernizers explain that the winning Democratic statewide strategy has always required the muting of economic differences in the electorate. This normally successful formula failed Jim Hunt only because of two special circumstances that came together in 1984: the enormous political strength of President Ronald Reagan, who led the GOP ticket against the unpopular Walter Mondale; and the unique appeal of Jesse Helms, aided by the Congressional Club's nasty but effective anti-Hunt media campaign.

According to modernizers, Democrats may at most need to make *symbolic* populist appeals, as Terry Sanford did in 1986 when he ran against Republican Jim Broyhill for a seat in the U.S. Senate. Sanford's winning strategy, a possible model for Democratic modernizers, is discussed in the remaining two chapters. The next chapter examines the process of white voters' dealignment from the Democratic party from the 1960s to the 1980s.

10

Dealignment in North Carolina Politics: Decline of the Democrats and Opportunity for Republicans

In the 1960s, white Southerners, including Tar Heel whites, began to abandon their century-long commitment to the Democratic party. In 1972, North Carolina Republicans won a U.S. Senate seat, the governor's office, and nearly one-third of the seats in the General Assembly. By 1984, any Republican candidate running statewide could expect to gain a majority of the white vote. Black voters, nearly one-fifth of the electorate, supported the Democratic ticket overwhelmingly. Democrats needed the strong black vote as well as 40 percent of the white vote to win. If Republicans won 60 percent or more of the white vote, they would be elected. In short, the swing voters in the 1980s' statewide elections were whites with weak partisan identification. Many of these voters pulled for the entire statewide Republican ticket, but maintained their affiliation as registered Democrats. North Carolina in 1984 elected a Republican governor and U.S. senator and decisively supported Ronald Reagan simply because several hundred thousand registered Democrats crossed over to vote Republican, primarily at the top of the ticket.

The gradual weakening of Democratic loyalties by white Southerners is known as dealignment. Dealignment means that many North Carolina whites have lost their commitment to the Democratic party, but have not yet transferred their loyalty to the Republicans. Republicans would prefer to see more whites switch their party registration to the GOP, or at least to identify with the Republican party. This process is known as realignment (Black and Black 1987, 237). But dealignment, not realignment, characterized the white electorate in the 1980s. For

156

example, while Jesse Helms received 62 percent of the white vote against Jim Hunt in 1984, just 42 percent of whites considered themselves Republicans. Another 42 percent of white North Carolinians identified with the Democrats, although 38 percent of them supported Helms (CBS News 1984). The governor's race between Jim Martin and Rufus Edmisten showed a similar pattern of dealignment; 37 percent of self-identified Democrats voted for Martin.

Dealignment as Southern White Reaction

During the 1960s, the struggle and success of blacks to achieve racial equality shocked most Southern whites. While white Southerners were aware that institutional discrimination was viewed negatively by many Northerners, few whites in the South believed that the series of laws and customs known as Jim Crow would disappear overnight. Early in the decade, blacks across the South challenged Jim Crow with sit-ins, street demonstrations, and economic boycotts. The first protest occurred in Greensboro on February 1, 1960, when students from the city's public black college, North Carolina A&T, sat at the Woolworth's lunch counter. Many Tar Heel whites were outraged by the students' actions and by the subsequent inability of politicians and police across the state to prevent these protests (Nathans 1983).

The protests proved to be a major dilemma for Governor Terry Sanford. Elected in 1960 as a forward-looking leader and yet as a supporter of North Carolina's Jim Crow laws, Sanford in 1963 sought a middle ground by establishing community forums, called "Good Neighbor Councils," where the conflicting views of whites and blacks could be aired. He tried to please traditionalist whites by speaking out against demonstrations, calling the protests counterproductive. But the fact that Sanford refused to condemn the protests strongly made him suspect in the eyes of many white Tar Heels (Chafe 1981, 139).

Sanford had won the Democratic nomination for governor by finessing his positions on racial change. In the June 1960 runoff, he defeated I. Beverly Lake, Sr., a strong segregationist professor at Wake Forest Law School, in classic modernizer fashion by capturing the center and urging those to his left to join him against the threat from the party's segregationist right wing. Specifically, Sanford persuaded blacks and their few white supporters that he was by far the candidate most sympathetic to civil rights, and he won the overwhelming majority of their votes. (Compared to the 1980s, of course, blacks were a much smaller segment of the Democratic electorate.) In speaking to traditionalist whites, his sympathy for civil rights was necessarily muted. His supporters emphasized that he was an eastern North Carolinian who understood the importance of the state's racial mores. They reminded skeptical whites that Sanford had supported the antischool integration Pearsall Plan (see Chapter 7) in 1955 (Chafe 1981), and implied that he opposed racial change (Spence 1968, 12). Sanford himself argued that the difference between him and Lake was moderate versus militant segregationism: "The people of North Carolina do not want integration and we cannot afford to close the schools, but this is where the (racial extremism of the) Professor would lead us" (Black 1975, 73–74). As much as possible, Sanford campaigned on nonracial issues, pledging to modernize North Carolina through improved education and economic development. Sanford beat Lake by 56 to 44 percent. It was one of only two times in the South between 1957 and 1973 that a moderate segregationist defeated a militant in a Democratic runoff primary (Black 1976, 241).

By 1964, however, the Sanford wing of the Democratic party was under attack for its alleged racial liberalism. Sanford ally Cloyd Philpott, elected lieutenant governor when Sanford won the governorship, would have been a logical choice to run for governor in 1964. But Philpott unexpectedly died in office in 1961 and the Sanford forces were left without a candidate. Consequently, Sanford's friend, Greensboro federal judge Richardson Preyer, resigned his post to enter the governor's race, informally representing the Sanford constituencies in the Democratic primary. Because federal judges were, in the eyes of many white Tar Heels, symbols of forced racial integration, Preyer began the race at a disadvantage. He was opposed by the hard-line segregationist Lake as well as by Dan Moore, a less traditionalist western North Carolina corporate lawyer. Moore joined Lake in attacking Preyer as a liberal, but he also claimed that Lake was too extreme. Moore's campaign worked. Preyer won 37 percent of the vote in the first primary of May 1964, and Moore placed second with 34 percent. But in the June runoff, Preyer gained hardly a vote. Moore exchanged his middle-of-the-road segregationism of the first primary for a "militant" stance in the runoff, attacking Preyer for accepting the "bloc Negro vote" (Black 1975, 74–75). Moore held onto his first primary vote and added Lake's segregationist supporters. He won in a landslide, taking 62 percent of the vote and ninety-three of the state's one hundred counties (Spence 1968).

The Preyer defeat, fueled by the politics of race, foreshadowed the splintering of the state Democratic party. Moore supporters and especially Lake voters constituted the core of white voters who, beginning in 1968, would question their commitment to the state and national Democratic ticket. But 1964 was still a good year for Tar Heel Democrats. Both Dan Moore and fellow Southerner Lyndon Johnson won the state easily.

By 1968, black power and anti–Vietnam War protests had replaced civil rights in the news. In North Carolina, these issues had the potential of hastening Democratic dealignment. The Democratic nominee for president, Hubert Humphrey, was not in fact sympathetic to either issue, but his long-standing commitment to civil rights was unpopular with all but strongly partisan Democrats. Both Republican presidential nominee Richard Nixon and American Independent candidate George Wallace sought the votes of white Democrats. A 1968 survey of Tar Heel voters indicated that these white Democratic defectors were more likely to choose Wallace than Nixon (57 to 43 percent). Stated differently, 74 percent of Wallace's votes came from Democrats, compared to 35 percent of Nixon's support (Beyle and Harkins 1975, 100).

Building on strong support from Mountain, western Piedmont, and metro Piedmont counties, Nixon became the first Republican to carry the state since Herbert Hoover in 1928. Nixon captured 40 percent of the vote, compared to 31 percent for Wallace and 29 percent for Humphrey. Wallace won rural eastern North Carolina and eastern Piedmont counties where white Democrats appeared to feel strongly about racial issues. In a pattern remarkably similar to Walter Mondale's showing in 1984, Humphrey won only the metro Piedmont counties of Durham and Orange (Chapel Hill) and the rural eastern counties where blacks made up more than 40 percent of all registered voters.

The white defection away from Humphrey portended a pattern for future presidential races in North Carolina. But political analysts Thad Beyle and Peter Harkins concluded at the time that the switch of white Democrats to Wallace and Nixon did not constitute a movement toward realignment with the Republican party. Rather, they viewed the vote as a rejection of national Democratic politics (Beyle and Harkins 1975, 102). In other words, 1968 was a major year of dealignment.

The 1972 presidential vote, with George McGovern facing Richard Nixon, offered white Democrats an easy opportunity to cross over to the Republican candidate. Nixon's 1972 totals correlated strongly with the combined 1968 totals for Nixon and Wallace. Unlike in 1968, however, enough white Democrats voted Republican in other races that James Holshouser was elected governor, Jesse Helms won a U.S. Senate seat, and fifty Republicans were sent to the General Assembly. Never before in the twentieth century had a North Carolina Republican served in the governor's office or the U.S. Senate.

Fortunately for the Democrats, the Watergate scandal broke the momentum of Tar Heel Republicans. The lengthy public investigations, culminating in Nixon's resignation just three months before the 1974 legislative elections, decimated the GOP delegation in Raleigh. In 1976, Democratic gubernatorial candidate Jim Hunt and Southern Democratic presidential candidate Jimmy Carter kept the Republicans at bay. Both Hunt and Carter won the state comfortably. Not until 1984 did the Republicans field a slate, including president, governor, and U.S. Senate, that had widespread appeal to white Democrats.

Sanford as Loser and Winner: Political Symbolism in 1972 and 1986

In spring 1972, shortly before he was crippled in an assassination attempt, George Wallace decisively defeated Terry Sanford in North Carolina's first presidential preference primary, 50 to 34 percent, with 8 percent of the vote for black congresswoman Shirley Chisholm and the other 8 percent divided among minor candidates (the candidacy of George McGovern had blossomed too late for him to be on the ballot). Significantly, Wallace ran as the antiestablishment candidate who sought to defend traditionalist values around race, law and order, and "the little guy."

At a campaign rally at Dorton Arena on the North Carolina Fairgrounds in Raleigh, shortly before the May vote, Wallace stirred the crowd with his appeals to standing up for "what's right." Country music and large Wallace banners created a festive atmosphere, and enthusiastic supporters were inspired by his determination.

By contrast, Sanford's advocacy of gradual racial and economic modernization of North Carolina fell flat in 1972. He could not generate the same level of enthusiasm as his charismatic opponent. Nor could he persuade voters that adapting to the inevitable decline of Jim Crow segregation made more sense than the hard-core resistance that Wallace pledged. Dogged by criticism of the food tax he had promoted in 1961 as governor, Sanford tried unsuccessfully to convince voters that Wallace had enacted similar programs as governor of Alabama.

At Dorton Arena, the crowd was uninterested in detailed policy proposals. Wallace was their candidate because he was willing to send the establishment a message. Wallace cornered Sanford into an uncomfortable position as a defender of racial change *and* the power elite. The Wallace vote in 1972 once again indicated major white Democratic discontent with the state party. It raised serious questions about whether most whites supported the modernizer ideology advocated by Sanford. Was North Carolina's reputation as change-oriented really warranted? (Beyle, Black, and Kemple 1975, 126). At the symbolic level, Wallace kept Sanford on the defensive. Wallace, not Sanford, came across as the "man of principle." In 1986, Sanford would switch roles and would attack his opponent as the guardian of the power elite.

Terry Sanford was the 1986 Democratic nominee for the U.S Senate against Republican Jim Broyhill, an eleven-term veteran of the U.S. House of Representatives. Two months before the November election, Sanford's campaign was foundering. Running on the theme of "a very special leader," who had served North Carolina for a quarter century as governor and as president of Duke University, Sanford hoped to convince the electorate that his kind of moderate Democratic platform was worth supporting. Unfortunately for Sanford, this general evocation of modernizer-Democrat ideology produced little enthusiasm. By September 1986, his campaign appeared quite similar to his losing race against Wallace in 1972 (Luebke 1987b).

But Broyhill, unlike Wallace, was himself a colorless candidate. The North Carolina congressman was the scion of a western Piedmont furniture family, and his promotion of free enterprise made him a favorite of both business political action committees and Tar Heel businesses. Contradicting his abstract economic ideology, Broyhill supported protectionist legislation to aid the U.S. textile industry. He was in the uncomfortable position of defending President Reagan's veto of the textile bill. But overall his business credentials were in perfect order.

On social issues, Broyhill differed from fellow Republican Jesse Helms. As a congressman, he had supported the Martin Luther King holiday and did not oppose abortion in all circumstances. In a bitter Republican primary in spring 1986, which Broyhill won over the National Congressional Club candidate, David Funderburk, Broyhill's credentials as a "true" (read, social) conservative were challenged in countless television ads. Despite Broyhill's strong economic conservatism, his moderate-conservative views on social issues denied him vigorous support from New Christian Right activists. This was in marked contrast to the religious right's work for Helms in 1984 (Luebke 1985–86) or for Pat Robertson in the 1988 North Carolina presidential primary. Broyhill's greatest asset was Ronald Reagan's popularity among white North Carolinians. Throughout the late summer, Sanford's and Broyhill's campaigns of generalities produced great yawns within the electorate. By mid-September, Broyhill was maintaining a lead in the polls that Broyhill's advisers believed could not be surmounted.

But to most everyone's surprise, Sanford in late September took a leaf from George Wallace's book. He began an aggressive campaign as the friend of the farmer and factory worker, playing on the theme of Democrats for the "little guy." He took a slap at Broyhill's upper-class background, always referring to him as "James" and evoking themes of linen napkins and wealthy stuffiness (Luebke 1987a). Sanford made it appear—just as Wallace had against Sanford in 1972 and Helms had against Hunt in 1984—that he was the principled politician who cared more about the average North Carolinian (Luebke 1987c).

In fact, Sanford had not abandoned his modernizer ideology. He remained closely aligned with many Tar Heel and national corporate leaders, and he continued to defend the food tax. But by asserting that Broyhill and the GOP were out of touch with the needs of the average citizen, Sanford was able to make the Democratic party more appealing to white voters. Especially in eastern North Carolina, enough whites who had supported Reagan, Martin, and Helms in 1984 "came home" to the Democrats that Sanford upset Broyhill by 52 to 48 percent. Populist symbolism became Sanford's asset in 1986. In other key races, going back to 1968 or 1972, it was not modernizer Democrats like Sanford, but traditionalists like Wallace and Helms who captured the turf of the "little guy." Both Democrats and Republicans can learn from Sanford's turning of the tables in 1986. It was the Democrats' first U.S. Senate victory since 1974.

The Racial Protest, 1968 and 1972

In a 1968 poll, only 23 percent of white North Carolinians said they would "like to see white and Negro children go to the same school." Only 17 percent favored "letting Negroes move into white neighborhoods" (Beyle and Harkins 1975, 97). George Wallace and Jesse Helms did not need such an opinion poll to know that racial equality, and especially the black power rallying cry of more militant blacks, offended most whites in North Carolina. It was a political issue waiting to be tapped. Although Wallace was much more of an economic populist than Helms (Frady 1976; Furgurson 1986), their racial appeals in 1968 and 1972 were remarkably similar. Further, Helms as a TV editorialist had over the years praised Wallace's opposition to the many egalitarian movements of the 1960s. Race, especially before the 1973 Supreme Court decision establishing women's abortion rights, stood out as foremost among a constellation of issues that included the Vietnam War, long hair, and drugs.

Wallace and Helms shared a knack for capturing the resentments of whites in well-turned phrases and paragraphs. As Helms editorialized in 1965 about Martin Luther King's nonviolent movement, "It is about as nonviolent as the Marines landing on Iwo Jima, and it is a 'movement' only in the sense that mob action is moving and spreading throughout the land" (Nordhoff 1984, 53). Voting for Wallace or Helms could, in Wallace's phrase, "send them a message." The "them" was the national Democratic party and the political and cultural protestors of the 1960s. In short, the target was "liberalism," real and imagined (cf. Bartley and Graham 1975, 132).

The Wallace vote in 1968, when voters could choose among three major candidates, correlates strongly with the level of black political participation in the state's one hundred counties. The higher the proportion of registered blacks in a county, the more likely that county's voters gave Wallace a majority. Wallace did not win a single county where blacks made up less than 10 percent of the electorate (thirty-seven counties). By contrast, excluding the six counties of the metro Piedmont (won by Hubert Humphrey in Durham and Orange, and by Richard Nixon in Forsyth, Guilford, Mecklenburg, and Wake), Wallace won 64 percent of the twenty-eight counties with a 10–25 percent black voter registration, and carried 79 percent of the counties where blacks constituted more than 25 percent of the electorate. Thus, racial resentment fueled the 1968 Wallace campaign.

In 1972, Wallace's social-political base was wider than in 1968. The percentage of his vote in the Democratic primary was, according to survey data, nearly identical to the total percentage of both Nixon and Wallace support among registered Democrats in 1968. Those who had voted for Wallace or Nixon in the 1968 general election were willing to unify behind Wallace in 1972 (Beyle, Black, and Kemple 1975, 123). The Wallace voters of 1972 were dealigned Democrats who were protesting the liberalism of the national Democratic party. Terry Sanford, in fact, ran for the Democratic nomination as a southern moderate alternative to northern liberalism (a strategy that Jimmy Carter successfully pursued four years later). But in the eyes of Wallace voters, Sanford's moderation was just as suspect as Yankee liberalism. Regardless of his actual views, Sanford for many white Tar Heels symbolized the disreputable national Democratic party.

When Jesse Helms decided to seek the Republican nomination for the U.S. Senate in May 1972, he feared his opponent in the November election might be Democrat B. Everett Jordan, a seventy-five-year-old Old South anti–civil rights incumbent with whom Helms agreed on many issues. But Durham congressman Nick Galifianakis, a modernizer who had been critical of military spending, upset Jordan in the May 1972 primary. As a result, it was Helms's good fortune to be able to tap the antiliberal themes in his general election campaign. Out on the stump, Helms linked Galifianakis none too subtly with the unpopular Democratic presidential nominee, George McGovern. Helms supporters also rallied around the ethnocentric claim that, unlike the Greek-American Democrat, Helms was "one of us." Galifianakis recalled that Helms's campaign even cast aspersions on his Greek Orthodox faith, noting the similarities to Russian Orthodoxy and thus to communism (Galifianakis 1987). Such farfetched linkages fit neatly with the truth that Galifianakis had questioned the wisdom of President Nixon's anti-ballistic missile proposal. Exaggeration of his opponent's positions was a Helms trademark; its effectiveness would be emphasized a dozen years later when used against Jim Hunt in their bitter race for the U.S. Senate.

A comparison of Wallace's 1968 vote and Helms's 1972 totals indicates that Helms's statewide support was built on more than the racial resentment of whites. Helms received the votes of many Republicans in the metro Piedmont, the western Piedmont, and the Mountains who in 1968 supported Nixon rather than Wallace. But Helms's success in eastern North Carolina, especially in counties within the WRAL-TV viewing area, points to a special finding for that part of the state. There Helms's well-known opposition to civil rights as well as his critique of the egalitarian movements of the 1960s won him votes from whites who were unwilling to cast their ballots for an unknown Republican gubernatorial candidate, Jim Holshouser. These white Democratic Helms supporters would become known as Jessecrats, because of their willingness to abandon the Democratic candidate in order to support Helms. Overall, on the Coastal Plain and in the eastern Piedmont, Holshouser won just 44 percent of the vote compared to 54 percent for Helms. In short, many eastern North Carolina whites who supported Helms over Democrat Galifianakis remained loyal to Skipper Bowles, the Democrats' gubernatorial candidate.

By contrast, in the metro Piedmont cities, the western Piedmont, and the Mountains, Helms's support was mostly party-line voting. In these regions the difference between him and gubernatorial candidate Holshouser was far less than in the east. Holshouser's campaign lacked the racial-traditionalist, antiestablishment edge of Helms's. While this racial moderation hurt him in the east, it made no difference or helped him elsewhere, especially in the metro Piedmont. Overall, in these three regions, Holshouser won 55 percent of the vote, compared to 52 percent for Helms. Holshouser's greatest lead over Helms was around Winston-Salem and Charlotte.

Helms's strong showing in the eastern parts of North Carolina was testimony to his personal appeal. Although Jessecrats abounded across North Carolina, they lived disproportionately in the east, where from 1960 until 1972 they could have watched Helms's daily editorial on the evening news. His editorials constituted an exercise in "keeping the faith." As a journalist, he had sought to build a countermovement to oppose the egalitarian tendencies of the civil rights and antiwar movements as well as the general attack on dominant values that became known as "the counterculture." According to Helms, citizens needed to unify against those changes. In running for the Senate in 1972, he allowed those who sympathized with his perspective to take political action at the ballot box.

The Emerging Republican Appeal, 1972 to 1980

Wallace's support in 1968 and 1972 and Helms's victory in 1972 are clear examples of white dealignment from the Democrats. But because both politicians had strong personal appeal in those elections, their vote tallies are an incomplete indication of voters' willingness to jettison the Democrats in favor of the Republican party. By contrast, two uncharismatic politicians, Jim Holshouser, a mainstream Republican state legislator from Boone who unexpectedly won the 1972 governor's race, and John East, a traditionalist college professor from Greenville who upset the incumbent U.S. senator in November 1980, provide a clearer picture of the growing Republican appeal.

In the June 1972 Republican runoff primary, Holshouser defeated Jim Gardner, a former congressman (1965–66) and former gubernatorial candidate (1968). It was a victory of a Republican modernizer over a Republican traditionalist. Holshouser's support of economic diversification and improved race relations—hallmarks of modernizer ideology—were hardly distinguishable from the views of his Democratic opponent, Greensboro businessman Skipper Bowles. Holshouser publicly urged black voters to split their ticket by supporting him for governor (Black 1975, 76). In marked contrast to Holshouser's modernizer politics, John East was a right-wing ideologue handpicked by the National Congressional Club to run a long-shot candidacy against incumbent U.S. Senator Robert Morgan. Morgan appeared unbeatable because of his decades-long involvement in the state Democratic party and political ties to all stripes of Tar Heel Democrat, but especially to traditionalists (he had, for example, managed I. Beverly Lake's campaign against Terry Sanford in 1960) (Spence 1968, 15).

Despite ideological differences between Holshouser and East, their patterns of voter support were remarkably similar. Statewide, Holshouser won 51 percent of the vote in 1972 and East eked out slightly more than 50 percent in 1980. The sources of their support, which differed from Helms's statewide bases, suggest a more stable indication of GOP strength. They also provide a picture of Republican voting when popular presidential candidates (Nixon in 1972, and Reagan in 1980 and 1984) have led the ticket. First, many loyal GOP voters live in the rural, small-town areas of the Mountains and western Piedmont. This is historical Republicanism, rooted in the antiplanter feelings of nineteenth-century small farmers who had nothing to gain from a slave economy. Holshouser won 57 percent of the Mountains and western Piedmont vote in 1972, and East took 56 percent in 1980.

Second, in the Piedmont's growing metropolitan areas around Charlotte and the Triad, the steady influx of northern business-oriented voters since World War II has enabled Republicans to expand grassroots party organizations. In 1952, the Charlotte-area congressional district supported Dwight Eisenhower (the state went for Adlai Stevenson) and, more importantly, elected North Carolina's first Republican congressman since the turn of the century (Bartley and Graham 1975, 90). Since 1980, this business in-migration has increased markedly, especially in Charlotte. During the 1980s, both in Charlotte and the Triad cities of Winston-Salem, Greensboro, and High Point, Republicans defeated Democrats regularly in contests for the county commission and the state legislature. The Republican trend was far less pronounced in Raleigh, where state government employees have historically favored the Democrats. However, business-oriented voters moving to the Research Triangle Park have added to GOP strength in Wake County (Raleigh). In Durham and Orange counties, the in-migration has had a university flavor, and these two counties have retained their Democratic strength. Holshouser's vote totals in 1972 reflected this varying GOP strength in the metro Piedmont: 55 percent in Mecklenburg/Forsyth/Guilford, 53 percent in Wake, and 45 percent in Durham/Orange. In a similar pattern, East won 52 percent in Mecklenburg/Triad, 47 percent in Wake, and 40 percent in Durham/Orange. Overall in the metro Piedmont, Holshouser captured 53 percent of the vote, while East was held to 49 percent. East's lower level of support probably reflects urban voters' preference for mainstream rather than Congressional Club Republicans.

The third area of Republican strength since 1972 has been in the small towns and rural areas of eastern North Carolina. Helms's particular success among white voters here, the Jessecrats, was, as noted above, especially tied to his personality. As a rule, in most of these eastern counties Republicans did not even file for county and legislative offices. Although ideologically similar to Helms, East's vote in eastern North Carolina resembled Holshouser's. Holshouser won 43 percent in the Coastal Plain and eastern Piedmont in 1972, while East was held to 44 percent in 1980. By contrast, in these same counties Helms received 54 percent in 1972 and 53 percent in 1978.

The parallel totals in eastern, western, and small-town Piedmont North Carolina for Holshouser and East contrast with East's poorer showing in the metro Piedmont. This suggests that the Congressional Club's heavily ideological, traditionalist campaign against Morgan in 1980, especially in thirty-second TV spots, may have been a case of overkill. The anti-Morgan advertising (for example, attacking Morgan for the alleged "giveaway of the Panama Canal"), for all the publicity it afforded the Congressional Club (Greenhaw 1982, 167), appears to have cost East votes in the metro Piedmont, where voters are the least sympathetic to traditionalist campaign themes. At the same time, Holshouser's modernizer brand of Republicanism in 1972 seems to have won him as many votes in the non–metro Piedmont as did East's Congressional Club traditionalism in 1980. In short, it appears that in most of North Carolina's counties, a slight majority of voters was prepared to support a Tar Heel Republican for statewide office in 1972 and 1980, regardless of candidate ideology.

The GOP Hope: White Flight from the Democrats

Tar Heel Republicans were euphoric after the November 1984 election. They swept the presidential, gubernatorial, and U.S. Senate races, took five of the eleven congressional seats, and sent more legislators to Raleigh than at any time since the 1972 Nixon-Holshouser-Helms sweep. But the real evidence that North Carolina had become a two-party state emerged in November 1986. On the stump Governor Martin urged voters to expand Republican representation in the General Assembly and to elect Republican judges statewide to the state supreme court. But Martin's goals, if serious and not just campaign rhetoric, were unrealistic for several reasons. First, Republican Senator Jim Broyhill's campaign—the lead race on the ballot—never stirred the voters and indeed Broyhill lost to challenger Terry Sanford. Second, in a non-presidential year, Republican candidates could not benefit from the coattails of a charismatic, popular candidate like Ronald Reagan.

At the federal level, North Carolina Republicans took a drubbing in 1986. Not only did Sanford upset Broyhill, but also Democrats regained two congressional seats (the Fourth surrounding Raleigh and Chapel Hill, and the Eleventh surrounding Asheville) that they had lost to Republicans in 1984. But significantly for state politics, the GOP did not lose ground in the General Assembly and even gained seats at the county commission level. In almost all of the state west of Raleigh, including most of the large cities, Republicans provided stiff challenges to Democrats. Statewide in 1986, Republican judges won about 45 percent of the vote, totals similar to those of Republican Council of State candidates (from lieutenant governor to insurance commissioner and auditor) in 1984. Thousands of Democrats crossed over to support Reagan, Martin, and Helms in 1984 and Broyhill in 1986.

Republicans can be optimistic about the future for a number of reasons. All result from the attractiveness of the Republican party to white voters. First, since the early 1970s the number of registered Republicans has increased steadily across the state. Second, the percentage of white voters who identified themselves as Republicans was, by the mid-1980s, almost as high as the percentage of whites who considered themselves Democrats. Third, the younger the white voters, the more likely they identify with the Republican party. Fourth, increasingly Republicans are winning local elections.

In 1972, when Republicans first swept the presidential, gubernatorial, and U.S. Senate races, only 542,000, or 23 percent, of Tar Heel voters were registered Republicans. In 1984, Republicans numbered 839,000, or 26 percent of the electorate. New white voters in this twelve-year period registered Republican and Democrat in almost equal numbers. The Republican registration trend is particularly pronounced in fast-growing counties characterized by high levels of in-migration from outside North Carolina. While GOP registration increased statewide by 55 percent between 1972 and 1984, in Wake County—the fastest-growing county in the metropolitan Piedmont—Republican registration increased 116 percent. In resort areas of the Mountains and the Atlantic coast that are popular with retirees, Republicans also fared well. Between 1972 and 1984, Watauga County (Boone) saw a 99 percent increase in the number of Republican registrants; in Dare County at the Outer Banks, the figure was 207 percent. In all these counties, Democrats still substantially outnumber Republicans because of the historic domination of the Democratic party. But, unlike registered Democrats, registered Republicans almost always support their party's ticket. Thus, Republicans in North Carolina are increasing the size of the party's core vote in every election.

The number of unaffiliated voters has also grown in North Carolina since 1972. The percentage of registered Independents is generally small (4.2 percent in 1986), in part because North Carolina historically has had a closed primary election system that prohibits participation by Independents. Especially in counties where the GOP is not well established, voters without strong allegiances to the Democratic party nevertheless register Democrat so that they can participate in the selection of the Democratic nominee. But in the fast-growing counties with high in-migration, Independents have been more prevalent. In 1986, these unaffiliated voters represented 6 percent of the electorate in Wake County, 9 percent in Watauga County, and 7 percent in Dare County. This benefits the GOP because self-identified Independents are more likely to vote Republican than Democrat. (In an effort to make Republicanism more attractive to registered Independents, the GOP changed its party rules in 1988 to allow Independents to vote in the Republican primary.)

A second indicator of Republican progress in North Carolina is the large number of whites who identify with the Republican party. The 1984 CBS exit poll found that white voters were equally likely to call themselves Republicans and Democrats (42 percent). The remaining 16 percent considered themselves Independents. (By contrast, black identification was 86 percent Democrat, 5 percent Republican, and 9 percent

Independent.) Upper-income voters were disproportionately likely to identify with Republicanism. For example, 35 percent of whites earning less than $12,500 were GOP identifiers, compared to 46 percent of those earning more than $35,000 (CBS News 1984). This is good news for Republicans, because upper-income voters are more likely to turn out on Election Day than the less affluent (Black and Black 1987, 189–92).

The CBS poll also showed that the generational issue favors Republicans. Among whites who are sixty and over, 38 percent chose the GOP and 49 percent supported the Democrats. As age declined, the percentage of Democratic identifiers also declined. Among whites under twenty-five, 46 percent identified with Republicans and 38 percent with Democrats. It is sometimes argued that Jesse Helms's three Senate victories were possible only because of support among older whites. The data show not only that younger whites supported Helms, but also that their commitment to Republicanism was more substantial than that of older whites.

Finally, Republicans in 1986 attained an all-time high in the number of county commissioners elected. This is significant because these local gains occurred without benefit of strong presidential coattails. Indeed, in 1984 Republicans won just 100 (20 percent) of the state's county commission seats, but in 1986 they captured 141 seats (28 percent). After the 1986 election, twenty-nine of North Carolina's one hundred county commissions were controlled by Republicans (Goodman and Betts 1987, 22). All seven of the counties where a majority of the registered voters were Republicans elected GOP majorities. But Republican majorities also won in four counties where one-third or less of the county's registered voters were Republicans. Although Mecklenburg County (Charlotte), the state's largest county, was 34 percent Republican in 1986, Republicans dominated the county commission by a six-to-one margin. Just 30 percent of Buncombe County's (Asheville) voters were registered Republicans in 1986, but Republicans held three of five seats. Republicans in Alamance County (Burlington) controlled four of five seats on the county commission, even though just 25 percent of county voters registered Republican in 1986. On the coast, Carteret County had an all-Republican board although only 30 percent of its voters were registered Republicans. But this last victory—in eastern North Carolina—has been a major exception for the GOP. In general, as will be discussed below, North Carolina Republicans have little local strength east of Raleigh.

The pattern of GOP success in North Carolina is consistent with

Republican gains across the South (Black and Black 1987). The Republican party began its offensive against the Democrats in the 1960s and 1970s by playing on the racial resentments of white voters. But over time, with help from the laissez-faire campaign rhetoric and program of Ronald Reagan, the Republican party increasingly became identified as protecting the white middle class from the alleged special-interest agenda of the Democratic party. This Democratic agenda was seen as taxing the voter to spend money on the demands of blacks, feminists, and other well-organized minorities. In advocating low taxes and laissez-faire government, Republicans in the South came across as supporting the economic aspirations of enterprising middle-class whites (Luebke 1984b).

In North Carolina, this Republican agenda has had special appeal at the presidential level. Between 1968 and 1984, forty counties, including five in eastern North Carolina and the four metro Piedmont counties of Mecklenburg, Wake, Guilford (Greensboro), and Forsyth (Winston-Salem), voted Republican in every presidential election (Goodman and Betts 1987, 33).

In contrast to Republican success, only ten Tar Heel counties went Democratic in virtually every presidential election between 1968 and 1984. Eight of these are heavily black rural counties of eastern North Carolina. The remaining two are bastions of citizen-power ideology in North Carolina: Orange (Chapel Hill) and Durham. The year 1972 represented the Democrats' low point in presidential elections: only Northampton, a predominantly black county on the Coastal Plain, and Orange gave a majority to Democratic nominee George McGovern.

The Decline of Democratic Traditionalism: Jimmy Green and Harold Hardison

The attempt of the Democratic party in the 1980s to respond to some of the political demands of citizen-action organizations constituted an important shift in North Carolina politics since the early 1970s. Gone from the Democratic party was the statewide candidate who unabashedly opposed the goals of blacks, feminist women, or environmentalists. The defeat of two once-powerful Democratic politicians as they sought higher office, former lieutenant governor Jimmy Green and former state senator Harold Hardison, typified the decline of the party's traditionalist appeal.

A tobacco warehouse owner from Bladen County in rural eastern

North Carolina, Green served in the legislature for more than a decade before becoming House Speaker for the 1975–76 session. He won contested primaries for lieutenant governor in both 1976 and 1980, and easily defeated his Republican opponent both years. In 1976 Green placed second in the Democratic primary, scoring 24 percent in a field of nine candidates as the most conservative on both economic and racial issues. The first-place finisher, with 28 percent, was Howard Lee, the former black mayor of Chapel Hill. In the runoff primary held four weeks later, Green took the unusual step of printing a picture of himself and his opponent in newspaper ads. It was a none-too-subtle racial appeal. Green won the runoff by a comfortable 54 to 46 percent margin (Luebke 1979).

Throughout his first term, Green was an ardent supporter of business interests and an opponent of environmentalists. Under his leadership, the state senate became a bulwark of anticonsumer legislation. In 1980, he won renomination as lieutenant governor promising more of the same. This time he defeated a white Democrat, House Speaker Carl Stewart, who ran as the modernizer candidate.

In 1982, Jimmy Green cast a tie-breaking vote in the state senate against the Equal Rights Amendment. When he sought the Democratic nomination for governor in 1984, Green believed his social traditionalism, illustrated by the anti-ERA vote, as well as his economic traditionalism, would ensure him continued support from the state's corporate community. But in a crowded Democratic field, most corporate leaders chose Lauch Faircloth, who blended probusiness economic ideology (similar to Jim Martin's Republicanism) with a modernizer's appeal to both blacks and feminist women.

No doubt Green's candidacy was weakened by a 1983 state indictment for accepting bribes, even though he was acquitted on the charge. Further, Faircloth, a large landowner in Sampson County in eastern North Carolina, had married into the socially prominent Bryan family of Greensboro (Jefferson-Pilot life insurance) and had had extensive contacts with North Carolina corporations while serving as secretary of commerce during the Hunt administration. Faircloth's ties to the business establishment were much more direct than Green's.

Green's second hope in 1984 was to win the votes of traditionalist Democrats who had become disenchanted with the growing power of blacks in the Democratic party and with the gains of women's rights advocates (for example, the General Assembly's continued appropriations for a state abortion fund for poor women). He made a strong pitch to the social traditionalists of the New Christian Right, declaring his opposition to the state abortion fund for poor women and affirming his anti-ERA position. In short, he sought the votes of Jessecrats, Falwell followers, or both. But confirming the weakened base of traditionalists in the Democratic party, Green won just 8 percent of the vote in the 1984 gubernatorial primary. He switched his allegiance in the November election to Republican candidate Jim Martin, and was rewarded with a well-paid legislative consultant position in the Martin administration. Martin hoped that Green, a symbol of the discontent of traditionalist Democrats in a modernizer-dominated Democratic party, would encourage traditionalist Democrats to cross over to the Republicans.

The 1988 candidacy of state senator Harold Hardison for the Democratic lieutenant governor's nomination illustrated how traditionalist candidates became convinced by the late 1980s that they had to adopt modernizer symbols in order to compete in a Democratic primary. Despite the modernizer veneer, Hardison lost decisively to a modernizer Democrat, Tony Rand.

A powerful state senator from rural eastern North Carolina, Hardison openly supported business interests against environmentalists in the 1970s and 1980s. In the early 1970s he worked in the state senate to pass the Hardison amendments, which stipulated that no North Carolina air or water quality or hazardous-waste standards could be more exacting than those of the federal government. Beginning in 1981, the Reagan administration weakened environmental standards. When Tar Heel environmentalists attempted to maintain strict state standards despite the president's action, the Hardison amendments stood in the way. Hardison opposed the environmentalists at this point, leading the fight to keep his earlier amendments on the books.

As a state senator, Hardison consistently favored the insurance industry in its unsuccessful effort to restrict corporate liability in damage suits (the so-called tort reform bills). He also voted against the ERA and the state abortion fund. Consequently, Hardison won the support of many corporate interests, including some modernizers, as well as backing from antiabortion activists. Nevertheless, Hardison's campaign tried hard to change his image as an economic and social traditionalist. Despite the Hardison amendments, his supporters defined him as "moderate and reasonable" on environmental issues (O'Connor 1987a). He added a well-known ERA advocate to his campaign staff and touted the names of black Democrats who had endorsed his candidacy. There was a stark contrast between the open traditionalism of Jimmy Green's campaigns in 1976 and 1980, and Hardison's camouflaged traditionalism of 1988.

Hardison recognized the changes in the base of the North Carolina Democratic party. As elsewhere in the South during the 1970s and 1980s, blacks were becoming an increasingly significant part of the Democratic electorate, especially in primaries. Segregation and even coded antiblack messages were no longer acceptable in the party (Black and Black 1987, 292–96). Further, as the Democratic party became more aligned with the environmentalist and women's issues promoted by many white middle-class urban activists, any candidate who sought to win a statewide primary election found it necessary to pay at least lip service to these issues. Because of greater population growth, including in-migration, in many of the state's urban counties, a traditionalist image became a liability for Democrats like Hardison who sought statewide office.

Hardison's attempts to posture himself as a moderate between traditionalism and modernism failed. Fayetteville state senator Tony Rand defeated Hardison 43 to 26 percent in a three-person race, and Hardison decided against challenging Rand again in the runoff primary. Hardison's defeat, coupled with Green's four years earlier, signaled the death knell of traditionalism in the North Carolina Democratic party.

The Democrats' New Face: Modernizers in Action

The dominant tone of the Democratic party in the late 1980s was expressed by Lieutenant Governor Bob Jordan. Modernization themes became especially clear in Jordan's 1988 race against incumbent Governor Jim Martin. His gubernatorial campaign emphasized three issues: education, economic development, and the environment. Both Tony Rand and Parks Helms, a former state legislator from Charlotte who was the third major candidate in the 1988 Democratic primary for the lieutenant governor nomination, shared Jordan's political philosophy.

Education and economic development were classic modernizer issues. Both Terry Sanford in the 1960s and Jim Hunt in the 1970s had placed these themes at the center of their campaigns. In Jordan's view, the state should play a major role in expanding jobs and people's qualifications for those jobs.

Jordan's third issue, the environment, reflected a newly found constituency for the Democratic party. Supporters of the Sierra Club and the Conservation Council of North Carolina had convinced Jordan as

well as Rand, a key state senator, not only that environmental legislation such as a ban on phosphates was necessary to prevent algae pollution of North Carolina rivers, but also that it would be politically profitable for Democrats to distinguish themselves from an antiphosphate-
ban Republican like Martin. Jordan and Rand championed the phosphate ban in the 1987 General Assembly and could justifiably campaign
as friends of the environment.

In the 1988 lieutenant governor's race, modernizer candidates Tony
Rand and Parks Helms both sought the environmentalist vote by expressing their commitment to watershed protection and other environmental issues. Rand's 43 percent of the primary vote against Hardison,
coupled with Helms's 18 percent, suggested that a majority of Democrats favored strict environmental enforcement. To be sure, not all
Democrats made their choice simply around the environment. But environmentalists took the risk of targeting Hardison as a kind of public
enemy number one. They publicized his record widely and developed a
series of "Stop Hardison" radio ads. Had Hardison won, environmentalists' standing in the state senate would have plummeted in 1989.
Rand's victory in the primary did not guarantee repeal of the Hardison
amendments, but it ensured that environmental issues would receive
serious treatment in future General Assembly sessions.

Hardison's defeat and Jordan's environmental emphasis reflected the
increasingly urban base of the Democratic party. Successful Democrats
began to respond to the problems that unplanned development was
generating in most of the state's growing metropolitan and coastal
areas. Air, noise, and water pollution—previously ignored as problems confined to New York, Denver, or Los Angeles—were becoming
sources of Tar Heel political conflict. Environmentalism, a potential
challenge to corporate dominance of North Carolina politics, had taken
root by 1988.

Bob Jordan's decision to advocate an environmental program constituted a significant concession by a leading modernizer that these issues,
unlike either progressive tax reform or utility rate reform, had such
potency within the electorate that he was willing to part temporarily
with big business. Unlike Sanford's symbolic appeals to factory workers, Jordan's environmental positions—for example, his support of the
phosphate ban—were substantive. Nevertheless, on most other issues
on which large corporations perceived an interest, Jordan tended to
agree with the corporations' positions. Republican Martin's business
ties were so strong, however, that it was uncertain whether it made

practical sense for Democrats like Jordan to follow such probusiness policies. Yet Jordan's own background as a lumber company executive in the eastern Piedmont made it hard for him to do otherwise. He competed vigorously with Martin for the financial support of corporate executives. In the 1988 gubernatorial race, Jordan was supported by some business people who in 1984 had preferred Martin over Democrat Rufus Edmisten. In sum, Jordan sought to balance his procorporate inclinations with a commitment to environmental protection. If followed by other modernizer Democrats, his approach provided a basis for a local revival of the Democratic party, at least in North Carolina's urban counties where many citizen activists worried about environmental damage at the local and state levels.

11

The Future of North Carolina Politics

Since the first Republican sweep in 1972, the style of North Carolina politics has changed. In the late 1980s it took on a more urban middle-class tone. The traditionalist views and style of the rural conservative Democrat increasingly lost favor in the General Assembly. And even as Republicans sought to capture the support of traditionalist voters in statewide elections, the dominant image of the party became the three-piece suit rather than the pick-up truck.

Beyond the shift in style, two changes in Tar Heel politics have been crucial. First, blacks have become a major, permanent force in the electorate. By 1986, 19 percent of all registered voters and 28 percent of registered Democrats were black. In part because of voting rights litigation by blacks against state and local governments in North Carolina, the number of black elected officials increased nearly fourfold between 1972 and 1986 (JCPS 1973, 1987).

Second, with increasing percentages of whites voting Republican, especially in statewide elections, North Carolina has become a two-party state. Although many of these whites retain their Democratic registration, they have joined new and long-standing Republicans to establish a competitive two-party system in statewide elections. The Republican party has appealed to voters' antitax and anti–big government sentiments, and openly argues that what's good for business is good for North Carolina voters. Especially since 1984, the Democratic party has been on the defensive, searching for a formula that will appeal to both white and black Tar Heels. Because of its core support from blacks—by far the Democrats' most loyal constituency—as well as from feminists, environmentalists, and moderate-to-liberal whites, Democrats feel compelled to offer some programs that are not part of the business agenda. Proposals to improve the poor's access to health

177

care, a ban on phosphate detergents, and stricter enforcement of child support agreements increasingly have become part of the Democratic agenda, particularly in the last few years.

The Republicans' Dilemmas and Hopes

North Carolina Republicans face a major dilemma in their effort to become a statewide majority party: in the eastern Piedmont and the east, too few Tar Heels register Republican. Although top-of-the-ticket Republicans in statewide elections almost always win a majority of the white vote in each of these fifty-three counties, in 1988 just 17 percent of the voters in these regions were registered as Republicans, compared to 35 percent of the voters in North Carolina's other forty-seven counties. Many of these voters in the eastern Piedmont and on the Coastal Plain are Jessecrats, white registered Democrats who regularly abandon the Democratic party to support Jesse Helms and, increasingly, Republican candidates for president and governor as well. The Jessecrats hold to traditionalist values which, in the high-visibility races, they see better represented by Republican candidates. But too often they support Democrats—from lieutenant governor to county clerk of court. In counties with few registered Republicans, there seldom is a strong local organization to remind white voters to support the entire Republican ticket. In many cases, Republicans may not even have filed for local or legislative races.

It appears that the GOP has a threshold problem. Unless a substantial minority, perhaps one-quarter, of a county's voters is Republican, serious candidacies to challenge Democrats for county-level races rarely emerge. Only five counties in the eastern Piedmont or the east have GOP registration above the statewide average of 30 percent, and in each of these (Brunswick, Carteret, and New Hanover on the coast; Moore County, a favorite of golfing retirees, in the eastern Piedmont; and Sampson County in the rural east, which has a long anti-Democratic tradition dating back to the 1890s) Republicans have held office in the 1980s. With several exceptions, Republicans have not been elected in any other county in the eastern Piedmont or on the Coastal Plain. How the state party can help local organizations to cross the apparent registration threshold is unclear. As long as no significant organizational strength exists, few local candidates will run as Republicans, even if ideologically they would be more comfortable in the Republican party. As long as no candidates run as Republicans, the conclusion of voters who sympathize with Republicanism is to keep their Democratic registration, because there is nothing to vote for in the Republican primary elections.

In other parts of the state, the party has much more visibility, although local success levels vary. In metro Piedmont cities like Charlotte, Greensboro, or Winston-Salem, GOP registration has grown enough in the past two decades to build strong party structures. In the Mountains and the western Piedmont, where Republicanism emerged after the Civil War as an alternative to the planter-based Democratic party, Republican county organizations also sustain themselves. In these two regions, more than one-third of voters are registered in the Republican party. The western Piedmont is the core of the Republican vote, having elected state legislators from these counties even in the post-Watergate debacle. In that election, held shortly after Richard Nixon's resignation, GOP strength in the General Assembly plummeted from fifty to ten seats.

A second dilemma for the party focuses on the ideological loyalties of those voters who have registered Republican. The question is whether mainstream Republicans and Republicans close to Jesse Helms's National Congressional Club can end their infighting in order to build stronger, more unified local parties. In part, this intraparty conflict centers on such personalities as Carter Wrenn, the club's executive director, and Phil Kirk, a Martin administration loyalist who previously worked with Congressman Jim Broyhill and Governor Jim Holshouser. Helms Republicans view Kirk as too pragmatic, and Martin Republicans see Wrenn as too ideological. But the party conflict also revolves around the relative importance of economic and noneconomic issues. Mainstream Republicans are so named because they are rooted in the long-standing economic ideology of the national Republican party. While critical of an activist state that promotes economic liberalism such as Franklin Roosevelt's New Deal, national Republicans historically have supported a less egalitarian activist state that promotes business prosperity. In more recent years, this is the Republicanism of Dwight Eisenhower, Gerald Ford, or Robert Dole. At the state level, the party's two successful gubernatorial candidates of the twentieth century, Jim Holshouser in 1972 and Jim Martin in 1984, typified mainstream Republicanism in North Carolina. Congressional Club Republicanism is virtually synonymous with the club's honorary chairman, Jesse Helms.

Two examples illustrate the intraparty conflict. First, mainstream Tar Heel Republicans are willing to consider government investments in infrastructure as legitimate, whereas the club perspective is strongly antigovernment. On the role of government vis-à-vis the economy, mainstream politicians like Holshouser and Martin are often hard to distinguish from modernizer Democrats. In 1985, Jim Martin fought for an increased state gasoline tax, a new tax that the Congressional Club did not support. In his 1988 reelection campaign, Martin reminded voters of his commitment to increased state expenditures for public schools, highways, and economic development. In general election contests against Democrats, mainstream Republicans consider this governmental spending a GOP asset, but Congressional Club Republicans do not have such a benevolent view of the activist state.

Second, Congressional Club Republicans focus on noneconomic aspects of traditionalist ideology. Examples of these are prayer in the public schools or an active antiabortion position. Mainstream Republicans typically agree with these points of view, but they rarely promote such issues as the basis for their political involvement. Martin, for instance, with little fanfare sent a mailing to evangelical Christians across the state during spring 1988, reminding them that he, unlike his Democratic challenger, opposed the state abortion fund for low-income women.

Congressional Club Republicans usually turn their antitax ideology and social traditionalism into a broadside attack on the alleged liberalism of political foes. Helms successfully ran three such campaigns for the U.S. Senate against Democratic opponents. But when the club took sides in subsequent Republican primaries between 1986 and 1988, it was defeated decisively. U.S. Senate candidate David Funderburk could not convince GOP voters in the May 1986 primary that his mainstream opponent, Jim Broyhill, was a "closet liberal." As the club's television spots pointed out, Broyhill had voted for a congressional budget also supported by Speaker of the House Tip O'Neill, a Massachusetts liberal and favorite whipping boy of New Right Republicans. Republican primary voters found this insufficient evidence to reject Broyhill. After twenty-two years as a congressman from western North Carolina, Broyhill enjoyed a reputation as dean of the state's Republicans; Funderburk's GOP credentials paled by comparison. Perhaps illustrating the relative strength of the two factions, Broyhill defeated Funderburk by a 67 to 30 percent margin (Ku Klux Klan leader Glenn Miller received 3 percent of the vote).

In 1987, the Congressional Club also promoted a challenge to Jack Hawke, Martin's choice for party chair. It selected Barry McCarty, then a professor at Elizabeth City Bible College, who promised to promote a more conservative party than the alleged pragmatism of Hawke. Open factional fighting erupted at numerous county conventions, but at the state convention Hawke held many more delegates than McCarty, a parallel to Broyhill's easy victory. As a face-saving device for the club, in the interest of party unity during the upcoming 1988 election year, Hawke was declared the victor by acclamation.

During the Republican presidential primary campaign of early 1988, club leaders Tom Ellis and Carter Wrenn backed New York congressman Jack Kemp. Yet the club did little to aid Kemp's flailing North Carolina campaign. Both Jim Martin and Jesse Helms remained neutral in the primary. Helms surprised many, however, when he hinted that his choice was neither of the strongly conservative candidates, Kemp or televangelist Pat Robertson, but rather his Senate colleague Bob Dole. These events further suggested the Congressional Club's desire to avoid public conflict with mainstream Republicans during 1988.

On Super Tuesday, the day in early March 1988 when virtually the entire South held its presidential primaries, Robertson and Kemp together won just 15 percent of the vote in North Carolina's election. Robertson was the favorite of the fundamentalist preachers who had backed Helms against Jim Hunt in 1984. Ironically, fundamentalist voters, many of whom the Congressional Club had first registered to vote before the Helms-Hunt election, were the major reason that Robertson defeated Kemp by 11 percent to 4 percent. The tiny vote for the "true conservative" candidates, in contrast to 45 percent for Vice-President George Bush and 40 percent for Dole, indicated again the relative strength of mainstream Republicanism in North Carolina. For the club and other Tar Heel partisans of the New Right, 1988 was a far cry from 1976, when Helms and Ellis saved Ronald Reagan from political oblivion by engineering the upset over President Gerald Ford in the state's Republican primary.

The Republican party's hopes for the 1990s center on two points: candidate recruitment and political program. First, the party needs to recruit candidates at both the local and state levels who appeal to registered Democrats and Independents. Unfortunately for Republicans, their limited success in local government and the General Assembly has led to a small talent pool. For example, when Governor Martin in 1987 appointed state senator Bill Redman of Iredell County (Statesville) to a vacancy on the North Carolina Utilities Commission, Redman's departure left a GOP leadership void in the senate. In 1988, the

Republicans failed to field a single candidate for the state house in Durham, Orange, or Cumberland (Fayetteville) counties.

Second, Republicans need to develop a more specific agenda that can enjoy wide appeal across the state's regions. The major source for such a program is in the General Assembly, where GOP legislators can take issue with Democratic initiatives. In the 1986 election, the Republican party chose to focus on the personality of Governor Martin, and GOP legislative candidates campaigned for office less on a specific program and more as part of a general appeal to voters to support Republicans. Their most specific appeal, to reject Democrats because they controlled special pork barrel expenditures of loyal Democratic legislators, may have helped to underscore the importance of Republicans as watchdogs.

Going into the 1990s, an option for the Republicans will be to identify policies that highlight their differences with the Democrats. For instance, the Democratic penchant to raise taxes provided Republicans with a potent opportunity in 1988. Other examples of party-line voting included the state Martin Luther King holiday and the state abortion fund for low-income women; both measures were generally supported by Democrats and opposed by Republicans. Taking a leaf from the Congressional Club, Republican candidates in the future could run on a statewide platform that sought to label Democratic legislators as liberals because of taxation, the King holiday, and the abortion fund. In other words, the party could field legislative candidates who intended to place Democrats on the defensive in much the same way as Jesse Helms successfully pinned the liberal label on Jim Hunt in 1984.

The Ascendancy of Mainstream Republicanism

Mainstream Tar Heel Republicans view Jim Martin's 1984 gubernatorial campaign as the model for the future. Almost two of every three whites in the state supported Martin. His dominant message was that he represented an alternative to the tax-and-spend policies of the Democrats. A poll conducted for Democratic party leaders after the election suggests reasons why Martin's economic message played well. More than 50 percent of white Tar Heels, in every region of the state, believed that the Republicans were doing a better job than the Democrats of "working for a fair tax system." Similar majorities thought the Republicans were more capable of balancing the federal budget. This perception of Republican fiscal expertise persisted despite record deficits rolled up in the first term of the Reagan administration. Even white Democrats did not feel the Democrats were fiscally more responsible. Republicans had won the symbolic battle as the better keeper of the purse strings.

This strategy of managerial competence worked for Martin in 1984, as he captured many more votes than either Helms or Reagan in some affluent liberal precincts in the Durham–Chapel Hill area. Voters there apparently did not know of Martin's antiabortion and anti–King holiday positions. By contrast, in 1986 former congressman Bill Cobey, from the Fourth Congressional District which includes Raleigh, demonstrated the dangers of public identification with evangelical Christians (cf. Wyman 1987). Elected to Congress as part of the 1984 GOP sweep, Cobey during his reelection campaign sent a strongly worded letter to fundamentalists in which he identified himself as an "Ambassador for Christ." As a consequence, it seems that many affluent Republican voters in North Raleigh and Cary stuck with U.S. Senate candidate Broyhill but, unhappy with Cobey's New Right image, switched to his challenger, modernizer Democrat David Price. Price easily defeated Cobey.

The 1988 mainstream GOP goal supposedly was a strong statewide ticket for all Council of State positions—lieutenant governor, attorney general, state superintendent of public instruction, labor commissioner, insurance commissioner, state auditor, and agricultural commissioner. Never in the twentieth century had a Republican won any of these seats. Would there be a coattail effect? Would the appeal of George Bush and Jim Martin lead to sufficient straight-ticket voting by dealigned Democrats for the GOP Council of State candidates to win office? The intended strategy was to present the Republican candidates as fiscal conservatives, committed to economic development and improved public schools and highways. In contrast to their Democratic opponents, they could not be labeled big spenders or, to use Republicans' favorite catch-all slogan, "liberals."

But after the Republican primaries in May, only one member of the GOP Council of State ticket, lieutenant gubernatorial candidate Jim Gardner, enjoyed any statewide reputation. This illustrated once again how talent-thin were Tar Heel Republicans. Gardner campaigned in 1988 as a mainstream Republican, a committed follower of Martin's blend of modernizer and traditionalist ideology. It was a remarkable political metamorphosis for Gardner, who in his early political life was widely viewed as a "militant segregationist" (Black 1976, 111). He was first elected to Congress at thirty-four, upsetting an incumbent Democrat in 1964 from the congressional district around Gardner's Rocky Mount home. When he ran as the Republican gubernatorial candidate in 1968, Gardner openly endorsed George Wallace, despite the fact that Richard Nixon was the Republican candidate. Asked during 1968 why a Republican would support Wallace, Gardner replied, "I've never heard [Wallace] say anything I disagree with" (Black 1976, 111). Reflecting on that campaign in a 1988 interview, Gardner said he was "an early Jesse Helms" (Sitton 1988). In the highly polarized 1968 election year, Gardner won 47 percent of the vote, garnering some support from both Wallace and Nixon voters. His Democratic opponent, Bob Scott, won— thanks to a biracial coalition that foreshadowed Democratic strategies of the 1980s. A majority of whites voted for Gardner, but Scott captured the black vote overwhelmingly and enough of the white vote to win the race.

In 1988, Gardner put racial issues on the sideline. A changed North Carolina seemed to suggest that, except for Jesse Helms, no Republican had a chance to win statewide by openly criticizing the growing power of the black electorate. For the GOP mainstream, the question was whether the party would build on the expanded power base that had begun with legislative victories and Martin's election in 1984.

The Democrats' Dilemmas and Hopes

The state Democratic party, built in the early to mid-twentieth century on the twin foundations of economic development ("progress") and racial segregation, confronts the challenge of how to build a winning political platform for the future. As part of the modernization process, Tar Heel Democrats, like other Southern Democrats in the 1960s and 1970s, abandoned their identification with old-fashioned racism. Since then the party has continued its commitment to an activist state by promoting and subsidizing private economic investment. Similar to their support in principle of racial equality, the Democrats also promise allegiance to women's equality. In short, the dominant positions in today's Democratic party are moderate and occasionally liberal on social issues like race and gender and conservative on economic issues.

This ideological mix constitutes a dilemma in general elections for several reasons. First, the Democrats' historic identification with Tar Heel economic development is endangered as Republicans increasingly claim responsibility for economic prosperity. At the top of the ticket, presidential candidates like Ronald Reagan, especially in 1984, conveyed a convincing image of Republicans as the anti–big government and pro-growth party. Further, a skilled Republican governor like Jim Martin, both as a candidate in 1984 and as an incumbent running for reelection in 1988, developed an economic program and rhetoric that blurred policy differences between him and modernizer Democrats like Bob Jordan, Jim Hunt, or Terry Sanford. Yet Martin retained a strong traditionalist identification with tax repeal. The Democrats were forced to defend existing taxes as necessary to fund North Carolina's major government programs, while Martin claimed an equal commitment to these programs but insisted that the state's economy could prosper even more if certain taxes affecting the business community were eliminated. Not surprisingly, North Carolina businesses during the 1980s increasingly identified with the state GOP, just as they had begun to do so years before in presidential elections.

Democratic candidates' tilt toward big business means that, conversely, the party lacks a commitment to a populist economic program that might stir less affluent voters, especially whites who do not have an overriding interest in either racial or gender issues. Certain Democrats have flirted with populism in response to Duke Power's and Carolina Power and Light's (CP&L) many requests to the State Utilities Commission for major rate increases. Most recently, Lacy Thornburg, attorney general since 1985, sounded those themes. But despite the unpopularity of power companies with voters, Thornburg's criticisms did not induce key Democratic legislators to push utility rate reform in the General Assembly. Nor did Democratic candidates running for governor develop specific policy proposals that favored consumers and challenged the utilities. The Democrats' second dilemma, then, is that less affluent voters lack reasons of economic self-interest to support the party on Election Day.

Similarly, leading Democrats have been unwilling, in populist fashion, to shift the burden of taxation to big business and the affluent. On the contrary, since Jim Hunt became governor in 1977, the state has become more dependent on the sales tax, a flat tax that impacts disproportionately on lower-income voters. Beginning especially with Martin's 1984 gubernatorial campaign, Republicans have tagged state Democrats as the "tax-and-spend" party. It is curious that as late as 1987, house Democrats, led by Billy Watkins, an interesting Democratic blend of modernism and traditionalism, overwhelmingly passed another penny increase in the sales tax. In asserting that the penny tax was needed for school construction, these Democrats fell back on the party's classic modernizer position: if the goal is praiseworthy, the source of the revenue does not matter. This, of course, was a reenactment of the 1961 decision of Terry Sanford and General Assembly Democrats to reinstitute the sales tax on food in order to aid public schools and community colleges.

House Democrats, perhaps feeling safe from GOP competition in their smaller legislative districts, foresaw no danger in passing the tax. But the vote provided the Republicans with more grist for their antitax mill; the 1987 penny sales tax increase was approved on close to a straight party-line vote. Although senate Democrats, led by Lieutenant Governor Bob Jordan, whose 1988 gubernatorial ambitions made him more sensitive to statewide political effects, refused to support the plan, the Republican party, including Jim Martin, had received another economic campaign issue from the Democrats, free of charge. Democratic support of higher sales taxes is a greater potential political liability than their waffling on utility rates, because GOP legislators are usually no more willing than their Democratic colleagues to criticize the power companies directly. But the Republicans' tendency to vote against sales tax increases makes the Democrats vulnerable to the charge that they, not Republicans, are responsible for higher taxes.

The Democrats' third dilemma centers on how hard party leaders are willing to fight for racial and gender equality. Their public commitment to support these goals, in contrast to their ambivalence and occasional open opposition to economic populism, gives the party a positive identification with blacks and women concerned about gender equality. Around such social issues, the distinction between Democrats and Republicans is clearest. The Republican party, in accord with its traditionalist ideology and recognizing that not all Tar Heel voters are concerned about race or gender equality, has paid lip service to equality but has not been supportive in practice. For example, the GOP in 1987 opposed the legislature's designation of a state Martin Luther King holiday and continued its attempts to abolish the state abortion fund for low-income women. Most General Assembly Democrats supported the King holiday and state abortion fund.

The problem for white Democratic leaders is that their positions on race and gender issues hurt them among white voters who are suspicious of equality, whereas blacks and women, especially the former, question whether the support for equality is more than just window dressing. In the 1980s, black Democrats believed that the abolition of the runoff primary, not the King holiday, was the true test of white modernizers' commitment to racial equality (Oleck 1988). Similarly, in 1985 equality-minded women were upset that the comparable worth issue received little backing from Democrats in the General Assembly. White Democratic leaders such as Bob Jordan and Tony Rand, the 1988 nominee for lieutenant governor, sought to address the criticism of blacks and women by supporting other desirable legislation. For example, the General Assembly in 1987 established ten new superior court judgeships in majority-black (or in Robeson County, black and native American) districts that almost guaranteed that minority candidates would become judges. General Assembly Democrats also increased financial safeguards for women in property and child support cases related to divorce, and strengthened legal protection against marital rape. If the party, consistent with modernizer ideology, emphasizes racial and gender equality rather than economic justice, it must be able to mobilize at election time the minority and feminist constituencies that care about these issues.

The Democratic victories in November 1986 provided a glimmer of hope for the next decade. Terry Sanford won the U.S. Senate race, two congressional seats lost in 1984 were returned to the Democrats, and the party turned back Republican attempts to elect supreme court judges and increase their strength in the General Assembly. Two key factors accounted for these gains: statewide party unity across the ticket and a winning strategy in the Sanford campaign.

Party unity mattered in 1986 because leading personalities had divided so harshly in 1984. The modernizer mix of social moderation and economic conservatism was offered by virtually all leading Democrats involved in the contested primaries for governor and lieutenant governor in 1984 and for the U.S. Senate in 1986. But following his loss to Attorney General Rufus Edmisten in the June 1984 runoff primary, former Charlotte mayor Eddie Knox focused his anger on Edmisten, whom he thought had campaigned unfairly, and Jim Hunt, his onetime close friend from college days at North Carolina State whom he accused of disloyalty during the primaries. In a move that influenced some of his supporters to follow suit or at least not to work hard for the 1984 Democratic ticket, Knox switched to the Republican party and specifically endorsed Hunt's Senate opponent, Jesse Helms. Blissfully for the Democrats, Terry Sanford won a clear majority in the May 1986 primary, and the party focused on a unified strategy for the fall campaign that could win back registered Democrats who had crossed over to the Republicans in the November 1984 election. Sanford's effective use of symbolic populism will be discussed later in this chapter.

North Carolina: The Enduring Plutocracy

For all of its reputation as a state tackling its social and economic problems, the reality of North Carolina remains far different. While Tar Heel politicians continually campaign on the importance of educational improvements, state and local expenditures have ranked near the bottom nationally (fortieth in 1985) and only near the middle among the southern states (National Education Association Datasearch 1987, 54). In the mid-1980s, plant closings exceeded openings, the infant mortality rate was sixth highest in the nation, and the illiteracy level ranked thirteenth (OSBM 1986). State and local expenditures for health care were twenty-ninth among the fifty states, and public welfare spending ranked forty-sixth, behind Mississippi and just above South Carolina (National Education Association Datasearch 1987, 48). North Carolina projects a national image of a state on the cutting edge of economic development. But this impression derives from several boom areas of the state, especially Charlotte and the Research Triangle Park where high-technology employment has been expanding. The image contrasts with the reality that there is much less economic opportunity in other parts of the state, and educational and health problems abound in both urban and rural areas. Even highway construction and maintenance, a program area in which North Carolina led the nation during the 1920s, had fallen below the national average. In 1985, the state ranked forty-fifth in per capita highway spending (National Education Association Datasearch 1987, 49).

How do North Carolina's dominant ideologies approach these problems? Traditionalist ideology, whether practiced by Democrats like Jimmy Green or Republicans like Jesse Helms, fails to address them at all. Traditionalism prefers low taxes and a government that provides a minimum of social services. It assumes that social ills are "natural" phenomena reflecting people's inability to achieve; government ought not to disrupt that natural social order. Statewide traditionalist candidates generally pay lip service to increased educational spending but avoid specific commitments to address the financial difficulties that confront school systems in the less affluent rural counties. While educational improvement is a cliché that all candidates feel compelled to support, traditionalist politicians can more easily ignore health care as beyond the purview of state government. When traditionalists control governments, as happened frequently during the 1980s in the state's small towns and rural counties, the existence of educational and health problems is hardly acknowledged. Given the challenges currently facing North Carolina, traditionalism stands as an outmoded testimonial to an earlier time.

Modernizer ideology endorses an activist state government to facilitate economic development. Nevertheless, by maintaining low levels of government spending and not focusing that spending on the problems of the less affluent majority, it too fails to address educational and health-care problems. Modernizer policy in North Carolina demonstrates a spending bias away from the needs of poor and working-class Tar Heels. For example, as noted above, in 1985 the state's per capita spending on primary and secondary public education was only fortieth in the nation. But its expenditures for higher education, programs from which the children of North Carolina's affluent minority are more likely to benefit, ranked eighteenth among the fifty states. During the late 1980s, modernizer Democrats like Bob Jordan and mainstream Republicans vied for credit for highway construction and maintenance, even though per capita spending on roads ranked near the bottom nationally. The budget of the state Department of Transportation's public transit division—the one most likely to aid low-income Tar Heels in both cities and the countryside—remained at less than 1 percent of the highway budget (King 1988).

Further, during the 1988 "short session" of the General Assembly, which by law must focus on budgetary issues, legislators expressed more concern for the complaints of corporations than for the economic problems of consumers. At the urging of R. J. Reynolds/Nabisco, which had announced plans to build a new cookie factory east of Raleigh, the General Assembly unanimously passed a revised corporate taxation formula that would give large corporations a $20 million tax break annually. Hardly a legislator questioned whether the new formula could hurt smaller corporations by raising their tax bill. Nor did legislators debate whether North Carolina's pressing educational and health needs should have precluded such a tax benefit to big business. Reynolds and other corporate lobbyists, as well as Jordan and Martin, who both supported the bill, claimed that this tax expenditure would encourage out-of-state corporations to locate their factories in North Carolina (Guillory 1988). But such statements are based on faith rather than evidence. Meanwhile, the General Assembly postponed funding on a health care program for indigent North Carolinians (Yeoman 1988b). These cases from the 1988 legislative session, as well as the examples of educational and transportation priorities, illustrate the basic thrust of modernizer ideology. Modernizer politicians address first the economic needs of corporations and the well-to-do. The less affluent majority benefits only if its needs coincide with the political agenda of big business and wealthier citizens.

Citizen Power: An Alternative Ideology

In the late 1980s, an alternative, more egalitarian vision for Tar Heel politics began to emerge. This alternative ideology presently lacks institutional position in state politics. It manifests itself in the work of political outsiders rather than insiders; it resembles the economic populism that flourished in North Carolina in the last decades of the nineteenth century.

The growth of this political alternative in North Carolina was preceded by similar developments in various other states—notably Illinois, Massachusetts, and Oregon—in the late 1970s. Known as the new citizen activism, the movement has characterized itself as empowering citizens against the excessive influence of large corporations on government policy (Boyte 1980; Boyte and Riessman 1986). Consequently, the alternative vision can be termed citizen-power ideology.

In North Carolina, the drive for increased citizen power has been amorphous. Not all those engaged in the struggle may recognize fellow activists as part of the same movement. The core value of citizen-power ideology is increased social equality. In North Carolina, citizen-power advocates generally view both traditionalist and modernizer ideologies as committed to political domination by affluent white males. Although citizen-power activists have more in common with modernizers than with traditionalists, they believe that modernizers are simply too beholden to the white male–dominated corporate establishment.

Examples of citizen organizing in North Carolina abound. Racially based citizen groups, like the state Black Political Caucus or local black organizations, have primarily aimed at more black political power. North Carolina's chapter of the National Abortion Rights Action League (NARAL) or county chapters of the National Organization for Women (NOW) have sought expanded rights for women.

In the early 1980s, the Sierra Club and the Conservation Council of

North Carolina began a drive to increase citizen control over the environment, primarily through lobbying in the General Assembly. They were joined several years later by North Carolina branches of two national environmental organizations, the Clean Water Fund and the Environmental Defense Fund. Both have received grants from the reform-minded Z. Smith Reynolds Foundation, which has identified citizen empowerment as one of its organizational goals. The various environmental groups, as they seek power to increase regulation of corporate activity, frequently are at odds with Tar Heel businesses such as Duke Power, CP&L, or developers along the Atlantic coast. Environmentalists question state government's bias toward corporations, both in appointments to and decisions of state boards and agencies.

The citizen-power movement includes groups whose focus is not limited simply to black, feminist, or environmental issues. The state AFL-CIO's primary goal is enhanced power for workers at the workplace, but it also lobbies for progressive taxation and against utility rate increases (see Chapter 6 for a fuller discussion). The Durham-based People's Alliance forged an interracial antiexpressway coalition in 1978 and 1979 that opposed the relocation of a low-income black neighborhood and asked the Durham City Council and the Hunt administration to support a nonhighway alternative to the $50 million, 1.6 mile-road project (Luebke 1981a). Although the highway was ultimately approved, the coalition forced local, state, and federal governments to relocate the black community intact, instead of implementing the governments' intended plan to pay each family a relocation sum and to destroy the community. Significantly, the antiexpressway movement led to the formation of a citywide interracial coalition that gradually won control of the city council between 1979 and 1987. This coalition included the People's Alliance, the Durham Committee on the Affairs of Black People (one of North Carolina's most influential black political organizations), and the Durham Voter's Alliance. Throughout the 1980s, coalition candidates, sensitive to the political goals of blacks, the poor, and environmentalists, defeated both traditionalist and modernizer candidates who shared the prevailing Tar Heel assumption that the chamber of commerce's agenda is the best agenda for any city government. As a result, developers' plans generally came under more scrutiny in Durham than in any other major North Carolina city. The more normal pattern in Tar Heel metropolitan areas is developer control of city councils, with an occasional white environmentalist or black expressing a dissenting point of view.

The Durham coalition defeated developers' candidates for two major reasons. First, both white and black citizen-power leaders took great pains to balance the sometimes conflicting interests of the white and black constituencies. In most local elections, the coalition's three citizen organizations endorsed the same interracial slate of candidates. Second, the social-political bases of the coalition were unusually strong. Both college-educated whites who had been schooled on the campus activism of the 1960s and early 1970s, and blacks, including a sizable community of black professionals, constituted a much higher proportion of the electorate in Durham than elsewhere in the metro Piedmont (Frazier 1925; Burgess 1962; Luebke 1981a, 1981c).

Whether they recognize their commonality or not, these citizen-power organizations, from the Black Political Caucus to the AFL-CIO or the People's Alliance, in fact constitute a challenge to a time-honored assumption of North Carolina politics. This assumption, dating back to the Democrats' defeat of the populist insurgency at the turn of the century, is that what is good for (white-male) business is good for North Carolina (Luebke 1979).

Modernizer Democrats, as earlier chapters have demonstrated, are more willing than traditionalists to respond to pressure from citizen-power organizations. Consequently, citizen advocates generally prefer a Democratic governor like Jim Hunt over a Republican like Jim Martin. They often agree with modernizers on the need to improve North Carolina's infrastructure, but they would prefer a more egalitarian distribution of government benefits and a more equitable tax system to pay for government investments.

Because citizen activists and modernizers often cooperate on issues, such as the phosphate-detergent ban or more judgeships for blacks, the distinction between the two ideologies can be fuzzy. The limits of modernizer concessions to citizen activists is well illustrated in the case of nuclear power plants. Despite considerable citizen protest against Duke Power's McGuire plant, just north of Charlotte, and CP&L's Shearon Harris plant, southwest of Raleigh, from the late 1970s through the early 1980s, neither the General Assembly, Governor Hunt, nor the State Utilities Commission took any steps against the nuclear proposals. North Carolina's pro–nuclear power policy stood in contrast to that of other states. For example, New Hampshire, Massachusetts (including its governor, Michael Dukakis), and New York helped citizens fight the opening of nuclear plants.

In spring 1986, after the Chernobyl nuclear accident in the Soviet

Union, a firestorm of citizen protest in the Triangle area arose against the Shearon Harris plant, even though the facility was almost finished. Symbolizing modernizer politicians' identification with corporate policy, former Governor Jim Hunt joined his Republican and Democratic predecessors going back to 1964 (Republican Jim Holshouser and Democrats Bob Scott and Dan Moore) in publicly declaring their continued support for CP&L. The citizens' group, CASH—Citizens against Shearon Harris—could not overcome the corporate and political power committed to opening the plant. Shearon Harris began generating electricity in 1987.

The nuclear power example provides an insight into citizen-power and modernizer relations. The more citizen demands cost corporations economically, the more likely modernizer politicians are to reject them. Thus, additional black judgeships, an abortion fund for poor women, or improved financial equity for divorced women are acceptable to modernizers if pushed by citizen advocates and if the costs to corporations are none or minimal. The phosphate ban was more complicated. Although detergent companies like Proctor and Gamble claimed the ban would cost them money, environmentalists gained the support of the North Carolina League of Municipalities because, without the ban, Tar Heel cities would have been required by law to spend considerable sums to remove phosphates at their sewage treatment plants. In this case, the cost issue favored the environmentalists.

The citizen-power movement in North Carolina differs from the historic pattern of economic populism in that citizen activists are more likely to be college-educated and from the middle class, not the working class. Although this is less true for blacks, the reality of white citizen activism in North Carolina is that it is dominated by the middle class. Black and Black (1987) have found a similar pattern throughout the South.

Conventional wisdom in North Carolina politics holds that lower-income whites participate less in the citizen-power movement because they are satisfied with the status quo. In particular, working-class whites are said to support corporate domination of state politics. Modernizer Democrats, in particular, offer this explanation to account for their cordial relations with corporate lobbyists. Another explanation is that less affluent whites are inactive because they are less likely to believe they can affect public policy (Botsch 1980). One important, but neglected poll of North Carolina public opinion from the mid-1980s supports this alternative view.

In November 1984 the state Democratic party suffered its worst defeat in the twentieth century. In the aftermath of the election, a group of Democratic candidates commissioned a mammoth statewide poll by William Hamilton (1984). It surveyed 10,000 North Carolinians to try to find out what went wrong. One of the key sets of questions concerned state tax legislation. Successful candidate Martin had campaigned on a three-plank tax reduction program: to eliminate the sales tax on food and nonprescription drugs, the tax on business inventories, and the tax on individuals' intangible wealth. The Democrats' poll asked voters which taxes they would like to see abolished.

By two-to-one margins, respondents favored abolishing the food tax and opposed repealing the business inventory tax. The data suggested strong sympathy for a populist economic strategy that would give tax breaks to "average citizens" rather than to business (cf. Luebke 1980). But no Democrat heeded the poll's results. On the contrary, General Assembly Democrats in 1985 actually increased the state sales tax from four and one-half cents to five cents and reduced the size of the business inventory tax.

The contrast between the findings of the poll and the policy decisions that followed indicate that the Democrats were guided by their own ideology rather than the economic preferences of the citizenry (cf. Luebke 1987d). The poll showed that citizens favored a populist tax policy. What was missing was not popular support but Democratic political leaders who were willing to challenge the ideological hegemony of party modernizers. Several citizen organizations that emerged in the 1980s across North Carolina have specifically sought to politicize less affluent whites. Among the most successful are the Pittsboro-based Rural Advancement Fund (RAF) and North Carolina Fair Share, based in Raleigh. The RAF mobilized small farmers who were about to lose their land by foreclosure. RAF activists challenged both the North Carolina and federal departments of agriculture to adopt foreclosure policies more sympathetic to the farmers' plight. North Carolina Fair Share, modeled after citizens organizations of the same name in states such as Massachusetts and Oregon, seeks to organize working-class whites and blacks around common economic issues. In 1987 and 1988, Fair Share opposed CP&L's rate hike request, which was largely based on construction costs at the Shearon Harris nuclear plant. By mobilizing affected citizens, Fair Share introduced hundreds of whites and blacks to the process of citizen pressure at Utilities Commission hearings.

Farm foreclosure and utility rates have a similar theme. They are issues that immediately affect countless citizens. Like foreclosure notices and power bills, the possibility of a radioactive waste landfill or health problems introduced by a chemical company located near residences have mobilized thousands of Tar Heels in recent years. Citizens of Rowan and Davidson counties in the western Piedmont turned out by the thousands at public hearings during 1987 and 1988 to oppose a state attempt to place a low-level nuclear waste storage facility in their counties. Residents of Buncombe and Caldwell counties organized against the health threat from existing firms using hazardous chemicals (Clean Water Fund 1988, 4, 7). Also in 1988, not wanting to be displaced from their homes or have high-tech development nearby, citizens of northern Durham County and adjacent Granville County launched a vigorous protest against a Martin administration proposal to the federal government to establish a federally funded Supercollider research center on a fifty-two-square-mile site about twenty miles north of downtown Durham.

The breadth of single-issue citizen protests during the 1980s raised a potential challenge to established modernizer power in state government. But for the citizen-action perspective to attain prominence in Raleigh, citizen leaders must convince many of the working-class whites who rallied against the single issue of farm credit or hazardous waste in their communities to take on regional and statewide issues as well. These citizens must also be willing to join a statewide movement for better health care for those who cannot afford it, or against such economic issues as the high cost of electricity or the 5 percent food tax.

At present, electoral participation by working-class black and white Tar Heels is lower than middle-class participation. Less affluent citizens will participate at higher levels only if they perceive that their political involvement can make a difference. In the 1984 race for the U.S. Senate, the Helms campaign convinced disproportionate numbers of working-class whites, especially in the western Piedmont, that it was in their self-interest to help reelect their senior senator. In a parallel fashion in 1988, Jesse Jackson persuaded working-class blacks, many of whom had never cared about politics, to register to vote so that they could support him in North Carolina's Democratic presidential primary on Super Tuesday. But the question remains whether, beyond charismatic personalities or a single issue in their own back yard, less affluent blacks and whites will become involved in electoral politics and, once involved, whether they will continue to be interested at the precinct, county, and statewide levels.

What Citizen Power Is Not:
Pseudo-Populists Edmisten and Ingram

When North Carolinians think of Tar Heel populists of the 1970s and 1980s, two sometimes successful statewide politicians come to mind, former attorney general Rufus Edmisten and former state insurance commissioner John Ingram. Both Edmisten and Ingram depended on their populist style to appeal to Tar Heel voters. Both were far less committed to the substance of citizen-power ideology than they were to its symbols.

Edmisten staged a comeback of sorts in 1988, when, based on name recognition, he won a three-way primary for the Democratic nomination for secretary of state. Although visible statewide, especially because just one person, Democrat Thad Eure, had held the post from 1936 through 1988, the secretary of state's office was primarily non-ideological. Edmisten's importance for a discussion of populism and citizen-power centers on his ten years as attorney general and his gubernatorial campaign of 1984.

Rufus Edmisten effectively used his position as counsel to U.S. Senator Sam Ervin during the 1973 nationally televised Watergate hearings to gain a statewide reputation. A year later, the Democratic State Executive Committee appointed him attorney general to replace Robert Morgan who had resigned to run for the U.S. Senate. Edmisten subsequently won three elections for attorney general (1974, 1976, and 1980) by comfortable margins. A native of Watauga County in the Mountains, he prided himself on his folksy ways. They brought him favor with many small-town and rural white Democrats across the state. Edmisten played the banjo and sang country and gospel tunes at political rallies, and he developed close political ties with most of the state's one hundred sheriffs.

Yet the substance of his populism was far less obvious than his style. Although as attorney general he directed his office to oppose rate increases proposed by the state's telephone and power companies, he never developed a systematic political campaign against the utilities. His critics claimed that his opposition to rate increases was strongest near election time. As the Democratic nominee for governor in 1984, Edmisten campaigned against the high cost of electricity. But no other potential citizen-power issue, such as the state's low level of industrial wages or its increasing reliance on regressive sales taxes, was part of his program. In fact, except for his criticism of utilities, Edmisten showed himself to be far more of a modernizer than a populist Democrat. For example, he supported rather than opposed the food tax.

But despite his true colors as a modernizer, Edmisten in the public eye was a country populist. A nasty runoff between him and former Charlotte mayor Eddie Knox, who campaigned as the urban middle-class candidate, left many Knox supporters embittered. After the Knox runoff, Edmisten was attacked for allowing his supporters to play "dirty" against Knox (*Greensboro News and Record* 1984). His campaign was dogged by the constant criticism that he lacked the "personal qualities" to be governor (cf. Snider 1984).

Edmisten lost badly in the 1984 general election. His defeat, however, cannot be viewed as voter rejection of citizen-power ideology. Edmisten's populist style made him attractive to white working-class Democrats. Exit poll data demonstrate that his appeal to that group was significantly greater than Jim Hunt's (CBS News 1984). But the style of populism was not sufficient to outdistance a Republican opponent who promised lower taxes for everyone. Given the unpopularity of the food tax, Martin's promise (which as governor he failed to keep) to repeal the sales tax on groceries probably had more appeal to undecided white working-class voters than Edmisten's good-old-boy symbolism.

While his populist style provided Edmisten with only limited gains against Martin's promise of tax cuts within the white working class, that very style alienated him from many in the urban middle class who preferred Martin's professional tone. In some urban precincts in the Piedmont, Edmisten's total for governor trailed Jim Hunt's vote for the U.S. Senate by twenty percentage points.

John Ingram's story resembles Edmisten's. Elected insurance commissioner in 1972 and reelected in 1976 and 1980, Ingram became the bête noire of state corporations. He campaigned as the consumer's friend against the excessive demands of insurance companies for increases in auto insurance rates. As insurance commissioner he regularly denied proposed rate increases, but the insurance corporations, on appeal to the North Carolina state courts, often won the increases anyway. Unlike Edmisten, Ingram's populism—though tied to the single issue of insurance—was substantive. His image as the people's candidate, "fighting for you," was secure.

In June 1978, Ingram parlayed his populist reputation into an upset victory over Charlotte banker Luther Hodges, Jr., son of the former governor. Running in the general election against Jesse Helms, however, Ingram faced three obstacles. First, Ingram found, as Edmisten would six years later, that affluent Democrats were unenthused about his populist style. Second, Helms himself campaigned as a populist, albeit around social issues like race and morality. White working-class voters sympathetic to a "little folks" appeal had two candidates to choose from. Helms styled himself a friend of the small tobacco farmer against the stop-smoking programs of President Carter's Department of Health, Education, and Welfare. Third, Helms, with the aid of the National Congressional Club, raised twenty times as much money as Ingram (Furgurson 1986, 127–30). Ingram attacked Helms as the "Six-Million-Dollar-Man" and the candidate of big oil contributors, a criticism that seemingly played well among white working-class voters in the textile counties around Charlotte. Ingram won several textile counties in 1978 that Hunt would lose to Helms in 1984. Overall, Ingram ran five percentage points better than Hunt against Helms in the eighteen industrial counties of the western Piedmont. But whether as a result of his poorly funded campaign, his limited appeal among affluent Democrats, or Helms's positive image among white Tar Heels, Ingram lost decisively.

When Ingram sought the Democratic gubernatorial nomination in 1984, he tried to run as both an economic and a social populist. On the economic side, he advocated the direct election of utilities commissioners instead of their appointment by the governor. Taking a page from Jesse Helms's book, he appealed to white working-class fundamentalists by opposing the state abortion fund for poor women. Ingram further confused voters by calling himself "the people's conservative." Such a label pushed away many black and white voters who had previously been attracted by his attacks on big corporations. Ingram's new message, primarily appealing to rural and small-town whites, in effect undermined a broader political base that he had developed among voters, both urban and rural, black and white, who had negative feelings about corporate power. Coupling the conflicting populist messages with little funding and a weak campaign organization, Ingram won only 6 percent of the vote in the gubernatorial primary, placing fifth and trailing, among others, Rufus Edmisten and Jimmy Green.

When Ingram filed for the U.S. Senate primary in early 1986, Sanford supporters worried that Ingram's populist appeal could deny Sanford a majority, much as he had when running against Luther Hodges in 1978.

But Ingram seemed burned out in that year, unable to articulate either a social or an economic populist agenda. The scourge of North Carolina's corporate elite in the 1970s and early 1980s, he ended the 1980s as a political has-been.

Terry Sanford: Modernizer Substance and Populist Symbolism

In recent years the most successful Tar Heel Democrat to use populist themes is not a populist at all. In his campaign for the U.S. Senate in 1986, Terry Sanford presented himself and the North Carolina Democratic party as the caring representatives of textile workers and tobacco farmers. Sanford drew a contrast between himself and the wealthy Republican interests who, according to Sanford, had only money on their side but did not bring government's benefits to the people. Sanford campaigned as if he were a citizen-power activist.

Three bits of evidence helped Sanford's case. First, his Republican opponent, Jim Broyhill, was the scion of an affluent North Carolina furniture family. Second, political action committees, mostly representing large corporations, showered Broyhill with $1 million in contributions, the third highest amount among the 66 candidates running for 33 U.S. Senate seats. By contrast, Sanford ranked forty-eighth in PAC contributions, with just $264,000. Third, a Washington research firm identified Broyhill as ranking next-to-last among the nation's 435 congressmen in the amount of funds brought into his western North Carolina congressional district. It was plausible to portray Broyhill, in campaign speeches and television spots, as the unresponsive Republican out of touch with average citizens.

Sanford added to his "just folks" credentials by rolling up his shirtsleeves and campaigning in a Duke windbreaker, whereas Broyhill rarely removed his suit jacket (Luebke 1987b). Sanford won the patriotism battle, an issue usually "owned" by Republicans, by reminding audiences that he had served as a paratrooper in World War II (he often wore his paratrooper insignia). He also pointedly contrasted his military credentials with those of Broyhill, who had received a deferment during the Korean War. Further, he criticized Broyhill's 1982 vote to raise taxes. Thus, Sanford came across as a patriotic man of the people who was critical of new taxes by big government and of political contributions by big corporations (Luebke 1987a, 1987c).

The populist image worked. Unlike Edmisten, Sanford could use populist symbolism without scaring off affluent Democrats, because his credentials as a modernizer Democrat who took *responsible* action were secure. As governor in the early 1960s he had been willing to impose regressive taxes, such as a sales tax on groceries in 1961, because he believed that North Carolina needed improvements in public education, including a statewide community college system. Second, as a former board member of ITT and president of Duke University, Sanford was hardly hostile to corporate America. At best, one could argue that he was a more liberal member of that elite than Broyhill. Broyhill's high level of PAC support reflected not only a conservative voting record, but also his standing as an incumbent who was expected to defeat Sanford in the November election. If Sanford runs for reelection in 1992, he will receive much more PAC support as an incumbent than he did as a challenger. Indeed, in 1987 PACs already had helped Sanford retire some of his 1986 campaign debt. In individual contributions, Broyhill's lead over Sanford—$2.5 million to $1.8 million—was much smaller. Broyhill ranked thirteenth and Sanford was twenty-second in this category (*News and Observer* 1986).

Sanford's campaign strategy blended populist rhetoric with his well-established record as a standard-bearer for modernizer Democrats. This blend may be crucial to give dealigned white Democrats a reason to "come home." In this view, the difference between the two parties is not tax-happy Democrats versus fiscally sound Republicans, but rather caring Democrats versus insensitive Republicans.

Whether Sanford would have done as well campaigning against a stronger candidate like Jesse Helms is unclear. But Sanford provides an important model for future Democratic modernizers: substantive commitment to the modernizers' trickle-down economic policy, but a symbolic campaign that presented him as a citizen-power advocate. In 1986, Sanford made it appear that he and the Democratic party were fighting a class war against the Republican plutocrats. Poll data suggest that such rhetoric, coming from Sanford, provided an image of change that made many white Democrats, regardless of income, switch their support from Helms in 1984 to Sanford in 1986 (CBS News 1986).

The Limited Prospects for Citizen Power in North Carolina

Citizen power could become a competitive ideology in North Carolina politics if significant numbers of voters believed that collective action would empower them to change society. The poll data available suggest that the familiar argument of Tar Heel Democrats that "the people" do not want a more aggressive stance against business is wrong. But responses to polls are an individual, privatized act. The link between individual preferences and collective action depends on a belief that collective action can make a difference in individual lives. For citizen-power ideology to be taken seriously in Raleigh, thousands of previously inactive Tar Heels would have to become politically active.

Three conflicting arguments have been offered to explain why less affluent citizens who believe that big business has too much political influence are not more active in politics. The first argument assigns primary responsibility to the citizens. If they cared, these less affluent voters could easily organize themselves to make a difference in local and state politics. After all, political parties in most North Carolina counties could use more, not fewer, volunteers. The lack of involvement from citizens indicates that they are more or less satisfied with the available alternatives.

The second argument centers on political uncertainty among working-class white voters. Botsch's (1980) interviews with furniture workers in the High Point area in the late 1970s revealed white support both for Ingram's economic attacks on insurance companies as well as Helms's social populism that criticized busing for school desegregation. In the first instance, the focus of political organizing is big business's ties to big government. In the second case, the problem is black influence on big government. The positions of both Ingram and Helms appealed to white workers' sense of powerlessness. Against which group should white workers concentrate their energies? Botsch concluded that workers' confusion over the most appropriate target undermined the prospects for an interracial economic populist movement.

The third argument for limited involvement among less affluent voters focuses on agenda-setting by the state's political elites. Voters stay inactive because they find that their anticorporate sentiments are not reinforced by North Carolina's dominant ideologies. In an earlier analysis of national data, Luebke and Zipp found that in the 1980 presidential campaign Ronald Reagan's attacks on big government set the agenda. Neither Republicans nor Democrats, including President Jimmy Carter, were willing to make the power of big business the issue, even though national polls had shown widespread citizen opposition to big business. Mass opinion revealed dissatisfaction with large-scale institutions, both business and government. But politicians chose to legitimize only the antigovernment part of citizens' critiques. The antibusiness attitudes were ignored (Luebke and Zipp 1983; Zipp, Luebke, and Landerman 1984).

In a similar way, North Carolina modernizer Democrats disregard the anticorporate sentiment of voters. Modernizers emphasize voters' concerns about jobs and education, but they do not respond to their discontent with the food tax or high utility rates because they wish to avoid a conflict with big business. The modernizer Democratic goal is to maintain state services at a level that will satisfy both business and the majority of voters. In presenting a vision of a society that seeks to unite business and average voters in a Democratic consensus, modernizers have decided that discussion of business power lies beyond the parameters of legitimate political debate (Luebke 1975). Because the decision does not take place on a roll-call legislative vote, Bachrach and Baratz (1963) termed this critical choice a "non-decision."

With this nondecision, Democrats ignore the citizens who, based on their everyday life experiences, doubt that such a consensus is possible. Poll data indicate that less affluent whites and blacks, regardless of income, are more likely than affluent whites to favor a redistribution of economic power (Risberg 1981; Luebke and Zipp 1983; W. Hamilton 1984). In other words, modernizer Democrats, in avoiding conflict with large corporations like Duke Power or R. J. Reynolds, reflect the political opinions of affluent Tar Heels like themselves, but they are discounting the political beliefs of a substantial minority if not a majority of North Carolinians. Feeling that Democrat-controlled government is unresponsive to their needs, less affluent Tar Heels can either not vote at all or vote Republican. For virtually all blacks in North Carolina, Republicanism is associated with cutbacks in government services and the personality of Jesse Helms. Thus, for blacks unmoved by today's Democratic party, the only immediate alternative is to stay home on Election Day.

By contrast, less affluent whites do not have such negative associations with Republicans. Republican calls for lower taxes in general or repeal of the food tax, themes that emerged in the 1984 and 1988 state campaigns, appeal to less affluent whites who cannot see how they benefit from the higher taxes that the Democratic majority in the General Assembly supports (Luebke 1984d). Consequently, Republican campaign appeals to throw out the Democrats in Raleigh can strike a chord with less affluent whites. Such voters, normally registered Democrats, may vote Republican, or they may not vote at all (Black and Black 1987).

The coming of the two-party system to North Carolina has not increased substantially the political alternatives facing Tar Heel voters. Before the emergence of a competitive Republican party in statewide elections, the political debate between leading gubernatorial candidates would have taken place within the Democratic party. Before dealignment, a strong statewide candidate with views similar to Governor Martin's would have run as a Democrat. The Martin-Jordan political sparring before the November 1988 election would in the past have occurred earlier in the calendar year. Republican strength in the 1980s has simply moved the crucial date of elections from the Democratic primary election in the spring to the general election in the fall.

Before the emergence of a strong two-party system statewide, Democratic primaries provided the forum for ideological debate among traditionalist and modernizer candidates. For example, Jimmy Green's traditionalism succeeded in both the 1976 and 1980 Democratic primaries for lieutenant governor. In 1988, in the Democratic lieutenant governor's race, traditionalist Harold Hardison's positions on the issues differed only slightly from those of Jim Gardner, the Republicans' major candidate for that office. In effect, Democratic voters chose between a modernizer and a traditionalist in their May primary; in November, all voters faced a similar race between Democratic modernizer Tony Rand, who defeated Hardison, and Gardner, the Republicans' blend of modernism and traditionalism. Citizen-power ideology and the challenge to big business remained beyond the parameters of legitimate political discussion.

The probable future of North Carolina politics lies in the limited debate between the dominant factions of the state's Democratic and Republican parties. Both parties are comfortable with a business-dominated, business-as-usual politics. A citizen-power alternative could emerge only if significant numbers of legislative Democrats were willing to break with the dominant Democratic ideology. Many of these legislators have challenged the corporate agenda on a variety of single issues during the 1980s. Representatives Dan Blue and Sharon Thompson, for example, have fought for improvements in workers' compensation; Harry Payne pushed through workers' right-to-know (about hazardous chemicals) legislation. Joe Hackney led the successful campaign to ban pollution-causing phosphates from laundry detergents, and Dave Diamant has sought to limit interest rates of banks' credit cards. But these legislators have been unwilling in a public way to challenge systematically the power of large corporations in the General Assembly.

These Tar Heel legislators fear that to advance a citizen-action agenda would be to invite political defeat. They believe that there is no mass constituency in North Carolina for economic fairness. While legislators support the citizen-power movement by passing bills that benefit some of the various constituencies—blacks, women, workers, the poor—they are afraid that if they publicize their victories, the corporate agenda will reassert itself and reverse the gains of the recent past.

As a consequence, less affluent voters rarely hear about economic fairness in political campaigns. They take for granted that politicians have no interest in such issues. Thus, legislators sympathetic to citizen power and less affluent voters across North Carolina with a self-interest in economic fairness fail to establish common ground. Although the successes of the citizen-power movement are notable, they are difficult for the general public to detect. As long as the citizen-action alternative remains hidden from the public, the political debate over business power in North Carolina will remain tepid. The North Carolina plutocracy will endure.

Afterword

The November 1988 Election
in North Carolina

"Republican Rule Continues" ran the banner headline on the first edition of the *Greensboro News and Record* on November 9, 1988, the day after the election. The headline was slightly overstated, in that both the state house and the state senate remained in the hands of the Democrats. Further, Democrats continued to hold eight of North Carolina's eleven congressional seats, as they had after the 1986 midterm election, despite vigorous challenges from Republicans in the Fourth (Raleigh and Chapel Hill area), Fifth (Winston-Salem area), Eighth (western and eastern Piedmont counties, from Yadkinville in the north to Hamlet on the South Carolina line), and Eleventh (the Mountains) districts.

But if Tar Heel Republicans did not rule, as the headline claimed, they had nonetheless attained an unprecedented victory in state politics. In November 1984, North Carolina Democrats had suffered their worst defeat of the twentieth century (Luebke 1984d), but November 1988 was even worse. The voters not only reelected Governor Jim Martin to a second term; they also preferred the GOP candidate for lieutenant governor, Jim Gardner, by a narrow margin. It was the first time in this century that a Republican was elected lieutenant governor, a position whose duties include the role of presiding officer in the state senate. Republicans won 10 more seats in the 120-member state house, which brought the GOP total to a historic 46 seats. Similarly, senate Republicans enjoyed a net gain of 3 seats, so that the 1989 session would open with a record 13 GOP senators compared to 37 Democrats. No legislature in the nation turned more from Democrat to Republican than did North Carolina's in the 1988 election.

Also for the first time in statewide races, two Republican judges, one on the state court of appeals and one in superior court, defeated their

205

Democratic opponents. Finally, in the one hundred races for county boards of commissioners, Republicans won sixteen more seats than in 1986 and had a net gain of one additional county board, bringing the total number of boards with a GOP majority to thirty-two. Most of the Republican-dominated county commissions were in the western Piedmont and the Mountains. But Republicans also won a majority on the county commissions of two of the state's fastest-growing counties, Dare and Brunswick, on the Atlantic coast.

After Election Day, Democratic leaders naturally sought to put a happy face on the results, pointing out that North Carolina voters had once again elected Democrats to the important Council of State positions such as attorney general, secretary of state, labor commissioner, and state superintendent of public instruction. But less partisan observers noted that, with one exception, the Republican candidates for these jobs had been political unknowns with no budget for media advertising. The Democrats simply had to be grateful that enough voters, 65 percent of whom were still *registered* Democrats, were willing to support the party ticket in those races where few citizens could remember even the names of either the Democratic or Republican candidates.

North Carolina Republican leaders were jubilant about their local and statewide successes. Immediately after surveying the 1988 results, they promised that in 1992 their Council of State candidates would be well funded and prepared to oust the incumbent Democrats. They pledged no longer to concede a single statewide race to the Democratic party. In sum, 1988 confirmed North Carolina as a two-party state, in which Democrats showed further evidence of decline, and Republicans seized the opportunity to persuade most Tar Heel voters that their party is the party of the future. The central question is why the two parties fared as they did. How important were candidate personalities, campaign themes, and media advertising in shaping the November 1988 outcome?

Republicans whipped the Democrats in North Carolina for several reasons. The most important is that the GOP coupled a strong incumbent governor's personality with a "let's keep a good thing going" nonissue message that conveyed normalcy and prosperity to voters. The Democrats sought to counter the Jim Martin pitch with the claim that he had been an ineffective and even absent governor (Democratic television spots pointed out that, while the General Assembly was meeting in Raleigh, Martin was out of town watching the Kentucky Derby or sailing in the Caribbean on a family vacation). The Jordan campaign expected that the voters would prefer a hard-working Democrat to an incumbent Republican who was, because Democrats controlled the legislature, necessarily less involved in legislative policy-making than Democrats. To their surprise on Election Day, Jordan and other modernizer Democrats learned that Martin's simple message of "reelect me" was compelling. It appears that many white voters, especially in affluent white precincts of the metro Piedmont, reacted negatively to incumbent Democratic power brokers like Bob Jordan, house speaker Liston Ramsey, and state senator Tony Rand, the candidate for lieutenant governor. The typical white Tar Heel in 1988 seemed to give the Democratic majority little recognition for passing educational, environmental, and highway programs in the General Assembly. Rather, white voters seemed to agree with Martin's assertions that he was, or at least should be, setting North Carolina's political agenda.

One unexpected outcome of the November 8 election was the toppling of eight-year House Speaker Ramsey. A coalition of forty-five Republicans and twenty dissident Democrats found common ground in their hostility toward Ramsey and his chief lieutenant, Billy Watkins, for excluding them from power and subjecting them to "arbitrary and petty" treatment (*Charlotte Observer* 1989b). By a 65–54 vote on January 11, 1989, the coalition elected Joe Mavretic, an outspoken Democrat from eastern North Carolina, as speaker. Republicans gained unprecedented power as chairs of several key house subcommittees (*Charlotte Observer* 1989a).

In the November election, Martin defeated Jordan by 56 to 44 percent, an improvement over his 54 to 46 percent victory over Rufus Edmisten four years earlier. Exit polls indicate that Martin received about two-thirds of the white vote, and he needed only 60 percent to win. As expected, more than 90 percent of blacks supported Jordan, even though Martin had advertised on black radio stations across North Carolina in hopes of taking black votes away from Jordan.

Martin ran an effective two-pronged campaign for the white vote. First, his overall theme of normalcy and prosperity permeated his television advertising, primarily emphasizing the goals of his administration and its alleged record of achievement. This television campaign highlighted Martin the modernizer politician, willing to use government to provide schools, highways, and environmental protection. His ads showed white and black children in classrooms together, as well as shots of the Cape Hatteras Lighthouse. An outsider watching the TV spots would have been hard pressed to know whether this sincere-sounding man in his dark suit and red tie was a New South Democrat or a New South Republican.

The Martin campaign's ability to neutralize Jordan's accomplishments as lieutenant governor constitutes a major Republican success. An analysis of environmental politics during 1987 and 1988, especially of the legislative ban on phosphate detergents, illustrates how the Jordan campaign contributed to its own demise. As mentioned in Chapter 10, in 1987 Jordan and other modernizer Democrats in the General Assembly, including lieutenant governor nominee-to-be Tony Rand, supported a legislative proposal to ban phosphates from household detergents. The legislation would have the environmental effect of preventing algae pollution in North Carolina's rivers, the fiscal impact of saving local governments the cost of additional pollution control equipment, and the political benefit to Democrats who supported the phosphate ban of a working alliance with North Carolina's growing environmental organizations (B. Hall 1988). In addition to the phosphate ban, Jordan and Rand in 1985 had backed a statewide worker and community right-to-know (about nearby hazardous chemicals) law, albeit a weakened version of the Durham right-to-know ordinance enacted by the city council as a result of intense pressure from citizen groups.

Because Governor Martin in 1987 had opposed the phosphate ban and in 1985 had charged that supporters of the right-to-know legislation were suffering from "chemophobia," Jordan supporters believed that they could count on electoral endorsements from the environmental groups. But in 1988 Jordan's campaign did not maintain good communication with the two major statewide environmental political action committees, the Sierra Club and the League of Conservation Voters (LCV). Although these groups endorsed Jordan's fellow modernizer, Tony Rand, over Republican Jim Gardner, they were neutral in the governor's race. The Sierra Club and LCV had concluded that, regarding issues of water quality and some board appointments in North Carolina, Martin was Jordan's equal in environmental commitment. Further, they recalled that Jordan had established a poor environmental record when he was a state senator, before becoming lieutenant governor in 1985. Finally, at a Conservation Council meeting in Raleigh in October 1988, Martin pressed hard for the environmentalists' support, emphasizing that he believed in a balance between environmentalists and developers. Jordan also asked for support at the same meeting, but did not speak as forcefully as Martin. Consequently, Martin's last-minute lobbying, despite his anti–right-to-know and antiphosphate ban positions of 1985 and 1987, neutralized Jordan's multi-year effort to win the backing of environmentalists. Because political observers generally assume that environmental PACs in the United States endorse Democrats, the North Carolina groups' decision to remain neutral in fact conveyed to the public the impression that a Republican was an acceptable choice for governor.

Martin further helped himself by running TV ads that affirmed his support for the environment. Jordan hurt his chances by declining to air a pro-environment television spot. Thus, despite the reality that Jordan had a stronger commitment to the environment, Martin appeared the better environmental candidate to voters who relied on TV commercials for their political information. A *Charlotte Observer* (1988) poll suggested that Martin's pro-environment ads and Jordan's failure to use them proved beneficial to Martin; by a 39 to 33 percent margin, most Tar Heels surveyed thought Martin would "do more for the environment."

Martin's first strategy to win the white vote, the campaign that saturated North Carolina's television markets in the weeks before Election Day, emphasized Jim Martin the modernizer governor. The second strategy was less public and stressed his traditionalist side. Throughout 1988, Martin targeted North Carolina right-to-life groups and fundamentalist Protestant organizations that also were strongly antiabortion to remind them by direct mail that he could be relied on to continue his fight against the state abortion fund for poor women.

While Martin was targeting the antiabortion constituencies, the Jordan campaign avoided the abortion issue, fearing that most voters did not agree with the lieutenant governor's 1985 vote to break a tie in the state senate and keep the state abortion fund alive. In fact, poll data consistently indicate that North Carolina voters favor a woman's right to choose an abortion. The failure to campaign on his pro-choice record left many pro-choice voters with no knowledge that Jordan and Martin had differing positions on the abortion rights issue. Exit polls among white voters in Guilford County (Greensboro) demonstrate what could happen if Jordan's pro-choice stand remained a secret to most of the public. Among fifteen pro-life voters surveyed, 80 percent supported Martin, suggesting that the Martin campaign had successfully alerted the antiabortion electorate. But among thirty pro-choice voters, only 40 percent voted for Jordan. How many additional pro-choice votes might Jordan have won if he had targeted a mailing to, for example, all registered Democratic and Independent women in the six metro Piedmont counties (Luebke and Yeoman 1988)?

Governor Martin's personality and the normalcy/prosperity themes of his reelection advertising were probably the major reason Republicans did so well in 1988. But a second reason was the coattail impact of Martin and presidential candidate George Bush on other Republicans, especially on Jim Gardner's narrow 51 to 49 percent victory over Tony Rand.

Tar Heel Republican strategists recognized by summer 1988 that, unlike in 1984, when incumbent President Ronald Reagan was significantly more popular than the relatively unknown candidate Jim Martin, the coattails of Martin would be virtually as long as Bush's. The November results support that insight. In 1984, Reagan defeated Walter Mondale by a 62 to 38 percent margin, while Martin won by 54 to 46 percent over Rufus Edmisten. But in 1988, Bush's victory over Michael Dukakis, 58 to 42 percent, was four points closer than Reagan's 1984 win, while Martin defeated Jordan by two points more, 56 to 44 percent, than he had beaten Edmisten in 1984. Recognizing Martin's popularity and his wide lead over Jordan in the preelection polls, the Martin team scheduled tandem campaigning by Martin and Gardner during the week before Election Day in the state's Republican heartland, the western Piedmont, and adjoining metro Piedmont cities like Charlotte and Greensboro. Martin specifically asked his campaign audiences to be sure to support the Republican candidate for lieutenant governor as well as himself.

The strongest region for both Martin and Gardner was the western Piedmont, where Martin took 62 percent and Gardner won 58 percent of the vote. Martin's second best region was the metro Piedmont; he won between 55 and 64 percent of the vote in Guilford, Forsyth, Wake, and Mecklenburg counties. The only metro Piedmont counties to deny Martin a majority were the two Democratic strongholds, Orange and Durham. Gardner won Forsyth, Wake, and Mecklenburg, but by substantially smaller margins.

The results suggest a Democratic party in disarray. Jordan won a majority of the November vote only in the eastern Piedmont and on the Coastal Plain, areas that have shown the least population growth since 1972. Those two regions were also Rand's strongest. The modernizer-led Democratic party has, since 1972, lost key statewide elections time and time again. But each time, party leaders have had an excuse. In 1972, the losses to Jesse Helms and Jim Holshouser were blamed on Democratic presidential candidate George McGovern. In 1984, the Reagan, Helms, and Martin victories were explained away by references to candidate Mondale, Helms's media advertising, and the intraparty rivalry that resulted from Edmisten's hard-won success in the two Democratic primaries. In 1988, however, modernizer Democrats had no easy scapegoat. It was time to take a good look in the mirror.

If the Democrats, in planning for 1990 and 1992, bring forth the same old appeals about education and economic progress, they will lose again. Such generalities worked for Tar Heel Democrats before 1972, but they are no longer effective. Jim Martin has shown clearly that he can take those issues away from the Democrats. If white voters, who constitute the swing vote in North Carolina, are asked to choose in the 1990s between two somewhat dull political parties, the Republicans—who promise both government investment in necessary infrastructure and lower taxes—and the Democrats—who make vague promises to "do more" with citizens' tax dollars—it will not be a close contest. Republicans will win hands down.

In the 1990s, the state's Democratic leaders will gradually transfer control of North Carolina politics to the Republicans unless they offer specific taxation and policy programs (for example, in education, health care, the environment, or transportation) that draw clear distinctions between Democrats and Republicans. If dealigned white Tar Heel voters, typically registered Democrats who lack strong allegiance to either political party, cannot easily see how they directly benefit from state government policies that are passed by the Democratic majority, they will vote against the Democrats. As Tar Heel Republicans are fond of reminding white voters, Democrats can easily be made out to stand for political bosses like former house speaker Liston Ramsey, special interest groups like blacks and feminists, and "tax-and-spend" policies that benefit "somebody else." Only specific campaigning by Democrats can counter that Republican message. It remains to be seen whether North Carolina Democrats can speak to the electorate as clearly and successfully as have, in recent years, their counterparts in the North Carolina Republican party.

Bibliography

Abrams, Douglas Carl. 1978. "A Progressive-Conservative Duel: The 1920 Democratic Gubernatorial Primaries in North Carolina." *North Carolina Historical Review* 55: 421–41.

Adams, Jerry. 1981. "That Freakish Thing: A Memo Dooms the Labor Center." In Eric B. Herzik and Sallye Branch Teater, comps., *North Carolina Focus*. Raleigh.

AFL-CIO Legislative Report. 1987. Raleigh.

Ashby, Warren. 1980. *Frank Porter Graham: A Southern Liberal*. Winston-Salem.

Bachrach, Peter, and Morton Baratz. 1963. "Decisions and Nondecisions: An Analytical Framework." *American Political Science Review* 57: 632–42.

Baker, Frances. 1986. "North Carolina Elite Attitudes toward Women, Blacks and Labor." Paper presented at annual meeting of Southern Sociological Society, New Orleans, April.

Bartley, Numan V., and Hugh D. Graham. 1975. *Southern Politics and the Second Reconstruction*. Baltimore.

Bass, Jack, and Walter DeVries. 1976. *The Transformation of Southern Politics*. New York.

Bell, John L., Jr. 1982. *Hard Times: The Beginning of the Great Depression in North Carolina, 1929–1933*. Raleigh.

Betts, Jack. 1985. "Rendering unto Caesar: A Taxing Problem for the 1985 Legislature." *North Carolina Insight* 7: 2–7.

Beyle, Thad. 1981. "How Powerful Is the North Carolina Governor?" *N.C. Insight* 3: 3–11.

————, and Merle Black, eds. 1975. *Politics and Policy in North Carolina*. New York.

————, Merle Black, and Arlon Kemple. 1975. "Sanford vs. Wallace: Presidential Primary Politics in North Carolina." In Thad Beyle and Merle Black, eds., *Politics and Policy in North Carolina*. New York.

Beyle, Thad, and Peter Harkins. 1975. "The 1968 Elections in North Carolina." In Thad Beyle and Merle Black, eds., *Politics and Policy in North Carolina*. New York.

Billings, Dwight B., Jr. 1979. *Planters and the Making of a "New South": Class, Politics and Development in North Carolina, 1865–1900*. Chapel Hill.

Black, Earl. 1975. "North Carolina Governors and Racial Segregation." In Thad Beyle and Merle Black, eds., *Politics and Policy in North Carolina*. New York.

————. 1976. *Southern Governors and Civil Rights*. Cambridge, Mass.

———, and Merle Black. 1987. *Politics and Society in the South*. Cambridge, Mass.

Botsch, Robert Emil. 1980. *We Shall Not Overcome: Populism and Southern Blue-Collar Workers*. Chapel Hill.

Boyte, Harry. 1980. *The Backyard Revolution: Understanding the New Citizen Movement*. Philadelphia.

———, and Frank Riessman, eds. 1986. *The New Populism: The Politics of Empowerment*. Philadelphia.

Budget. 1959. *Summary Budget of the State of North Carolina*. Raleigh.

Burgess, M. Elaine. 1962. *Negro Leadership in a Southern City*. Chapel Hill.

Calhoun, Craig. 1988. *North Carolina Today: Contrasting Conditions and Common Concerns*. Raleigh.

CBS News. 1984. *CBS Election Day Election Poll (North Carolina)*. New York.

———. 1986. *CBS Election Day Election Poll (North Carolina)*. New York.

Chafe, William. 1981. *Civilities and Civil Rights*. Reprint. New York.

Charlotte Observer. 1987. "Why Myrick Beat Gantt: 2 Local Political Experts Examine the Mayoral Election." November 8.

———. 1988. "Martin Holds Steady; Jordan Slips in New Poll." October 16.

———. 1989a. "Ramsey Ousted as House Speaker." January 12.

———. 1989b. "Revolt Was 10 Weeks in Making." January 12.

Clean Water Fund. 1988. *Clean Water Update*. Vol. 2. Raleigh. June.

Clotfelter, James, and William R. Hamilton. 1972. "Beyond Race Politics: Electing Southern Populists in the 1970s." In H. Brandt Ayers and Thomas H. Naylor, eds., *You Can't Eat Magnolias*. New York.

Cobb, James. 1984. *Industrialization and Southern Society, 1877–1984*. Lexington, Ky.

Conway, Mimi. 1979. *Rise Gonna Rise: A Portrait of Southern Textile Workers*. New York.

Corporation for Enterprise Development. 1987. *Making the Grade: The 1987 Development Report Card for the States*. Washington, D.C.

Crow, Jeffrey J. 1984. "Cracking the Solid South: Populism and the Fusionist Interlude." In Lindley S. Butler and Alan D. Watson, eds., *The North Carolina Experience: An Interpretive and Documentary History*. Chapel Hill.

CTJ (Citizens for Tax Justice). 1987. *The Sorry State of State Taxes*. Washington, D.C.

Doty, Mercer, and Doris Mahaffey. 1979. "Which Way Now?" In Eric B. Herzik and Sallye Branch Teater, comps., *North Carolina Focus*. Raleigh.

Dowd, Edward. 1976. "Respondent to 'Earnings, Profits, and Productivity in North Carolina.'" In Jane A. Begoli, ed., *Proceedings, Employment-Management Relations: Issues in the South*. University of North Carolina at Charlotte. November.

Durden, Robert F. 1984. "North Carolina in the New South." In Lindley S. Butler and Alan D. Watson, eds., *The North Carolina Experience: An Interpretive and Documentary History*. Chapel Hill.

Durham Morning Herald. 1987a. "Cities-Highways Bill Gets House Approval." July 1.

_____. 1987b. "Senate Approves Bill on School Spankings." July 1.

_____. 1988. "U.S. Labor Groups Lost 62,000 Members in 1987." January 24.

Earle, John R., Dean D. Knudsen, and Donald W. Shriver, Jr. 1976. *Spindles and Spires: A Re-Study of Religion and Social Change in Gastonia*. Atlanta.

Edmonds, Helen G. 1951. *The Negro and Fusion Politics in North Carolina, 1894–1901*. Chapel Hill.

Ehringhaus, J. C. B. 1934. "The Sales Tax Has Its Virtues." In Lindley S. Butler and Alan D. Watson, eds., *The North Carolina Experience: An Interpretive and Documentary History*, 394–95. 1984.

Elazar, Daniel. 1972. *American Federalism*. New York.

Employment Security Commission. 1987. "Employment and Wages in North Carolina, Second Quarter 1987."

Ephron, Seth. 1987. "Breaking New Ground in Economic Development Subsidies." *Greensboro News and Record*. August 2.

Escott, Paul D. 1985. *Many Excellent People: Power and Privilege in North Carolina, 1850–1900*. Chapel Hill.

Fahy, Joe, and Ford Reid. 1986. "Money Machine Rakes It In, Spends Little on Candidates." *Virginian-Pilot*. Norfolk. May 11.

Feeney, Patrick. 1983. "At-Large Elections, Black Political Representation, and Social Change: A North Carolina Case Study." M.A. thesis. University of North Carolina at Greensboro.

Ferguson, James S. 1981. "Progressivism in Decline." In Eric B. Herzik and Sallye Branch Teater, comps., *North Carolina Focus*. Raleigh.

Finger, Bill. 1981. "Forces of Paradox." In Eric B. Herzik and Sallye Branch Teater, comps., *North Carolina Focus*. Raleigh.

Fox, Rosemary K. 1982. "Social Action against Injustice: Impact of the United Church of Christ Movement in Support of the Wilmington Ten." Unpublished paper. Department of Sociology, University of North Carolina at Greensboro.

Frady, Marshall. 1976. *Wallace*. New York.

Frankel, Linda Jean. 1986. "Women, Paternalism, and Protest in a Southern Textile Community: Henderson, N.C., 1900–1960." Ph.D. dissertation. Harvard University.

Frazier, E. Franklin. 1925. "Durham: Capital of the Black Middle Class." Reprint. 1968. In Alain Locke, ed., *The New Negro: Studies in American Negro Life*. New York.

Friedlein, Ken. 1986. "Selling Industry on North Carolina." *North Carolina Insight* 8: 43–49.

Furgurson, Earnest. 1986. *Hard Right: The Rise of Jesse Helms*. New York.

Galifianakis, Nick. 1987. Interview with author. Durham, May 9.

Goldman, Robert, and Paul Luebke. 1985. "Corporate Capital Moves South: Competing Class Interests and Labor Relations in North Carolina's 'New'

Political Economy." *Journal of Political and Military Sociology* 13: 17–32.

Goodman, Vanessa, and Jack Betts. 1987. *The Growth of a Two-Party System in North Carolina: A Special Report (North Carolina Center for Public Policy Research)*. Raleigh. December.

Goodwyn, Lawrence. 1976. *The Populist Moment*. New York.

Greenhaw, Wayne. 1982. *Elephants in the Cotton Fields: Ronald Reagan and the New Republican South*. New York.

Greensboro Daily News. 1978. "Winston Policemen Eye Union Affiliation." September 20.

———. 1980. "Ward Choice Up to Voters for Fourth Time." May 4, May 7.

———. 1982. "Council Adopts District Rule in Greensboro." June 24, November 16, December 17.

Greensboro News and Record. 1984. "Knox Won't Back Edmisten in Race." June 29.

———. 1985a. "Martin Restates Proposals for Some Tax Elimination." January 23.

———. 1985b. "State Ranks 8th in Survey on Business Climates." June 8.

———. 1987a. "Assembly Isn't Cross Section." February 8.

———. 1987b. "Job Recruiter Incentive a Switch." August 3.

Greensboro Record. 1977. "This Time, ERA Fight May Be More Gentlewomanly." January 19.

———. 1979. "Study Sees More Union Support in South." June 13.

Grisson, Eddie, and James Grisson. 1983. Interview with author. Henderson, N.C., September 17.

Guillory, Ferrel. 1988. "Lawmakers Give Green Light to Tax Giveaways." *News and Observer*. Raleigh. July 8.

Hall, Bob. 1985a. "Jesse Helms: The Meaning of His Money." *Southern Exposure*. Durham. February.

———. 1985b. "The 1984 North Carolina Voter Registration and Turnout." Unpublished memorandum. Institute for Southern Studies, Durham.

———, ed. 1988. *Environmental Politics: Lessons from the Grassroots*. Durham.

Hall, Jacquelyn, et al. 1987. *Like a Family: The Making of a Southern Cotton Mill World*. Chapel Hill.

Hamilton, Richard. 1972. *Class and Politics in the United States*. New York.

Hamilton, William. 1984. "The Political Views of North Carolinians: A Report to North Carolina Democratic Candidates." Unpublished report. Washington, D.C.

Hammer and Company Associates. 1961. *The Economy of Western North Carolina*. Atlanta.

Harvin, Lucius, III. 1983. Remarks at Helms-for-Senate dinner, Henderson, N.C., September 17.

Hellman, Mark. 1988. "Durham's Progressive Coalition." In Bob Hall, ed., *Environmental Politics: Lessons from the Grassroots*. Durham.

Helms, Jesse. 1976. *When Free Men Shall Stand: A Sobering Look at the Supertaxing, Superspending Superbureaucracy in Washington*. Grand Rapids.

_____. 1983a. Interview with author. Henderson, N.C., September 17.

_____. 1983b. Speech at Helms-for-Senate dinner, Henderson, N.C., September 17.

Hobbs, Samuel Huntington, Jr. 1930. *North Carolina: Economic and Social.* Chapel Hill.

Hodges, Luther. 1962. *Businessman in the State House.* Chapel Hill.

Hughes, Joseph T., Jr. 1982. "Targeting Desirable Industries." *N.C. Insight* 5: 27–35.

Hunt, James Baxter, Jr. 1981. "Microelectronics: The Key to the Future." *N.C. Insight* 4: 17.

_____. 1982. *Addresses and Public Papers of James Baxter Hunt, Jr., Governor of North Carolina, Volume I, 1977–1981.* Raleigh.

JCPS (Joint Center for Political Studies). 1973, 1980, 1985, 1987. *Black Elected Officials: A National Roster.* Washington, D.C.

Judkins, Bennett M. 1986. *We Offer Ourselves as Evidence: Toward Workers' Control of Occupational Health.* Westport, Conn.

Key, V. O., Jr. 1949. *Southern Politics in State and Nation.* New York.

King, David D. 1988. Interview with author. Raleigh, September 7.

King, Wayne. 1978. "North Carolina's Leaders Worried by Blemishes on State's Image." *New York Times.* February 22.

Lamis, Alexander P. 1984. *The Two-Party South.* New York.

Lavelle, J. M. 1981. "We Were All Bigots: Election '81 Decided by City-Wide White Backlash." *North State Reader* 1.

Lefler, Hugh Talmage, and Albert Ray Newsome. 1973. *North Carolina: The History of a Southern State.* 3d ed. Chapel Hill.

Leiter, Jeffrey. 1986. "Reactions to Subordination: Attitudes of Southern Textile Workers." *Social Forces* 64: 948–74.

Liner, Charles D. 1979. "The Origins and Development of the North Carolina System of Taxation." *Popular Government* 45: 41–49.

_____. 1981. "State and Local Government Finance over the Past Fifty Years." *Popular Government* 46: 32–36.

_____. 1982. "Government Spending and Taxation: Where Does North Carolina Stand?" *Popular Government* 48: 30–41.

Lo, Clarence. 1982. "Counter-movements and Conservative Movements in the Contemporary U.S." *Annual Review of Sociology* 8: 107–34.

Luebke, Paul. 1975. "Political Attitudes in a West German Factory: A Political-Sociological Analysis of Chemical Workers." Ph.D. dissertation. Columbia University.

_____. 1979. "The Social and Political Bases of a Black Candidate's Coalition: Race, Class and Ideology in the 1976 North Carolina Primary Election." *Politics and Society* 9: 239–61.

_____. 1980. "Repeal Food Tax; Raise Taxes on Liquor, Corporations." *Charlotte Observer.* May 11.

_____. 1981a. "Activists and Asphalt: A Successful Anti-expressway Movement in a 'New South City.'" *Human Organization* 40: 256–63.

————. 1981b. "Corporate Conservatism and Government Moderation in North Carolina." In Merle Black and John S. Reed, eds., *Perspectives on the American South*, vol 1. New York.

————. 1981c. "Neighborhood Groups vs. Business Developers in Durham: Expressway Politics in the Scarce Energy Age." *Carolina Planning* 7: 42–48.

————. 1984a. "Dear Senator Helms; Dear Governor Hunt." *The North Carolina Independent*. Durham. August 31.

————. 1984b. "The Helms-Hunt Race in North Carolina." *St. Petersburg Times*. August 12.

————. 1984c. "State of Competition: North Carolina's Senate Race and the Newspapers' Battle to Cover It." *Washington Journalism Review* 6: 21–23.

————. 1984d. "Carolina Democrats after the Deluge." *The Sun*. Baltimore. December 5. Reprint. *Greensboro News and Record*. January 22, 1985.

————. 1985. "North Carolina: Still in the Progressive Mold?" *News and Observer, 400th Anniversary of North Carolina Special Edition*. Raleigh. July.

————. 1985–86. "Grass-roots Organizing: The Hidden Side of the 1984 Helms Campaign." *Election Politics* 3: 30–33.

————. 1987a. "Newspaper Coverage of the 1986 Senate Race—Reporting the Issues or the Horse Race?" *North Carolina Insight* 9: 92–95.

————. 1987b. "Style, Substance and Symbolism: The Sanford-Broyhill Race of 1986." *Election Politics* 4: 11–14.

————. 1987c. "Take to the Stump; Hit Issues Hard; That's Sanford's Lesson to Democrats." *Atlanta Constitution*. January 28.

————. 1987d. "The Food Tax Epitomizes Tar Heel Tax Inequality." *Greensboro News and Record*. April 19.

————. 1989. "Southern Politics: Past and Future." In Joseph Himes, ed., *The South Moves into Its Future: Studies in the Analysis and Prediction of Social Change*. Tuscaloosa.

————, and Patrick Feeney. 1981. "Sophisticated Gerrymandering? At-Large Districting and Black Political Representation in the North Carolina General Assembly." Paper presented at the annual meeting of the Southern Sociological Society, Louisville, Ky., April.

Luebke, Paul, Bob McMahon, and Jeff Risberg. 1979. "Selective Industrial Recruiting in North Carolina." *Working Papers for a New Society* 6: 17–20.

Luebke, Paul, Steven Peters, and John Wilson. 1986. "The Political Economy of Microelectronics." In Dale Whittington, ed., *High Hopes for High Tech: Microelectronics Policy in North Carolina*. Chapel Hill.

————, and Jeff Risberg. 1983. "Jesse Helms: Leader of the Countermovement Pack." Paper presented at the annual meeting of the American Sociological Association, Detroit, September.

Luebke, Paul, and Joseph Schneider. 1987. "Economic and Racial Ideology in the North Carolina Elite." In James C. Cobb, ed., *Perspectives on the American South*, vol 5. New York.

Luebke, Paul, and Barry Yeoman. 1988. "Democrats Ignore Pro-Choice Vote." *Greensboro News and Record*. November 27.

Luebke, Paul, and John Zipp. 1983. "Social Class and Attitudes toward Big Business in the United States." *Journal of Military and Political Sociology* 11:251–64.

Luger, Michael. 1986. "The States and Industrial Development: Program Mix and Policy Effectiveness." In J. Quigley, ed., *Perspectives on Public Finance and Policy*. New York.

Mahaffey, Doris, and Mercer Doty. 1979. *Which Way Now? Economic Development and Industrialization in N.C.: A Report by the North Carolina Center for Public Policy Research*. Raleigh.

———. 1981. "Which Way Now? Economic Development and Industrialization in North Carolina." In Eric B. Herzik and Sallye Branch Teater, comps., *North Carolina Focus*. Raleigh.

Malizia, Emil, Robert E. Crow, et al. 1975. *The Earnings of North Carolinians*. North Carolina Office of State Planning. Raleigh.

Marshall, F. Ray. 1967. *Labor in the South*. Cambridge, Mass.

MCNC (Microelectronics Center of North Carolina). 1985. *Annual Report*.

MDC. 1986. *Three Views of Rural Economic Development in North Carolina*. Chapel Hill.

Minority Report to the 1988 Democratic Platform, Democratic National Convention, Atlanta.

Molotch, Harvey. 1976. "The City as a Growth Machine: Toward a Political Economy of Place." *American Journal of Sociology* 82: 309–32.

Moore, Barrington. 1966. *Social Origins of Dictatorship and Democracy*. New York.

Morse, Lawrence. 1978. "Wages in North Carolina: An Evaluation of the Potthoff Report." *North Carolina Review of Business and Economics* 4: 3–9.

Mullins, Terry, and Paul Luebke. 1982. "Symbolic Victory and Political Reality in the Southern Textile Industry: The Meaning of the J. P. Stevens Union Contract." *Journal of Labor Research* 3: 81–88.

———. 1984. "The Corporate Campaign against J. P. Stevens: The Impact on Labor Relations in the 1980s." *North Carolina Review of Business and Economics* 8: 23–27.

Myerson, Michael. 1978. *Nothing Could Be Finer*. New York.

National Education Association Datasearch. 1987. *Rankings of the States, 1987*. Washington, D.C.

NCDOA (North Carolina Department of Agriculture). 1986. *Agricultural Statistics*. Raleigh.

NCDOC (North Carolina Department of Commerce). 1986. *Blueprint on Economic Development*. Raleigh.

———. 1986–87. *Business North Carolina*. Raleigh.

———. 1988. *North Carolina Economic Development Report, 1987*. Raleigh.

NCDOT (North Carolina Department of Transportation). 1988. *Transportation Improvement Program, 1988–1996*. Raleigh. December.

News and Observer. 1977a. "Person Industry Hunters Quit." Raleigh. August 10.

_____. 1977b. "Hunt Cites Industrial Growth." Raleigh. December 23.

_____. 1977c. "Citizens Fight 'Power Structure' to Lure Philip Morris into Area." Raleigh. December 25.

_____. 1978a. "Hunt Defends '10' Decision as Correct." Raleigh. February 12.

_____. 1978b. "PPG Employees Will Vote on Union." Raleigh. July 6.

_____. 1981a. "Trio Tied to Congressional Club to Fight Tax Hike." Raleigh. May 12.

_____. 1981b. "Motor Fuels Tax Supporters, Opponents Continue Attacks." Raleigh. May 30.

_____. 1981c. "Ads Attack 'Cronyism' among Hunt Supporters." Raleigh. June 4.

_____. 1981d. "UAW Fights for a Place in the Sun (Belt)." Raleigh. April 12.

_____. 1981e. "Voting Rights: Is U.S. Law Still Needed?" Raleigh. August 23.

_____. 1983. "Helms, Falwell Begin North Carolina Voter Registration Drive." July 6.

_____. 1986. "Broyhill, Sanford, Top Spenders." Raleigh. November 4.

_____. 1988a. "Sanford Reports Assets of $2 Million; Helms Declares $325,000." Raleigh. June 5.

_____. 1988b. "Nomination Blocked as Helms Battles State Department." Raleigh. June 26.

Nordhoff, Grace, ed. 1984. *"A Lot of Human Beings Have Been Born Bums": Twenty Years of the Words of Jesse Helms.* Durham.

North Carolina Center for Public Policy Research. 1986, 1988. *Rankings of the Lobbyists.* Raleigh.

O'Connor, Paul. 1987a. "Hardison's Pro-Business Record May Block His Nomination." *Durham Sun.* May 5.

_____. 1987b. "When It Comes to Economic Development, Jim Martin and Bob Jordan Have Big Plans." *North Carolina Insight* 9: 40–43.

Oleck, Joan. 1988. "Runoff: To Its Foes, It's a Primary Concern." *Virginian-Pilot.* Norfolk. May 29.

Orth, John V. 1982. "Separation of Powers: An Old Doctrine Triggers a New Crisis." *N.C. Insight* 5: 36–47.

OSBM (Office of State Budget and Management). 1986. "State Rankings 1986." 1st ed.

_____. 1987a. *Population Counts for North Carolina Counties.* Raleigh.

_____. 1987b. *Revised Estimates of North Carolina Population.* Raleigh.

_____. 1988. *Revised Estimates of North Carolina Population.* Raleigh.

Parramore, Thomas C. 1983. *Express Lanes and Country Roads: The Way We Lived in North Carolina, 1920–1970.* Chapel Hill.

Payton, Boyd. 1970. *Scapegoat: Prejudice-Politics-Prison.* Philadelphia.

Peters, Mason. 1986. "New Right Crusaders Hunt Liberal Prey in Sen. Helms' National Political Holy War." *Virginian-Pilot.* Norfolk. May 11.

Peterson, Bill. 1984. "Jesse Helms' Lessons for Washington: Big Bucks, Street Fighter Skills, Racist Appeals and Charisma Still Work." *Washington Post.* November 18.

Pinsky, Mark. 1977. "Wilmington 10: The Trial They Never Had." *The Nation* 224: 754–56.

Pope, Liston. 1942. *Millhands and Preachers*. New Haven.

Reid, Ford. 1986. "Fundraising." *Virginian-Pilot*. Norfolk. May 11.

Risberg, Jeffrey Earl. 1981. "Social Class, Race, Education and Liberalism-Conservatism in the South: An Analysis of North Carolina Survey Data." M.A. thesis. University of North Carolina at Greensboro.

Roach, Janet H. "The Voting Rights Act: Dilution of Black Voting Power." *Campbell Law Observer*. February 24.

Robinson, W. S. 1950. "Ecological Correlations and the Behavior of Individuals." *American Sociological Review* 15: 351–57.

Rosenfeld, Stuart. 1983. *After the Factories*. Southern Growth Policies Board, Research Triangle Park, North Carolina.

Roy, Donald. 1975. "Fear Stuff, Sweet Stuff and Evil Stuff: Management's Defenses against Unionization in the South." Unpublished manuscript. Durham.

Sampson, Gregory. 1986. "Employment and Earnings in the Semiconductor Electronics Industry: Implications for North Carolina." In Dale Whittington, ed., *High Hopes for High Tech: Microelectronics Policy in North Carolina*. Chapel Hill.

Schneider, Joseph. 1985. "Preachers and Politics: New Christian Right Ideology among North Carolina Fundamentalist Ministers." M.A. thesis. University of North Carolina at Greensboro.

Sitterson, Joseph Carlyle. 1957. "Business Leaders in Post–Civil War North Carolina, 1865–1900." In Joseph Carlyle Sitterson, ed., *Studies in Southern History*. Chapel Hill.

Sitton, Claude. 1988. "It's Too Soon to Say This Is a New Jim Gardner." *News and Observer*. Raleigh. May 15.

Snider, William D. 1984. "What Did the 'Mecklenburg Thing' Mean?" *Greensboro News and Record*. June 17.

_____. 1985. *Helms and Hunt: The North Carolina Senate Race, 1984*. Chapel Hill.

Spence, James R. 1968. *The Making of a Governor: The Moore-Preyer-Lake Primaries of 1964*. Winston-Salem.

Sternlicht, Ann, and Bill Finger. 1986. "Who Makes State Economic Development Policy?" *North Carolina Insight* 8: 22–35.

Stevenson, David E. 1975. "Gubernatorial Transition in a Two Party Setting: The Holshouser Administration." In Thad Beyle and Merle Black, eds., *Politics and Policy in North Carolina*. New York.

Stoesen, Alexander R. 1984. "From Ordeal to New Deal: North Carolina in the Great Depression." In Lindley S. Butler and Alan D. Watson, eds., *The North Carolina Experience: An Interpretive and Documentary History*. Chapel Hill.

Stuart, Brad. 1981. "Making North Carolina Prosper." In Eric B. Herzik and Sallye Branch Teater, comps., *North Carolina Focus*. Raleigh.

Tilley, Nannie M. 1985. *The R. J. Reynolds Tobacco Company*. Chapel Hill.

Tolbert, Charles, Patrick Horan, and E. M. Beck. 1980. "The Structure of Economic Segmentation: A Dual Economy Approach." *American Journal of Sociology* 85: 1095–1116.

Troy, Leon, and Neil Shaeflin. 1985. *U.S. Union Sourcebook.* West Orange, N.J.

U.S. Department of Commerce. 1986. *Major Shippers Report.* Washington, D.C.

U.S. Department of Labor. 1970. *Employment and Wages, 1970.* Washington, D.C.

———. 1987. *Employment and Wages, 1987.* Washington, D.C.

Vogel, Ezra F., and Andrea Larson. 1985. "North Carolina's Research Triangle: State Modernization." In Ezra F. Vogel, *Comeback, Case by Case: Building the Resurgence of American Business,* 240–62. New York.

Wheaton, Elizabeth. 1987. *Codename GREENKIL: The 1979 Greensboro Killings.* Athens, Ga.

Whittington, Dale. 1986. "Microelectronics Policy in North Carolina: An Introduction." In Dale Whittington, ed., *High Hopes for High Tech: Microelectronics Policy in North Carolina.* Chapel Hill.

Whittle, Richard. 1983. "Jesse Helms Has a Problem: He's Destined to Lose in '84." *Washington Post.* October 23.

Wood, Phillip J. 1986. *Southern Capitalism: The Political Economy of North Carolina, 1880–1980.* Durham.

Wrenn, Carter. 1987. Interview with author. Raleigh, March 27.

Wyman, Hastings, Jr. 1987. "Yes, But Then Again, No: Social Issues and Southern Politics." *Election Politics* 4: 15–18.

Yeoman, Barry. 1988a. "More Dreams than Dollars." *The North Carolina Independent.* Durham. June 30.

———. 1988b. "The Convention TV Didn't Cover." *The North Carolina Independent.* Durham. July 28.

Zingraff, Rhonda, and Michael Schulman. 1984. "The Social Bases of Class Consciousness: A Study of Southern Textile Workers with a Comparison by Race." *Social Forces* 63: 98–116.

Zipin, Paul. 1982. "North Carolina's Individual Income Tax." *Popular Government* 48: 24–29.

Zipp, John F., Richard Landerman, and Paul Luebke. 1982. "Political Parties and Political Participation: A Reexamination of the Standard Socioeconomic Model." *Social Forces* 60: 1140–53.

Index

Abortion, 161, 180; modernizer-traditionalist differences over, 21, 41–42, 54, 55–57; and Hunt, 28, 142; and Helms, 124, 138, 146, 148, 149, 151
—state fund for, 172–73, 193, 198; and Hunt, 33, 34, 142; and Martin, 33–34, 180, 183, 209; Democratic-Republican differences over, 34, 55, 182; and Jordan, 45, 209
Accuracy in Academe, 136
Accuracy in Media, 136
Activist government. *See* Government activism
Advisory Budget Commission, 43
Affirmative action, 19, 21
AFL-CIO, 31, 39, 89, 134, 148; and proposed Labor Education Center, 90, 91; lobbying efforts of, 100–101; and citizen activism, 191, 192
Agriculture: and traditionalism, 18–19; regional distribution of, 61, 67; place of in North Carolina's economy, 62, 66–67; importance of tobacco cultivation in, 64, 66, 67
Alamance County, 170
Alexander, Bill, 41
Alexander, Kelly, Jr., 114
Amalgamated Clothing and Textile Workers Union (ACTWU), 97–98
American Airlines, 82, 83
American Federation of Labor (AFL), 13. *See also* AFL-CIO
American Federation of State, Municipal, and County Employees (AFSMCE), 92
American Textile Manufacturers' Institute, 98
Amnesty International, 113
Antiwar movement, 25, 27, 129, 165
Apparel industry: traditionalism of, 25, 32, 74, 86; opposition of to high-tech industry, 25, 32, 75; and Martin, 32; place of in North Carolina's manufacturing sector, 62, 63, 64, 70; wages in, 64, 70, 74, 75; regional distribution of, 67, 68; problems facing, 75; labor relations in, 87. *See also* Low-wage industries

Asheville, 66, 69, 79, 168, 170
Atlantic coast, 58–59, 61, 169, 191, 206
Atlantic Committee for Research in Education (ACRE), 51
Aycock, Charles B., 7, 8

Ballenger, Cass, 90
Banking and finance industry, 23, 32, 37, 59–61, 63, 65, 86, 203
Baptist church, 19, 96, 126, 129, 138
Basic Education Plan (BEP), 34, 46, 49–50
Bayh, Birch, 128
Beilman, Don, 78
Bennett, Bert, 28–29
Berry, Harriet Morehead, 9
Bertie County, 152
Bickett, Thomas, 13–14
Big business. *See* Business community
Black Political Caucus, 190, 192
Blacks: exclusion of from political life, 2, 7, 13, 14, 102, 117; in fusion forces, 4–6, 22; in General Assembly, 5, 112, 115, 116, 117, 118; disfranchisement measures used against, 6, 7, 8, 102; spending on schools for, 7, 8, 48; affirmative action for, 19, 21; and traditionalists, 19, 35; and modernizers, 21, 33, 35, 78, 104, 192, 193; and Helms, 25, 104, 202; and Martin, 33, 207; and Jordan, 45, 207; and women's issues, 55, 56; as percentage of population regionally and statewide, 61; and Hunt, 78, 104, 137, 143, 147, 149, 150, 152; lack of economic opportunities for, 83, 102; and unions, 91, 96, 97; as Democrats/Democratic voters, 104, 113–14, 147, 148, 156, 169, 174, 177, 202, 211; politi-

75, 76, 86–101 passim; strikes by, 13–14, 72; business community's opposition to, 13–15, 76, 86–98 passim; and furniture industry, 14, 86; and traditionalists, 19, 76, 86–99 passim; and modernizers, 21, 75, 86–99 passim; and right-to-work law, 39, 71, 88; and General Assembly, 39–40, 95; in core vs. peripheral industries, 63; and wages, 76, 88, 93–94; Helms's opposition to, 85, 91, 131, 140–41; and apparel industry, 86; and Republicans, 91; and representation elections, 95–97; and contract negotiations, 97–98; and citizen activism, 100–101. *See also* Labor; Labor relations
United Automobile Workers (UAW), 92, 95
United Church of Christ: Commission for Racial Justice, 112
United Rubber Workers, 95
United Textile Workers (UTW), 13, 14, 91
Universities, 1, 9, 21, 48, 59, 71, 85, 136, 189
University of North Carolina at Chapel Hill, 16, 21, 24, 28, 71, 77, 78, 88, 153, 155
University of North Carolina at Charlotte, 78
University of North Carolina System, 89–90
University Park, 82
Utilities, 63, 65, 87, 186
Utilities Commission, 181, 185, 192, 194

Valentine, Tim, 118
Vance County, 67, 132
Verbatim, 82, 83
Vietnam War. *See* Antiwar movement
Viewpoint, 128–29
Voter registration: black, 114, 141, 147, 148, 163, 177, 195; fundamentalist Protestant, 147–48; Republican, 147–48, 168–69, 178–79; Democratic, 169, 178–79
Voting Rights Act (1965), 110, 116
Voting Rights Act (1982), 117–18, 119, 120

Wachovia Bank, 71
Wages: industrial, 29, 30, 63, 64–65, 72,

73–77, 79, 87, 88, 93–94; as issue in economic development, 73–77, 79, 93–94
Wake County, 59, 67, 115, 152; Republicans and Republican support in, 163, 167, 169, 171, 210
Wake Forest University, 127
Walker, Russell, 52
Wallace, George, 25, 159, 160–61, 162–64, 184
Warren County, 67, 152
Warrenton, 67
Washington, Harold, 141
Washington Post, 131, 137
Watauga County, 59, 169, 196
Watergate, 40, 160, 179, 196
Water/sewer lines: and economic development, 21, 30, 81, 82, 84
Watkins, Billy, 42, 187, 207
Wayne County, 152
Western Piedmont, 4, 198; Republicans and Republican support in, 40, 148, 149, 151–52, 159, 164, 165, 166, 179, 195, 206, 210; traditionalism in, 42, 61; region defined, 59; blacks in, 61; agriculture in, 61, 67; manufacturing in, 62, 67–68, 152; educational levels in, 69, 152
White Government Unions, 5
Whites: disfranchisement of poorer segment of, 6, 7, 8; deference to authority among, 19; Helms's support among, 24, 25, 137, 139, 141–42, 144, 147–48, 149, 150, 157; racial traditionalism among, 32–33, 108–13, 157–59; Republican appeals to racial traditionalism of, 32–33, 141–42, 171; and desegregation, 103, 110; representation of blacks by, 104, 108; reaction of to black political participation, 107–8, 141–42 (*see also* Democrats/Democratic party: dealignment of white voters from); and electoral cooperation or confrontation with blacks, 112, 113–21; as swing vote, 150, 156, 207, 211; voting patterns and turnout of in 1984 senatorial election, 150–55; and cooperation with blacks in citizen activism, 191–92; efforts at politicization of less affluent segments of, 193–95, 200–202, 204
Whiting, Albert, 89